AROUND THE WORLD
ON THE QE2

AROUND THE WORLD ON THE QE2

Alfred Armand Montapert
and
William David Montapert

QUEEN ELIZABETH 2
10th Anniversary World Cruise

PRENTICE-HALL, INC. ENGLEWOOD CLIFFS, N.J.

Prentice-Hall International, Inc., *London*
Prentice-Hall of Australia, Pty. Ltd., *Sydney*
Prentice-Hall of Canada, Ltd., *Toronto*
Prentice-Hall of India Private Ltd., *New Delhi*
Prentice-Hall of Japan, Inc., *Tokyo*
Prentice-Hall of Southeast Asia Pte., Ltd., *Singapore*
Whitehall Books, Ltd., *Wellington, New Zealand*

© 1981, by

Alfred Armand Montapert and
William David Montapert

Library of Congress Cataloging in Publication Data
Montapert, Alfred Armand.
  Around the world on the QE 2.

  "Queen Elizabeth 2, 10th anniversary world
cruise."
  1. Queen Elizabeth 2 (Ship)   2.   Ocean travel.
I. Montapert, William David.
II. Title.
G550.M6   910.4'1   81-5921
ISBN 0-13-046615-8   AACR2

Printed in the United States of America

Other Books by Alfred Armand Montapert

Distilled Wisdom: Thoughts That Successful Men Live By

Supreme Philosophy of Man: The Laws of Life

Personal Planning Manual: How to Increase Your Worth

The Way to Happiness: Formulas to a Better and Happier Life

ADDITIONAL COPIES MAY BE ORDERED FROM

BOOKS OF VALUE
2458 Chislehurst Drive
Los Angeles, CA 90027

PARADE OF PORTS

PICTURES OF THE TRIP

PICTURES OF THE TRIP

AROUND THE WORLD
ON THE QE2

The Queen's Room on the QE2

THE BEGINNING

You're tired. You've been working too hard. Just for a lark you stop by a travel agency and pick up a load of brochures. You know the kind—South Sea Island dream stuff. When you get home, no one's there. You settle down in a comfortable chair and start to read. One brochure catches your eye.

"Why travel?" it asks. "Why travel around the world by ship?" You reply cynically, "Because I have a lot of both time and money." As if reading your mind, the brochure answers back impertinently, "Certainly time and money are the prerequisites, but not the reasons."

Then the brochure goes on to say, "Travel can help you be a whole person, living a rich, full life." True wholeness takes time— a lot of living and seeing and being. Above all, it requires contact with others—other people, other times, other places—stretching out to complete ourselves. We can't understand life or the world from just one point. We have to go out, looking for the rest, the beyond...the earth, the heavens, and finally God. Then the other, the beyond, will make us whole, make us understand not only where we've been but what we've left. Where we are when we return—not only who we were but who we might become.

You close your eyes for a second and there are images of palm trees, white beaches...a calm and tranquil sea. Wouldn't it be great to turn off the burners on the day-to-day pressure-cooker routine of your life just for a week or two? Just the thought of getting away acts like a shot of adrenalin.

Travel provides a change of climate and scenery which is often more necessary for your well-being than medicine.

Although travel may be considered the richest of all pleasures, it may also be thought of as a good investment. If we have eyes to see, ears to hear, patience to understand, a whole new life is in store—through travel. We are all travelers on the highway of learning. Through experience and observation we learn the fine art of living. The purpose of this book is *not* how to build a career, *but how to live.*

"That may be true," you say, "but why write a book about it?" Simply, the answer is this: Sharing our experience may, perhaps, impart a desire for you to do the same, and your new adventures will bring us closer, proving that we are all travelers—traveling endlessly inside and out, and only our names are different.

You think about it. No, don't think. Dream about it. You know you can't get away but it's still fun to dream. Then your dreams kind of get out of hand and become an obsession. In the morning you find yourself rereading the brochures. And as you turn one over, you see it. The words jump out at you from the page:

CUNARD OFFERS ITS 10TH ANNIVERSARY
AROUND THE WORLD CRUISE

"No," you say, "it's ridiculous. I can't afford it." Then you catch your subconscious whispering, "You can't afford not to. You may never have another chance again."

"But I can't get away."

"Sure you can. It'll all be there waiting for you when you get back."

You give in and decide to say yes to your secret desires—the ones that are inside everyone who is afraid to say, "By

George, I'll consider it. I've worked hard and been blessed. What better way to spend my money than to invest in myself?"

For a long time now you have longed to simplify your life. Paradoxically, you propose to launch the pursuit of your goal by taking a luxury world cruise on the QE2. You feel it would enable you to get out from under the pressure—to have more freedom. The eighty days of rest and change would give you time to think and plan ahead. And there's plenty to think about.

The world appears to be sick—its morality moronic, its crime a cancer. The government cannot stop the inflation that is making the dollar worth less every day—probably because the government itself is causing it. The world, as you see it, is becoming a violent, dangerous, and uncertain place—all speed and no direction. Just the thought of getting away from your daily routine acts like a shot of adrenalin.

But you have other reasons for taking this voyage. You begin to realize that this voyage of the QE2 will probably be one of the last vestiges of seagoing luxury in our time, a priceless opportunity to savor the greatest cuisine and enjoy the most outstanding service that money can buy. It is a chance to share the gaiety of others and contribute some of your own.

Your health is another consideration. Nothing can match an ocean voyage as a tonic for body and spirit. Your doctor has told you that travel can provide a change of climate and scenery which is often more necessary to your well-being than medicine. When you return for your next physical examination, you can expect your doctor to say, "When you left, you were as sick as a dollar. Now you are as sound as a Krugerrand."

"Today," you think, "we are gradually losing all the good things, so let me hang my hat in the Queen and live like a King!"

Your banker tells you that a trip may also be a good investment. Your head tells you, "If you have eyes to see, ears to hear, patience to understand, travel can be more than an adventure; it can help you learn the fine art of living." Your heart tells you, *"Go!"*

But how can you get away? You have so many respon-sibilities—there's this to do, so-and-so to see, what's-his-name depending on you.

You decide they'll all just have to wait.

You have learned that if you want to find time to do anything, you have to make time.

You discovered long ago, after attending a few funerals and looking into open graves, that your little day would soon be done, just like everyone else's. So many of your friends were VIP's, but they are gone and forgotten, and nobody mentions their names anymore.

So you have to seize every opportunity to take time out to live. That is why you decide to take a vacation and *enjoy life,* and in the process perhaps help others to enjoy theirs.

All of us greatly benefit in our general well-being, as well as in our work, by an occasional complete change of scenery and new places. Such is the adventure of taking a vacation. The benefits accruing from a vacation—any vacation, not just a world cruise—are many.

A vacation gives an opportunity for an overhaul of the physical mechanism. To get the best results, plan a regular rest period during the day in which you completely relax. Let the world go by and hang loose.

There is a song titled "You Light Up My Life." If you have someone going along with you who lights up your life, you are a very lucky person. Life is either a daring adventure, or nothing.

The right mental attitude will do much to make any vacation enjoyable and beneficial. Cheerfulness, gratitude, and optimism are upbuilding influences. The good thoughts you radiate to others will come back to you in increased measure.

Ninety-nine percent of what you do is done by *habit.*

Getting away from the daily routine is like getting a shot of adrenalin. It really makes you come alive. Most important of all, a vacation is a break in routine. It offers a change, a rest, variety, and a time to relax, to unwind, to release the tension. New ideas then come freely to the mind. Vacations are shunned by some people because they entail a break in routine. But that is exactly the most important reason for taking them. To keep things inside you from going stale, you need a new, fresh look now and then. An occasional break in routine is essential to your well-being. If you want to fully enjoy the superb luxury and gaiety of a sea voyage on the QE2, you should not put it off. It may be later than you think!

You decide to take the plunge. *"What better way to spend my money than to invest in myself?"* A call to the travel agent and you're booked! Suddenly you feel jubilant, but there is much to do, like checking your passport to see that it is up to date, getting traveler's checks, packing, and so on....

ON LUXURY LINERS: END OF AN ERA?

Gone is the dirigible
The train
Soon gone the ocean liner
The music grinds to a stop.
The lights flicker
They will soon be gone too.
As we approach
Inexorably
The uniworld
Of unwanted trivia, sights and sounds
Propelled at us
At unbelievable, galling, ghastly speed
A miracle of science and credulity.

THE RESEARCH

You want to know all you can about where you're going and the ship that will carry you there. You take your stack of books and begin your reading, starting with ocean liners. You find that luxury liners, superb combinations of solid comfort and slow splendor, were unrealistic, impractical, uneconomical, and magnificent. Being all of these things in an age of frenetic mediocrity, they seem undoubtedly destined to disappear, like the dirigible before them.

But before you have a chance to contemplate what we have lost, you're attracted by the romance of ships, by how the era of the liners began in the first place. You find that it was probably because there was a North Atlantic, a Europe on one side and an America on the other, a need to get from one place to another in the shortest possible time. Competition decreed that most passengers would gravitate to the ships that made sure they traveled in the most comfortable way.

The whole thing wouldn't have gotten off land, so to speak, had Mr. Samuel Cunard not received a mail contract from the British government in the 1840s. From there on came a succession of ships, one bigger and better than the other, ships that became a source of national pride and competition. The most famous of these became household names: *Lusitania, Mauretania, Majestic, France, Normandie, Queen Mary* and *Queen Elizabeth, United States.* These later ships were not really ships at all, but floating cities, the length of three football fields, with dining rooms longer than the Hall of Mirrors at Versailles.

But crises are common to every noble undertaking, and as you read on you find that in 1958 the first crisis struck the superliners in the form of air competition. That was the first year air travel exceeded sea travel across the North Atlantic. (In 1957, more than one million passengers crossed the North Atlantic on seventy steamers. This declined to 50,000 on one liner, the QE2, in 1980.) By the mid-sixties, the jet airliners had won the race with the public. And in 1974, the death knell sounded for the few remaining ships with the advent of the age of high-priced fuel. Oil that had cost two dollars a barrel in 1970 was suddenly eleven dollars. Now it is three and four times as much.

On May 8, 1967, the *Queen Mary* and *Queen Elizabeth 1* were both retired. But in that same year, the *Queen Elizabeth 2,* the fastest and most luxurious of them all, was launched in a defiant assertion that the time of the great superliner was not yet over. In April of 1969, the QE2 embarked on her maiden crossing of the Atlantic.

Today, the QE2 rules the waves virtually alone. The thirteen-story, 67,000-ton superliner would cost perhaps $300 million to duplicate, assuming today's mentality would support the grandiose idea of spacious cabins, all with private baths and all air-conditioned, an acre of open deck space, dozens of lounges, four swimming pools, synagogue, gymnasium, miniature golf course, shopping arcade, five nightclubs, six bars, four dining rooms, casino, and full-size theater, all moving across the sea at over thirty miles per hour, driven by engines of 110,000 horsepower, more power than 5000 cars.

But how long can the QE2 survive? The fuel for its engines, which cost only $2 million in 1973, is worth over $20 million now, with no end in sight. Nor is that the only cost that's soaring.

Up until the beginning of this century, iron men navigated wooden ships by the stars. Now steel and aluminum ships chart their courses by satellites which relay information to computers. Gone with celestial navigation is the old hard life of the sailor. And, there's a little thing called the Maritime Union.

The crew of the QE2 has its own movie theater and three lounges, ranging from the Pig and Whistle Pub to the Castaways, where coats and ties are *de rigueur.* In the old days, sailors often spent a year or more aboard, but now they get 140 shore days a year and are never at sea for longer than two months at one time. No one would object to this bit of progress, but it has its costs.

Cunard spends $2 million on plane tickets alone each year "bussing" employees back to England for shore leave. After three years, a crew member can bring his or her spouse along for up to thirty days on a cruise, proving that, for the crew at least, the good old days are...today.

So, costs alone may soon drive the QE2 to port. But whatever her destiny, she is yours to claim for the next eighty days on a magnificent voyage around the world, bringing her tradition of unsurpassed luxury to those of you lucky enough to join in this new adventure. As you arrive at your first port to begin your journey, you are eagerly looking ahead to the morrow, for here begins the fulfillment of a lifetime dream.

Next, you pick up the itinerary.

You smile. If the world is not yet your oyster, one of its pearls, New York, is your point of departure. Each of the thirty ports you will call on will be full of grand and glorious adventures.

So...let's get on with it.

World Trade Towers—New York City

NEW YORK

PORT 1

New York

U.S.A.

Port Everglades

Gulf of Mexico

NEW YORK

You have given yourself a few days in the city of cities—New York, the Big Apple to which so many millions have come to get their bite, even if all you can hope to catch in your brief stay are glimpses, fragments, fleeting images to carry away with you.

Creative city
Chauvinistic city
Power broker to the nation
Working hard
Dreaming hard
Playing hard
City.

Nonstop city
Expect the unexpected city
Thriving on its own adrenalin
Rush of shopping
Crush of subway
3000 acres of ambition and expertise
550 miles of waterfront
725 miles of subway
Thousands going around in circles.

A new day dawns over Manhattan. Sprawled out under a ceiling of winter blue sky, the sleeping giant of a city awakens and with concrete fingers reaches out to God. He must be out there somewhere, beyond the World Trade Towers—maybe not even as high, for who ever saw him nudge clouds with spires that inspire and defy? Built on strength, founded on a rock, Manhattan stretches out and flexes its muscles—hard, big, brawny city of action, forced to prove daily what can be done with enough money and guts. Guts and money.

City surrounded by sea, giving a special washed texture to its granite beauties, its fragile concrete pavilions and shrines rising strangely out of the shallows. Cleansing sea. Though others count your shortcomings—your taxes, crimes, pretenses, and scams—all is not lost, New Yorker. Remember the sea around you. Breathe deeply and be forgiven. Anchored there, still watching over it, raising her torch above it all, stands the Green Lady, Begetter of a Trillion Hopes.

> *Ogle it from afar*
> *See it through the lights of Triborough Bridge*
> *Climb the hills of Brooklyn Heights,*
> *Or take a Staten Island Ferry,*
> *Or a Circle Line cruise.*
> *Or ride in caged cab, see what a tiger feels like,*
> *Or better yet walk.*
> *Move in close*
> *On your toes*
> *Like a boxer*
> *And watch, observe.*

But listen. You'll like the city's sights and sounds. Though it is winter along Seventh Avenue, men push racks of cotton frocks on slippery sidewalks, reminding us that spring will soon be here.

See the restaurants, the bars and hash houses. Nibble a pastrami sandwich at Wolff's or let the hot borsht and perojis warm you on a cold day at the Russian Tea Room. Dine with the present inhabitants of The Inn on the Park, or with some of the ghosts at Lindy's.

Why shouldn't New York be proud? Vichyssoise, Waldorf salads, Delmonico steak, Thousand Island dressing, chocolate fondue, Baked Alaska—they all originated here.

And afterwards, after the rare steaks and entertainment well-done, stroll along 59th Street by Central Park. See the glowing charcoal stoves warming top-hatted drivers' hands. Notice the row of handsome hansom cabs, still much in demand by doting gentlemen and susceptible ladies—dallying, susceptible, even in winter.

Stand in the shadow of great ships towering above the street and watch as a Yankee Doodle Dandy, a James Cagney of a tug, steams cockily under Brooklyn Bridge, tooting steam and insolence at the world, ready to push a grapefruit into the face of a lovely liner if she gives him any trouble.

From the waterfront, inhale the spicy smells from the warehouses nearby, or walk along Broadway and savor its special kind of star-struck hopes and egg cream dreams. See the racks of strange newspapers crying out the latest bad news in mercifully unreadable print. Careful now! Watch your step. A snarling taxi driver knocks you down but, looking up, you see the blue sky and a skinny cat sunning itself on a narrow window ledge, and you are both glad to be alive.

Visit the UN. Eat with the delegates. Eavesdrop on history. Tour the General Assembly or visit the once-sacred chambers of the Security Council.

Exciting city. Nasty compendium of good and bad, life and death, and all other possible alternatives in between those that are explored here daily and nightly. A never-ending fusion of races—trading, talking, working, loving, fighting, breeding the always ever new, out of the never-changing old. It's like being everywhere at once. More Irish than Dublin, more Italian than Rome. Higher black population than any other city in the world. If New York is no longer a melting pot, it is at least a granite mixing bowl, with the world slopping over into the Hudson and the East River.

Many things don't change. The pretty girls still show off in the Rockefeller Center skating rink, practicing their soft, youthful magic, making young men's heads turn and old ones shed their unseen tears. In the background, a child doubles up in hilarity, struck down by the wondrous punch line of a teenager's joke. Some things can't change.

Merchants of Manhattan
Respecting the good and the beautiful—
Make this the
Money-can-buy-anything capital
Of the world.
Shamelessly they set their traps
Loading their stores with all manner of
   cultivated opulence
To catch the passersby
On Madison
Fifth Avenue
57th Street
More than places—ideas
Lifestyles—more than names
Is what they sell.
Witty city.
Imaginative city
Grumpy, rude, crude city
Fifth Avenue is enthralling
But your crime rate is appalling
Get on
Move over
Make way for tomorrow or get out.

City of superlatives. Biggest this. Biggest that. Beyond statistics are people. Those who have come to stay, those here for a day. The visitors come charging in like Merrill Lynch cattle— bullish on America—pushing and crowding into airports and bus terminals, looking for the action, hoping to exchange fifty-dollar bills for two pieces of cardboard on Broadway, get a decent meal, hear all that jazz in Harlem, or sip coffee in Greenwich Village. For him, it's Dreamtown USA. For her, it's Bloomingdale's-Bergdorf's-Macy's-Bendel's and all the other names you can print on a sack.

You know the stranger by his acts. He takes off his hat in an elevator, walks and misses the subway, doesn't kneel in Saint Patrick's but bows down at Rockefeller Center, lets the view from the Empire State inspire, but never takes time to stretch out end-to-end at Coney Island. He worships at the Metropolitan, gets dizzy at the Guggenheim, gargles the salt air as he rides the Staten Island Ferry for a quarter, telling you that it still has to be the city's biggest bargain, unless you take a peek at the Rockettes' legs for a few dollars more.

Still, for most, New York is a working giant of a city, with the inhabitants straining every nerve and muscle just to survive. Lift that broom, tote that mud, earn a little more and you'll be evicted by HUD, earn a little less and you'll really be in a mess. Work, work, sweat, swear, making it, brother, is really a bear. Give us jobs. Let us pull up streets with our bare Caterpillars, tear down depreciated yesterdays to build bigger and better tomorrows. The iron wrecking balls spew concrete and memories all over town, creating new piles of rubble, constructive destruction, so that a new concrete-and-steel phoenix can rise from a hole in the ground six stories deep. Let us bang and clatter, clatter and bang till we go home exhausted to our wives.

But the visitor cares not two whooping cranes for all this. He is busy seeking pleasure and bargains. Shopping till he drops, he spends till the end. Up Park, down Fifth. Careful you aren't flattened by a bus or a herd of charging shoppers at Bergdorf's or Macy's. Ready-to-wear capital of the world. Ready-to-tear-you-apart capital of the world.

But the visitor soon spends his last dime and so finishes off with a ride through Central Park. The horse paces off his practiced steps, contemplating through his oats another age when things were better—because he and you were younger.

Yet even when you have shopped and dined and ogled and applauded, there is always more to see, always more that there isn't time to see. How can anyone take it all in? You've never seen enough, never done enough...but it's almost time to leave.

The beginning or the ending. For those who have ended their Atlantic crossing on the QE2, it is the ultimate destination. But for you, it is the beginning of another adventure!

Your visit has been all too brief, but you have to go, to begin your trip around the world. Exhausted, exhilarated, you will carry the bright images of New York as part of you.

Open Decks and Swimming Pools on the QE2

BON VOYAGE

The Queen lies at anchor
Reigning majestically over dock and city
Dwarfing other ships
As your dreams dwarf reality.
There is a lump in your throat
As you see it
A certain inability to hear what
Those around you are saying.
New shipboard companions crowd the decks
But you do not see them.
Old friends call out goodbye
But you do not hear them.
So busy are you dreaming
Of foreign ports and places.
Suddenly over a loudspeaker
A voice rasps:
"All ashore that's going ashore."
It is your time to stay
Your time for shipping lanes
Sea air…sunshine
Eighty days to be spent
Making dreams come true…On the QE2.

DEPARTURE

Even the world seemed restless on the eve of your departure. After a night of turning, tossing dreams about the little boy who sleeps right through Christmas, you awaken, alarmed by the thought that somehow the ship would sail without you.

Finally, three o'clock comes and you start across town to the pier. Why does it seem that everyone wants to go to the same pier? You remember some wise man saying that we should all travel with as little luggage as possible—mental as well as physical. You wonder how come it took you eleven suitcases to store your gear...

All of a sudden there is the first view of the sea, the sea that reminds you of nature's dignity—its sea-lanes free of parking meters, the fish still masters of their own migrations. Somewhere out there, at the end of the pier, grand things always seem to be happening.

Then there is your first view of the ship, with its gleaming white superstructure and sleek black hull. It's the Tenth Anniversary Voyage of the QE2, and it's so magnificent that you decide any excuse to celebrate this ship will do. It is love at first sight.

There are flowers, music, check-in, and, finally, the gangplank. By four o'clock, a few assorted loved ones, business associates, and other friends are assembled in your stateroom, munching hors d'oeuvres and clinking glasses.

The cabin is large and luxurious, as big as a living room, but it cannot hold you. The wonder of the great ship calls. You start exploring: the Queen's Room, the Double Down nightclub, the Columbian dining room where you will eat, the Queen's Grill where the really rich will dine. Orchestras seem to be playing wherever you go. Friends seem to be casting about for places to stow away. One says, "I never envied anyone anything before, but I envy you this trip."

Suddenly a voice says over a loudspeaker, "All ashore that's going ashore." Like most calamities, it catches everyone flat-footed and has to happen four more times before it is believed.

There are *au revoir*'s and *adieu*'s. No one says "goodbye" to New York.

From the engine room comes the metallic song of 110,000-horsepower turbine engines turning over. It is a thrill-packed, breathtaking, numbing, wobbly-kneed, glorious moment as the "Seven Seas" seems suddenly more than just a phrase.

When the gangplanks have been pulled away and the last line cast off, you join the throng of fellow passengers on some top deck, elbow to elbow, and frantically begin sending sema-phoric messages to the people on the dock below. Why do they all seem so strangely happy to see you go?

The moment of departure is unforgettable. It is early evening but already dark as the great ship swings slowly away from shore into the Hudson. As you move further away and slide along the river, you are treated to one of the world's most spectacular views: the New York skyline on a winter evening.

And as the city slips past, its million tiny twinkling lights cloaked in misty halos, you realize suddenly that you are on your own—at sea—in another world, one more bubbly and intoxicat-ing than any champagne. Your eyes are suddenly moist. Must be the sea air, you think, but you are too wonderfully excited or numb to care. You go below.

The cabin seems strangely quiet, a still life of cigarette butts, empty glasses, and a score of strangely mutilated petit fours that have been bitten into but not eaten. You see what kind of friends you really have—they're nibblers.

From your porthole you look out across the widening expanse of water. The lights of Manhattan slide silently by, the ceaseless racket miraculously stilled. Its skyline remains disdainfully aloof, as if only too willing to dismiss anyone so foolish as to turn his back on its magic. You bid goodbye to the Statue of Liberty, shivering suddenly with pride at being an American.

Soon the towers of the great city are gone. Your world-shrinking journey to the storyland places of your childhood has begun.

All your life you have dreamed of taking a trip on a great ship around the world. Now you are under way. Your bags are in your stateroom and will stay there until you land in New York eighty days later. You will visit the storied lands and places that have peopled your imagination since childhood...the Great Pyramids, the Taj Mahal, the Great Wall of China, the Holy Land. You will stand in the shadow of the Acropolis and the Parthenon in Athens, tour the beautiful harbor of Hong Kong, visit Tokyo and observe the culture of the Orient, set foot at last in a thousand other places of your dreams...dreams that are coming true.

For the next eighty days, except when you will leave for land tours at each port, the ship will be your home. You will enjoy soft beds with fresh white sheets, thick rugs, and beautiful surroundings. You will enjoy the luxury of leisure, good health, the clean and invigorating ocean air, and a great sense of peace of mind.

You remember the statement of a good friend, Dr. Robert Scott: "Something great and wonderful is happening today and I am part of it." Here, on the QE2, are all the ingredients of the good life. It is up to you to enjoy them.

FIRST DAY AT SEA

Stewards' jackets starched to the end
Creaking woodwork
Noon whistle
Morning bouillon
Hum of rigging
The clack of shuffleboard discs on
The boat deck

Smells of tea, floor wax, and salt air
An urge to prove
The world decidedly not flat
If it's all there.
You're either at sea, in love,
Or both.

The first morning you awaken in a large bed, startled by the mahogany paneling and green felt wall-covering. You lie there, wondering where you are. Then you see the sea light dancing on the cabin ceiling.

A voice over the public address system commands all passengers on deck for the lifeboat drill. You are up and looking out the porthole at the North Atlantic. It doesn't look like the world's most dangerous ocean, yet you know that it's a graveyard of ships whose names read like a catalog from Hell. The ship's horn sounds stridently, recalling similar sounds heard by passengers on the *Titanic,* the *Lusitania,* the *Andrea Doria.* In each cabin there are prominent notices which describe instructions for all emergencies—lifeboat station, location of life jackets, how to put them on, and so on.

But there is no actual worry here. The QE2 has double hulls with flow-through bulkheads. She will never go "belly up" like some of her predecessors.

That night all thoughts of disaster are drowned as Captain Robert Arnott throws a large party. The big man has an amusing twinkle in his eye and sounds like fun as he exchanges pleasantries with the passengers crowded around him. He reminds you that there are three sides to a ship—port, starboard, and social.

A ship is an island society and one doesn't waste much time making friends. After what seem like a hundred handshakes, you seek out a corner and just observe. On board ship there is no more commonplace pastime than passenger watching.

Female passengers
Eager for information
On the workings of a ship
And ways of the sea
Unduly detain
Brassbound young officers
Acquiring knowledge
Or a dancing partner.

All is not always what the travel ads indicate. You overhear a woman saying to the chief steward, "I'd like to be placed at a mixed table." She means, of course, one at which men and women are seated alternately.

"Lady, there are none," he replies. "The ratio of women to men is two-to-one, and that's including the married ones."

You commiserate about the lack of justice in the world and wonder where it will all end.

After the party comes your first formal dinner at sea. As you open the menu, you decide that travel by ship is rather pleasant. There is caviar, king crab, sturgeon, smoked Scotch salmon, foie gras, roast duck, Beef Wellington, Soufflé Rothschild—and, pleasantest of all, there is no check.

"But maybe it can't last. Maybe it was a one-shot deal," you think in sudden panic. "What if you run out of food?" you ask your steward, Jonathan.

He launches into a long explanation of the impossibility of such an occurrence. When challenged, he produces the following reasons:

In the United States of America, much of the meat has been taken onto the ship for the cruise. This includes 180,000 pounds of beef, forequarter meat needed for the kosher kitchen on board, loin for steak, prime rib and rump for pot roasts, stews, and hamburgers. During a previous world cruise, the ship consumed 2850 tins of Portuguese sardines, 11,000 pounds of salt, 15,000 gallons of milk, 15,500 pounds of turkey, 25,000 pounds of butter, and 95,000 pounds of tomatoes.

Dishes have evolved to suit the ports of call that the QE2 makes. One may eat ratatouille while cruising off Cannes or drink Turkish coffee after a meal and a day out in Istanbul.

Lunch is also a good time to try many traditionally British recipes or curries. One can have simple things, like tripe and onions or bangers and mash (sausages and creamed potatoes), which Noel Coward adored on the Queens. Scouse is a rather unlovely name for a beef stew originating, like many of the ship's crew, in Liverpool. It is cooked with plenty of vegetables and is good on a cool day. One can finish with a chocolate soufflé made "all right" for dieters by using Sweet 'n Low as its sweetening, or this nursery favorite, Rusk Custard Pudding, long served on the QE2 and the *Queen Elizabeth 1* before her.

One thing is certain, no one will go hungry on the QE2 during any day's cruising. One can choose lighter diet-conscious foods from the lengthy menus and the chef will make dishes for special diets. But with so much good food around, it is a pity to pass up the chance to try it fully at least on some days.

The world cruise order list that has gradually built up on the ship over four to five months is an imbiber's paradise. There are 10,000 bottles of champagne, 27,000 bottles of still wine, 16,500 bottles of spirits, 5000 bottles of port, sherry, and liqueurs, and 45,000 cans and bottles of beer. And for the smokers, there are 2 million cigarettes.

You tell Jonathan you don't smoke.

Satisfied, you leave your table at last to wander forth to explore the ship's entertainment.

You see a library. "It's open," you say hopefully. But as you start to read, you are distracted by the laughing, happy noise of people having a good time coming from the card room beyond. You put the book down. Just as you are about to enter the card room, out of the corner of your eye you see a group of people standing around a map, betting furiously on how many miles the ship will travel in the next twenty-four hours!

Your equilibrium and faith in decorum are reestablished as you leave this group of nautical pirates and join a more sedate group gathering around a large jigsaw puzzle. But, drat, there is the distraction of first one, and then *two* orchestras playing noisily in the background. Past the dancing couples in the Queen's Room you climb to the Boat Deck to see where all the noise is coming from. It turns out to be applause from the Upstairs-Downstairs Nightclub. The room is full of people and the stage is full of beautiful women dancing in a way that is more naughty than nautical, while pretending to sing.

You decide instead to go see a movie. As you come out of the theater two hours later, a jewel-bedecked dowager precedes you. Emerging, she momentarily forgets she is on a ship, goes over to a steward and says imperiously, "Young man, call me a taxi."

You swallow hard to keep from laughing and duck through some swinging doors. You find yourself in the Casino, where you are startled to see crowds of earnest gamblers pushing and shoving to lose their money as they pursue their luck at the roulette and blackjack tables.

There is an old Arabic fable about a great ruler who was sick. A sage came to him and he asked the sage how he could recover from his illness. The sage replied, "You must find a happy man, a man who is really happy in life, and wear his shirt."

So the ruler sent around the world to find the happy man. At last he found one, but the man had no shirt. He had lost it in the Casino on the QE2!

As you start back toward your stateroom, you see banquet tables being spread for a midnight buffet. One thing is sure, you certainly won't starve to death!

LEARNING ABOUT THE SHIP

On your second morning at sea, you are up early, eager to learn how the QE2 works. You see a young, wind-burnished face over an officer's uniform, and naively ask to see the engine room.

"No one has been allowed in the engine room or on the bridge since 1974," he says patiently, like a father talking to an unruly child.

You grimace, but surmising that he's a kind officer—the knowledgeable kind—you push him to educate you: "I imagine the engine room is a maze of ladders, shafts, pistons, boilers, pipes, electrical conduit, switch panels, gauges, and mysterious plumbing. I'd probably get dirty down there, anyway," you suggest.

"No. It's more like an operating room in a modern hospital. There's no smoke or grease, and the whole thing is amazingly quiet."

"Oh," you say, "even when the engines are running?"

He then proceeds to tell you how the engines work. It seems that two sets of giant boilers heat water to steam. The steam drives giant windmill-like structures, creating a current of air, and this makes the propellers turn. There are two of them, each with six blades instead of the four-blade kind used on the old Queen.

"So, it's just like a steam kettle?" you suggest.

"More like two. One big and one little. The high-pressure boilers, the small ones, heat the water to around 950 degrees, and the low-pressure boilers, the larger ones, reheat it to about half that."

You nod thoughtfully to show you understand, and then ask, "Why is it so smooth? I hardly know I'm at sea."

"Side stabilizers automatically work off the gyroscope as the blunt, whale-shaped nose pushes the water away. That's why we literally glide through the sea."

"The ship is so tall—thirteen or fourteen stories—I'm surprised it isn't top-heavy," you observe wisely.

"An aluminum superstructure, from two decks up, is bolted to the steel hull. The lightweight top gives stability."

"Why is the number 736 everywhere? The name of the Casino, the plaque on the top deck, and so on?" you ask.

"That's the QE2's shipyard designation. It was called 736 when it was built by John Brown's in Scotland."

"And its speed?"

"Top speed is around twenty-nine knots. That's about thirty-three miles an hour."

"The ship seems immense. How big is it?"

"106 feet beam, 973 feet long," he answers tersely.

"How will we ever get through the Panama Canal?" you wonder out loud.

"We'll have five inches on each side to spare," he says proudly. "The big oil tankers only have three inches."

"Must cost a lot to run," you suggest.

"Burns a ton of oil a mile. Cost is now over 200 dollars a ton, so that makes over 200 dollars a mile."

"What about its water supply?"

"Can distill 1200 gallons of water a day from sea water."

He is a man of few words, but he manages to say a lot.

Standing on the boat deck after the officer is gone, you can't help but reflect on the old ships—the sailing ships that traveled these same waters. There is something about a ship that upsets one's brain, and you think of William Dana going to

California on a clipper ship, remembering all the adventure contained in *Two Years Before the Mast.* You look out and, in your mind's eye, you can almost see him.

The ocean is wide, the sea has room for all, but gone are the pulley, the flooded decks of the dear old sailing ships, their sailors singing at their work. Now there are only thumping, thudding engines, immune to wind and weather, run by technicians with nothing to do but navigate, fighting gallantly to keep aware of the machine. And, you think with regret, you have not two years to reach California, but two weeks. You must be incredibly romantic to miss what you never knew except in books. You look up at the wisp of black smoke trailing the sky and miss the mastheads all covered with sea-lace and the God-men who hoisted them into place, disappeared with the necessity of trade winds.

Now, as computers compile data from satellites and celestial navigation is done only by God, the boundaries of progress clearly crossed, you wonder what has been gained...and lost.

It is early afternoon as the great ship moves in toward Florida, riding the current of warmth that first caresses the coast above the luxury winter palaces of Palm Beach. The Gulf Stream has gentled the cold winds of the North Atlantic. The touch of the sun is warm on your cheeks as you hurry out on deck for your first docking. There is a new excitement in the air, the sense that you have just completed a sort of "shakedown cruise," getting your sea legs under you.

You watch the gleaming towers and the lush landscape of Florida's Gold Coast take shape on the horizon. You have reached Port Everglades!

Young Alligator—Fort Lauderdale, Florida

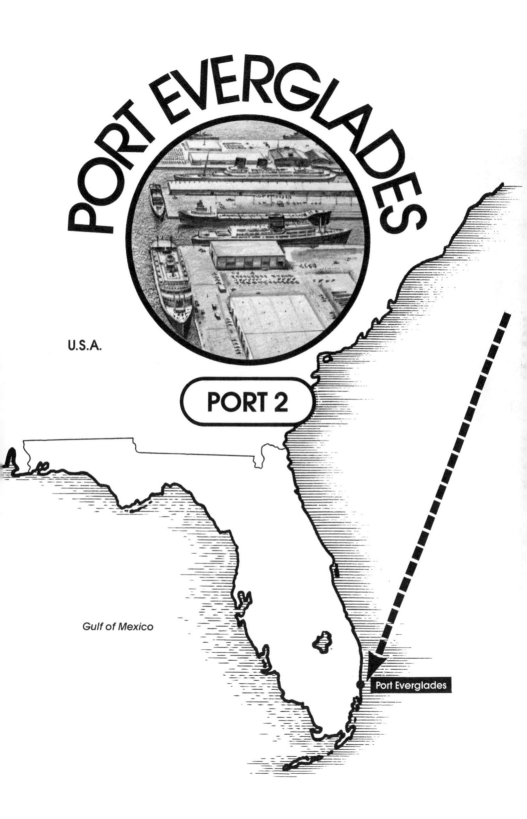

PORT EVERGLADES

U.S.A.

PORT 2

Gulf of Mexico

Port Everglades

The Double Down Room

PORT EVERGLADES

You see it first from the Third Avenue Drawbridge, looking out to the Keys, to Cuba, to the litter of flat, melancholy islands that stretch all the way to South America. It's your first port of call—Port Everglades, or Fort Lauderdale.

When you arrive here, you are already in the Caribbean. Dozens of cruise ships use it as their starting point and each pays homage...and money.

Port Everglades is a modern waterfront town built to a purpose, designed for the cruise traveler. Situated by the sea, it serves as gangway to the Caribbean. Located at Fort Lauderdale on Florida's Gold Coast, at the confluence of three rivers, undisturbed by mountains or memories, it prospers in the sun, profiting from others' escapist pleasures through its contrived floating restaurants and modern shopping centers.

Its promenade is the waterfront, intermittently dressed up with esplanades and monuments, but in essence it is really a working quay. As you travel along Las Olas Boulevard and eagerly ogle the shops along this little Fifth Avenue, you learn that Port Everglades has the deepest moorings in Florida. The Bahia Mar Marina is not only the largest in Florida, but one of the largest in the world. (It also boasts some of the area's best restaurants.) If you ignore the Norfolk pine and paper trees and squint a little, the yachts, boats, and ships can be seen to stretch along 270 miles of slips and waterways, making Port Everglades seem like the Venice of America. You stop and shop and it seems more like Paris.

You wonder how it came to be and if Port Everglades was built on sound economic necessity or just some land developer's daydreams. Then you find the answer. In today's busy world, who would want to waste forty-eight hours on sunless skies and feel the brace of ice-cold real North Atlantic sea spray, douse their clothes, and ruin their hair? Why, no one, of course. No one who really counts—and that is why New York, a victim of its own disdain of boredom, has been knocked out of still another title— the busiest port in the country. That title now belongs to—you guessed it—Port Everglades.

But you have only a few hours here, and in the early evening, as lights begin to sketch the waterfront and to define the inland passage, new voyagers crowd the decks to bid land and friends goodbye. Even you, veteran already of the excitement of departure, are not immune.

Quietly you cruise out of the inlet, past gleaming new high-rises that crowd the ocean's edge, until at last you break free once more, riding into the open sea. You turn your face toward the south, eager now, your spirit already looking past the white towers of Miami, past the sand-dollar islands of the Keys, toward the sun-drenched Caribbean.

Winter lies behind you, its tenacious grip broken at last. A festive atmosphere fills the QE2's four gracious restaurants this evening. Seventy-eight days to go...your party has really begun!

For three nights and two days, you sail the Caribbean, glorying in the brilliance and warmth of sun-drenched decks, blue skies, and matching seas. At night the ship seems caught between two brilliant deep-blue mirrors, sea and sky. The Caribbean, far from January's cottony bluster, is like soft, warm silk.

You marvel that Columbus sailed these same waters in three ships smaller than today's tugboats. Though you sail in your own luxurious resort-hotel-at-sea, all the pristine adventure is still there.

There is time now to discover the ship, the passengers, the view—and perhaps to start rediscovering yourself. Eyes grow clearer and softer at sea. The lines of tension melt away as if by magic. The laughter heard along the decks and passages is more spontaneous, more free.

It is about this time that you've settled down enough to notice the other passengers, and certain familiar faces emerge out of the sea of shipmates.

There's the lady from Brazil you chat with one day. She tells you her son offered her a new apartment or a trip around the world. Smart lady—she took the trip.

Then there is a pair of pretty sisters—identical twins—who dress alike and look as if they might have done so all their lives. When they appear like a double vision at the Captain's cocktail party, you feel as if you might have had one too many. As the trip progresses, you come to look for them together and you would be doubly concerned if they failed to appear someday.

Then there's the fashion model, an amazingly beautiful woman who seems to have found the secret of eternal youth. You're told that she has married well and occupies two staterooms, one for herself and one for her clothes. You're also told that if you admire something she's wearing, she is in the business and can get it for you—for a price.

Another lady, you learn, was mugged in New York and decided to take this trip where she would be safe. If everyone could afford such a wonderful solution to the crime problem, New York would surely look like a nest of lemmings following each other off its granite rocks into the sea.

There are a lot of military people on board. One day a man is sitting in your deck chair and you shoo him off unceremoniously, only to discover later that he is an admiral. When you remember that you were only a seaman apprentice second class, you begin to realize what a wonderfully democratic world the QE2 really is.

These are also the first days when the QE2's swimming pools on the two open upper decks are crowded with handsome men and beautiful women seeking to use the golden Caribbean sun to acquire their own 24-karat tans. With the bikinis and other fashionably cut bathing suits on display, it is a good time for looking, as well as sunning.

An old man, bent with age and arthritis, his face lined with wrinkles from too many wars and winters, makes his cane-directed way across the deck and you wonder if he spent his health to gain his wealth and is now busily engaged in spending his wealth to get back his health. You ponder whether that is his story or just your own perverse imagination. You make a mental note to watch your own weight, get enough exercise, maybe dance a little more tonight, and then take a walk around deck afterwards.

As you sail the Caribbean toward your next port of call, you feel you're really getting into the swim of things, not just in the pool, but through becoming more active and alive. The sun is still shining on an azure sea, and it is good to be and feel alive. You decide that the real entertainment on board is in you. In your eager desire to look ahead, you put your face to the wind and look out toward South America, scanning the horizon for new things yet to come!

Recreation on the QE2

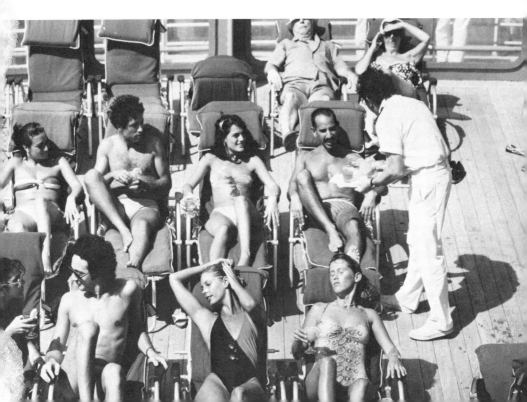

**Recreation
on the QE2**

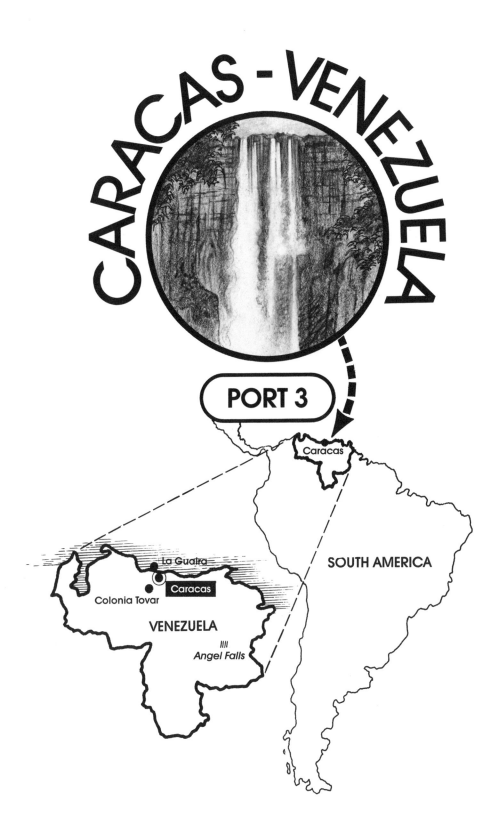

CARACAS - VENEZUELA

PORT 3

Caracas

SOUTH AMERICA

La Guaira

Caracas

Colonia Tovar

VENEZUELA

||||
Angel Falls

CARACAS, VENEZUELA

It is dawn in La Guaira, the hot place, and already a line of ships, both tramps and ladies, are fighting for a place at her sand bar, hoping to get loaded, as you arrive.

You dock thirty miles east of the city, feeling the trade winds blowing from east to west, constantly erasing the clouds, wiping clear the crayon blue sky along the Spanish main.

You come ashore, the anticipation of a full day of sightseeing ahead of you. A bus is waiting and soon you're climbing from the port, 3000 feet up. Above are red hills, beyond are roads that lead to freeways, freeways that lead to Caracas. On both sides are green growing things that look as if they might grow across the road and reclaim the whole scene if you just look away for an instant. Mesquite plants poke their heads above the rest, pretending they didn't really belong there.

From the mountaintop, it almost takes your breath away as you see a hundred flamingos flying in a scarlet cloud from the beaches of Estación del Mar, heading south over the dense jungle rain forests, green valleys, and exuberant architecture of pastel painted towns to Lake Maracaibo—little Venice—where the oil is. Where the money is. Or maybe they're heading beyond to the tall blue mountains of the Andes.

You arrive at the top of the coastal finger of mountains and observe Caracas itself, sprawling eastward and westward for about ten miles in a freeway-bisected valley by the sea. It's a town that's been both advantaged and disadvantaged by an oil boom, a town still searching for its El Dorado.

City of growing pains
City of people pains
Skeletons of buildings
Rising from jungle floors
Skeleton-like people in the dark
Cast shadows on lean-tos and worried politicians.

Cement city
Brick city
City of trucks and buses, cars and noises
And steel cranes
All working for the hill people
Hoping they will remain the still people.

Past and present and future crowd together in modern Caracas. Native houses cling like growing things to all the hills, in sharp contrast to the steel-and-glass towers of high-rises springing up everywhere, thrusting Caracas into the late twentieth century. The past lives, too, in rich colonial churches and castles, in the memories of pirates and Spanish dons—and most of all, Simón Bolívar.

In the early 1800s, Simón Bolívar, "The Great Liberator," led the first of the colonial rebellions against Spanish rule, a revolt that united people born in the New World by pitting them against the Old. Bolívar freed Venezuela, Colombia, Ecuador, and Panama from the Spanish yoke. He had a dream of one democratic, united republic for all of these nations, a dream that floundered for awhile after the Spanish were driven out in 1823, but one that still lives in the hearts of today's Caraqueños.

Bolívar is everywhere in Caracas…in his birthplace, Casa Natal, and his final resting place at the Pantheon…in the Plaza Bolívar at the center of the old city…in the heroic paintings on display at the capital and in the parade of monuments, street names, and place names. The sightseeing tour traces his modest memory at each of these historic sites, amid the spectacular luxury of the exclusive Country Club residential district, the lavish Officers' Club at Military Circle, the lushly landscaped beauty of Universal City, the gleaming towers of modern office buildings and luxury hotels.

Lunch is served in the restaurant of the Hilton, a welcome oasis after the striking contrasts of the busy city outside. Caracas offers many fine restaurants that reflect its cosmopolitan character today—French, Italian, and American cuisine equal to any found in the world's great cities. El Portón, on the Avenida Pichinchao, specializes in Venezuelan dishes. Most of Caracas's better restaurants are expensive, but worth it. Another stop of interest is Le Drugstore, in Centro Comercial Chacaito, a huge, crowded, and colorful shopping center as popular with native Caraqueños as with visitors.

Looking at the forest of cranes and Caterpillars working furiously to rehouse the hill people, one wonders if Caracas will find its El Dorado or just remain the Land of Eternal Promise, the tomorrow that can't quite become today.

While the battle to build a better tomorrow for the hill people rages on, millions of affluent Caraqueños—an open, casual people—live their lives in a forest of apartment houses, venturing forth to bullfights, art galleries, horse races, or just sitting in lavish restaurants or sidewalk cafés, gesticulating wildly about local gossip. If an orchid petal falls into their food...why, that's the risk they take.

ANGEL FALLS

For others among your fellow adventurers, the day held a different and equally spectacular excursion deeper into the heart of Venezuela. From La Guaira, the coach rides over the barrier range of mountains, offering its passengers striking views of Caracas before depositing them at Simón Bolívar Airport.

From there, a short plane flight carries you from modern city sophistication to one of the world's most spectacular unspoiled wonders—Angel Falls. The plane circles the falls again and again, its passengers unable to get their fill of this stunning vision. It is the highest waterfall in the world, fifteen times as high as Niagara Falls. Its first great fall plummets over 3000 feet in a dazzle of light and color and force.

Nothing can beat the rush of water
The exhilaration
Physically shaken
More an eruption than a fall.

Poets must tremble to capture its beauty and power, as the mountain itself trembles to its shuddering fall.

You land at Canaima, itself spectacularly situated on a bluff overlooking the lagoon, which is fed by seven separate cascading waterfalls, the lower falls called Hucha Falls. Surrounded by the dense green jungle with its brilliant flora and fauna, you lunch at a rustic lodge at the edge of the rose-colored lagoon. There is time here for the travelers to rest and relax, to allow the mind to cope with the beauty of the scene and the wondrous cataract, a vista hidden from all but a few for most of the world's history.

Angel Falls might have been named for heavenly visitors, or simply for its vision of beauty. It wasn't. It got its name from another adventurer, a busy pilot and gold prospector named Jimmy Angel. He had piloted another prospector into the area in the late 1920s when gold was found. Jimmy Angel came back in the mid-thirties, himself searching for the lost area. Instead, he crashed in the jungle, survived, and discovered Angel Falls.

Some discoveries are more precious than gold.

From Caracas you may choose, instead of riding back to the port by coach, to take the cable car that rises above the valley to the peak of Mount Avila, at the top of the coastal range. It is only a short ten-minute ride to the top from the Caracas side, and it is well worth the trip. There's a good restaurant and shops at the peak, but the view is the reason for going there. To the north is a panorama of the Venezuelan coastline, the port far below, the beaches, the blue mirror of the Caribbean. And to the south stretches the long valley. You're at an altitude of 7000 feet above sea level, and the entire city of Caracas opens out to your astonished gaze.

Reluctantly, you turn away and board the cable car again, a twenty-five-minute ride down the coastal side to the sea and the waiting ship.

Each return to the QE2 is like a homecoming. Here is the luxurious retreat of your cabin, also the excited meetings with your new friends, a sharing of experiences and memories and reflections upon what you have just seen. Here you can unwind, relax again, enjoy the serenity of being catered to, pampered, and entertained.

It is dark when the anchor is finally raised. The moon comes up over the Caribbean. There is music and the cool caress of the trade winds. You retire early but happy, your thoughts full of what you have discovered this day, of man's ceaseless energy and Nature's glory.

ENJOY NOW

People spend their lives in anticipation
Of being extremely happy in the future.
But all we own is the PRESENT...NOW
PAST opportunities are gone.
FUTURE opportunities may or may not come.
NOW is all we have...
We must enjoy each day—one at a time.
We are here on a short visit...
Be sure to smell the flowers.

Simón Bolívar Monument—Caracas

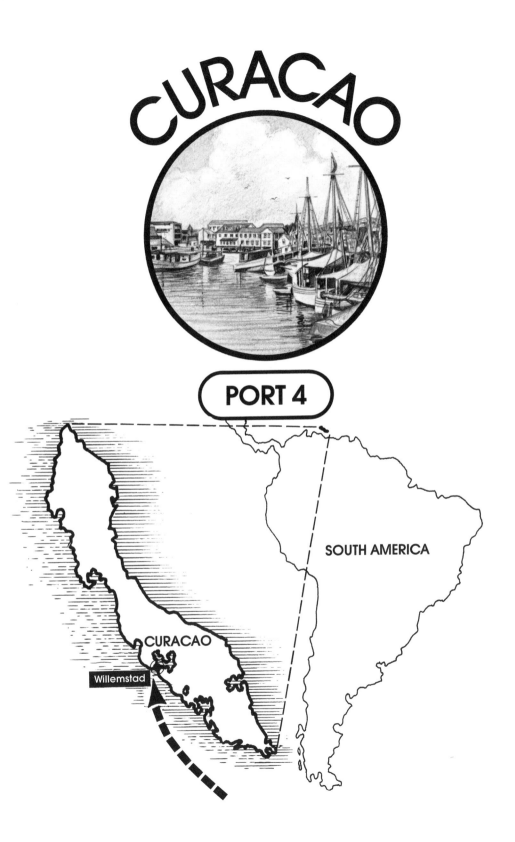

CURACAO

PORT 4

CURACAO

Willemstad

SOUTH AMERICA

CURACAO

Curacao (pronounced *cure-a-sow)* lies just forty miles off the coast of Venezuela. The QE2 makes the voyage at night across a serene span of tropical sea and dawn finds you abreast of the island, a twenty-four-mile-long sliver of sand, cactus and divi-divi trees that is the largest in the six-island group of the Netherlands Antilles.

In Willemstad, Curacao's principal city, gabled eighteenth-century Dutch houses, painted in all manner of pastels, evoke a tale of Hans Christian Andersen told in a provincial Papiamento accent—a happy fairy tale of a city. Legend has it that an early governor, a man given to headaches, blamed his affliction on the hot sun reflecting on the vibrant white used to paint the houses. Enraged and in pain one day, he had a law passed decreeing that only non-white paint was to be used—hence the variety of multi-colored houses that characterize the city to this day...or so they say.

The first Dutch governor of the island was peg-leg Peter Stuyvesant, who had his leg shot off in a clash with the Spanish. This same Peter Stuyvesant was later transferred to become governor of the new Dutch colony in North America, called New Amsterdam—and later New York. But today, a ghost from the past, old peg-leg is still there to greet visitors arriving at the waterfront. This is a coveted role among local actors—in spite of the one-legged performance required.

Among other novel sights is the Queen Emma bridge, built on pontoons, which swivels from one end, swinging out of the way to let ships enter along the passageway. The town is actually bisected by the waterway and smaller ships dock in the center of town. When the Queen Emma, which links the two parts of the city, swings open on its pontoons, pedestrians scramble and automobiles screech to an impatient stop.

Queen Emma was originally a toll bridge built in the nineteenth century, exacting a two-cent fee from each person walking across. There was a provision meant to exempt the poor from paying the toll; it exempted anyone who was not wearing shoes. In time the toll had to be abandoned because it didn't work out. It seems that the industrious but genuinely poor Dutch settlers would borrow shoes to cross the bridge rather than admit their poverty. The prosperous, on the other hand, were said to leave their shoes at home rather than pay the two-cent tolls!

The best place to see all this is from the new bridge, the Queen Juliana—a 185-foot-high archway looking down on the pontooned perch. It is the tallest span in the Caribbean. Nearby are some of Curacao's finest shops. It is not strictly speaking a "duty-free" port, but it is tax-free, and excellent buys can be found.

Two half-day motor coach tours of the island are set up for the QE2's visitors, one leaving in the morning and the other in the afternoon. You choose to wander the town yourself in the morning, visiting the stores and meeting some of the friendly people of the island. The official language is Dutch, but the people speak a polyglot *Papiamento,* a lively mixture of French, Dutch, Spanish, Portuguese, and Indian, a language that contains the whole history of the Caribbean. But everyone seems to speak English wherever you go.

The fairy tale atmosphere of Willemstad continues in the Floating Market, a romantic series of schooners and sailing vessels loaded with fruits and vegetables, silks and satins, with only a few glazed-eyed fish thrown in to give a touch of reality.

Eating fine food is one of the things the Dutch enjoy most and, as you learn at lunchtime, Willemstad is no exception. The restaurants here are proud of their "Dutch-size" servings—

meaning huge. Among the most popular choices is *rijsttafel*. It starts with rice and includes a rich variety of side dishes, more than you can eat. There are several small, inviting restaurants along the waterfront that offer charm and a view as well as good food.

In the afternoon, pleasantly overstuffed and relaxed, you take the coach tour leaving the pier at two o'clock. You drive past the home of the U. S. Consul General at Mount Arrarat, through Scharloo with its colorful Dutch houses, catching glimpses of divi-divi plants along the way.

In the center of town is the oldest synagogue in the Western Hemisphere, built in 1732. Fleeing the Spanish and then the Portuguese Inquisition, Jews were among the first settlers of the Western Hemisphere. Beth Haim, a cemetery that was set up in 1659, is still in use, and one can still see the stones placed by the faithful to mark their visits. Though the chemically laden air from the adjacent oil refinery is rapidly eating away at the inscriptions, one is sure they will not be forgotten.

A pretty guide explains that though the island was settled by the Dutch in 1634, and its leaders had the foresight to be the first sovereign power to recognize American independence in 1776, it wasn't until oil was discovered in nearby Venezuela in 1914 and Royal Dutch Shell built one of the world's largest refineries that Curacao really came into its own. Today its 160,000 people, 40,000 cars, and 30,000 goats still live off the 600,000 barrels-a-day refinery, only supplementing their income from the shops and tourist attractions. And it looks as if this will continue for some time. It is difficult to imagine ships almost five times the tonnage of the QE2, yet these do exist and their future is linked closely with that of Curacao. The natural depth of its harbor can accommodate these behemoths of the sea—the new Queens, the 300,000-ton supertankers that slip in and out on their way from the Mideast to the United States. Oil has made Curacao one of the major commercial ports, not only in the Caribbean, but in the world.

One of the highlights of the tour, as it is for every visitor to the island, is a stop at the famous Curacao Liqueur Factory on the northeast side of the harbor. The famed liqueur is still made from a secret family recipe in small quantities. Its principal ingredient is a small green orange called *laraha*, which is grown only on Curacao. It's said that attempts have been made to grow it elsewhere, but it turns into an ordinary orange when planted in other soil. You are given a paper cup to sample and, cradling it fondly in your hands, you return to the QE2.

Leaving the island is like closing the cover on a favorite fairy tale. You carry away (along with your tax-free "finds") memories of a prosperous, neat, and happy land—as Dutch as a place can be without windmills, tulips, and wooden shoes.

Largest Shell Oil Refinery in the World—Curacao

THINGS YOU CANNOT BUY

Life's richest treasures are within:
A heart full of love
A friendly word
A cheerful smile
A thoughtful kiss
An act of kindness

All of these must be developed by you. The greatest responsibility given to every man is the development of self.

THE PAMPERED LIFE

Years ago, a person who traveled around the world was considered something of a hero because he put up with so many hardships. As you cruise the Caribbean out of Curacao, enjoying two more nights and a warm day in the sun, you cannot help reflecting on how, traveling on the QE2, you are pampered every wave of the way. You may be called a globe-trotter but you are traveling in the lap of luxury.

The ship is like a floating hotel. You put your bags in your stateroom when you come aboard and they stay there until you disembark. It is the ideal way to go when you're going to stop at many ports. You can bring all the things you buy onto the ship— souvenirs, rugs, pictures, furniture, whatever. The QE2 hauls it free of charge if you are a passenger.

You have traveled over a million miles by air in the course of your lifetime and you have appreciated the speed of air transportation. But you have always been tired at the end of a long flight, wishing you could have gone to bed when you were suffering from jet lag.

The Queen makes it so much easier—and so much more fun. As you settle down to some serious sunbathing on the aft deck, the Caribbean—in fact, the whole world—looks pretty good. This, you think, is truly the pampered life.

If sunbathing and girl (or boy) watching is not your cup of tea, or if your aquatic abilities are something short of Olympian, there's a golf driving range and a miniature golf course that should suit you to a tee. Or perhaps skeet shooting or table tennis are for you, or exercise classes under the expert eye of Eric Mason, the QE2 Athletic Director.

If you're more the sedentary type, the bar opens early and should all those Piña Coladas make you hungry, there are hamburgers and hot dogs from 11:30 on to keep you from starving before the real buffet lunch on the quarter deck is served at 12:30.

If the sun holds no magic for you and your bridge and backgammon need improving, there are experts aboard who can hone your skills to a razor-sharp edge in a few lessons' time. Or maybe craft classes, lectures on the stock market or the places you'll visit, or demonstrations of flower arranging are more to your liking. Some of the lecturers on past trips have included Lillian Gish, Moira Shearer, Ludovic Kennedy, Lord Lichfield, and the Duke and Duchess of Bedford.

Better hurry. There's lunch, and after that...

You don't want to be late for the tea dance at four and somehow there's always, always more.

There are tea and biscuits in the afternoon, new movies every day, dancing every evening in the Queen's Room, nightly show acts in the Up-Down Room. There's a reading room, a card room, bingo games and other social activities, a library with an attendant, a gymnasium, a barber shop, a beauty shop, a chiropodist, a manicurist, and more. Barclay's Bank has two offices on the ship. Thomas Cook has a tour office. Every morning a "QE2 News" is put under your cabin door. Together with the daily bulletin, called "A Festival of Life," you are kept apprised of everything that is going on day or night.

There are religious services on ship for all faiths and denominations, including Roman Catholic services and Holy Mass, services for the Jewish faith, Episcopalian and Anglican services, Christian Science services, and Bible discussion groups.

This is the stress-free way to travel—which is what travel should be all about. Stress and worry are the biggest killers of mankind today. They're not part of your baggage on the QE2.

Casino on the QE2

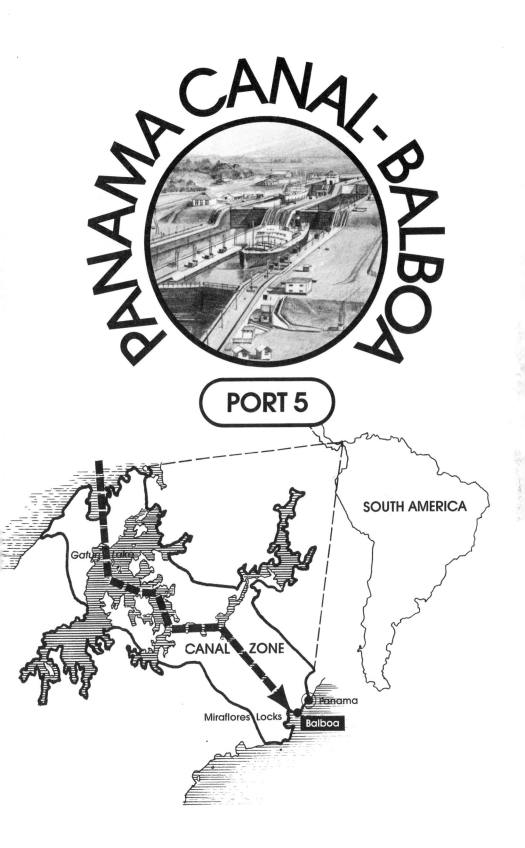

PANAMA CANAL · BALBOA

PORT 5

SOUTH AMERICA

Gatun Lake

CANAL ZONE

Miraflores Locks

Panama

Balboa

Gatun Locks on the Atlantic Side of the Panama

THE PANAMA CANAL—BALBOA

It is six o'clock in the morning when the QE2 gently eases into the first of the Gatun Locks at the entrance to the Panama Canal. You watch philosophically as two tour groups leave the ship in the early morning—one group bound for Old Panama by bus across the peninsula, the other scheduled to fly to the nearby San Blas Islands, home of the Cuna Indians. One cannot do everything. Travel on the Queen, like life itself, offers rich choices. But in this case there's no problem of choice. It's the Canal that interests you.

One doesn't take just a nine-hour voyage on the world's busiest waterway. To traverse the Canal is to travel back in time to when it all began...and to relive it all again, you quickly scan your history books...

On his fourth voyage in 1502, Columbus searches frantically along the coast of what he thinks is the Malay Peninsula, looking for a passage to India—to break the overland monopoly of Venice. Seeking silks and spice, he finds only impenetrable jungle and Indians. Brokenhearted, he returns to Valladolid to die, a failure's death.

Balboa comes with the extraordinary strategy of befriending the natives and, in 1509, is transported magically across the isthmus on their shoulders and allowed to gaze on the Pacific Ocean from a palm tree.

Spain's King Carlos V even contemplates building a canal in 1524, but finally decides imperiously that "no one should separate what God has joined together."

The city of Portobelo is built on the Atlantic coast as the join-up point for Peruvian gold—the destination of the donkey caravans that keep Spain strong. Then come the freebooters, the marauders, the pirates to cut this slender throat of Spain's power. By 1700, they burn and pillage and finally succeed.

Panama sleeps for centuries under the Southern Cross— nine degrees north of Hell. The humidity-soaked Indians watch dispassionately as the daily rains trickle brown soil into jade-green water. Swamp-bred night things, flying things, seek blood to quench their thirst, bright green slime to lay their eggs—progeny to protect their jungle for posterity—their posterity. Finally, the long sleep ends as Ferdinand de Lesseps, the builder of the Suez Canal, fresh from desert victories, decides to rend the land and join the seas. The mosquitoes hear of his pretension and buzz with laughter.

The mosquitoes make the desert sands seem hospitable, turning man's projects into idle boasts. They drive out the French but 22,000 corpses are left behind, victims of yellow fever, malaria, and madmen's dreams.

Finally, in 1903, America looks at this crossways of agony and in Congress boasts are heard of connecting the two oceans, cinching the wasp waist of the Americas with a belt of locks and canyons, uniting the nations, old world and new. What really cinches the vote is that Teddy Roosevelt thinks it's the best way to move a battleship from one ocean to another. The battle is fixed, man versus land. Man versus mosquito.

Engineers with a taste for dirt, sweating workers with a taste for rum and dollars, nameless faces unknown to fame, fight mosquitoes with a taste for blood in a decidedly tasteless jungle, fighting constantly to reclaim man's work. It's a win-a-few, lose-a-few battle—thirty-four years of pain and suffering driving toward an uncertain conclusion, a kind of old Vietnam—the Americans determined to finish what the French had started.

Man takes his first giant step into space. The yellow, hot space around each worker, filled with microscopic malevolence and other hardships too numerous to mention. The U.S. chooses Walter Reed to be its first explorer.

Through fifty miles of Yellow Jack, the ultimate hole in the ground is dug, its cost not measured in dollars but in men per mile.

Slowly, surely, the earth renders itself to untimid dreams, and the jungle beats a silent, sultry retreat. Broken, the land surrenders to man and his projects and lies back to receive half a million ships.

Walter Reed and Teddy Roosevelt frown from their graves when, in our time, Omar Torrijos Herrera says, "We, the Panamanians, did this. It is ours—give it back." And a billion young mosquito eggs listen to his boasts and wait patiently, malevolently hoping for a more fertile tomorrow.

In mid-afternoon, having climbed the watery steps of this engineering miracle, the QE2 descends into the Pacific, laying anchor off Balboa. For those who choose, there is a late afternoon tour of Balboa, of historic Panama City and its old colonial churches, of the ruins of Old Panama.

You go, but when, an hour before midnight that warm evening, the ship bears you out on the bosom of the new ocean, it is not the modern suburbs or the ancient cathedrals that linger in your mind, but the men who dug and fought and died, the men who made a miracle.

THE QUEEN'S MEASURE

Perhaps it was the memory of so much hardship behind you, that evening out of Balboa, that made you think with such affection of the sheer luxury you can enjoy on the QE2, this miracle of construction in her own right, almost 1000 feet in length and thirteen stories high.

The Queen is a beautiful ship. One look at her and you know that something *good* is about to happen to you. She is a perfect blend of artistry and design, complete with stabilizers to keep her steady and every modern technology—with a tradition of quality and service and, like the monarch whose name she bears, full of gaiety and regal charm.

On deck that evening you fill your lungs with clean, fresh ocean air. Just let the Queen chauffeur you around the world. The stress will melt off your body like icicles melting in the hot June sun.

When you go below, you look at your stateroom with fresh, admiring eyes. Staterooms on the QE2 are nothing short of lavish, designed by the best interior decorators on both sides of the Atlantic. Whether first class or transatlantic class, staterooms have wall-to-wall carpeting, individual climate control, and are ideal for living as well as gracious entertaining. Yours is, you think, so nice to come home to.

ENTERTAINMENT ON THE QE2

While cruising toward Acapulco, you settle down and start becoming an habitué of the Double Down Nightclub. Every night after dinner you make your appearance just in time to get a front row seat on a million dollars' worth of entertainment.

One night you meet Brian Price and become fully aware of what it means to have the job of keeping the passengers on a luxury liner like the QE2 from being bored.

Brian Price has been employed by the Cunard Lines for seventeen years, and he has been Cruise Director since 1974, prior to the QE2's first world cruise in 1975. He is thirty-six years old, married, with three children, and his home is in Wales.

Besides producing a formidable program of entertainment for the entire voyage, he is also responsible for the social director and for maintaining a liaison between Thomas Cook's shore excursions and the operation of the ship.

But his first and most important duty, in his own words, is "to make sure that, as best I possibly can, the passengers on board the QE2 are quite happy to be here," which means public relations, meeting and talking to passengers, solving problems, and coping with the strange and unexpected happenings that inevitably occur on board a great ship.

Price tells you that he oversees musicians and entertainers, crew staff and social staff, plus all the guest speakers and lecturers—well over a hundred in all. This is impressive enough but later on you learn that Price, with typical British understatement, modestly omits to tell you that the total number of entertainers employed during the course of a world cruise— dancers, singers, and others at twenty-nine ports of call—adds up to a cast of about a thousand people. Not only that, but he keeps passengers up to date on all that's happening with a four-page news flyer called "The Festival of Life on the QE2."

You decide to ask him how he finds the time to do it all.

"It's nothing, really," he says modestly. "To give people the fun they pay for, that's my job really. Let me tell you just a small part of what's available. For daytime there are golf lessons, clay pigeon shooting, deck sports tournaments with table tennis, shuffleboard, and swimming contests, and various other events on the outer decks. Inside, card parties and lectures, classes of various types—from painting to yoga to flower arranging—all taught in appropriate languages."

"And at night?" you ask, nodding toward a chorus line of beautiful women, trying to help him along.

"Nighttime entertainment also runs the gamut of taste. There is the cultural—lectures, plays, operas, and classical music performed by the artists on board."

"And the movies," you add helpfully.

"The theater is a focal point of the entertainment program. The QE2 is one of the few ships in the world that shows a different movie every day during the course of the world cruise. The popular theater is in use from nine o'clock in the morning until one, then again from two-thirty in the afternoon till midnight. On Sunday, the theater is used for religious services."

"And the nightclubs," you add, applauding as the girls move off-stage.

"Yes, the popular main shows play twice each evening, featuring well-known entertainers. Joe Loss's orchestra is one of the finest in the world, and let's not forget the Rob Charles Orchestra and two small bands in the nightclub. For the more trendy set, there is also a discothèque in the Theater Bar.

"The QE2, in short, has something for everyone and each show is changed every ten days to keep both the audience and the entertainers fresh. Which reminds me. I've got to freshen up for dinner."

Price leaves.

The girls dance back on-stage. You stay.

Dining Room—One of Five on the QE2

DINING WITH THE QUEEN

Feasting on the *Queen Elizabeth 2* is like being at an endless party where the elegant host and hostess have thought of everything. There are several large dining rooms: the Columbia Room, the Princess Grill, and the Queen's Grill. The Tables of the World dining room is assigned to the passengers in accordance with the cost of their staterooms. But wherever your table is, you will dine in elegant splendor.

Each meal is a gourmet event. Sample from the 20,000-bottle wine cellar, one of the finest on land or sea. The cuisine is decidedly Continental and includes five-course English breakfasts and seven-course luncheons. The head waiter will come to your table and ask if you would like something special for dinner that isn't on the menu. They delight in making something special for you.

And there's much more. You can have your room steward bring your meals to your room. You can have fresh fruit in your room at all times. There is a hot dog and hamburger stand on the Lido Deck that also serves salads and beverages. When you are "tired" of steak or lobster, you can have many a pleasant lunch *al fresco* on the open deck, at a table, or at your own deck chair.

And....

- "Earlybird" coffee is available on the One Deck Lido from 7:30 to 8:00 A.M. and from 11:00 A.M. to 3:30 P.M.

- An excellent buffet lunch is served on the Quarter Deck Lido from 12:30 P.M. to 2:00 P.M.

- Afternoon tea is served in the Queen's Room, the Double Down Room, and on the Open Decks, weather permitting. Tea Music by the Joe Loss Trio is an extra bonus.

- A Midnight Buffet is served in the Columbia Restaurant from midnight to 1:00 A.M. for all guests.

Best of all, perhaps, is the delightful knowledge that you can have all you can eat or drink for free. The bars are the only place you have to pay or charge the bill of fare to your account or room.

But too much good living has its own price, as you discover. Along about the time you are cruising past Central America on your way to the enchantments of Acapulco, your pants feel tight and you become worried about your waistline. There's a story making the rounds about a man who's already gained fourteen pounds. It prompts you to make a list of resolutions...

1. Don't overeat. Sooner or later you'll pay for it.
2. Eat fruits and juices, preferably some nonconstipating things like prunes.
3. Resist the sweets.
4. Swim every day.
5. Get enough sleep.
6. Participate in the exercise class.
7. Don't drink too much.
8. Take group dancing lessons.
9. Plan to have lunches on deck (buffet)—skip breads and desserts.
10. Try to eat more fish and less beef.

Having written this, you go off to a stoical lunch of caviar, king crab, smoked salmon, and lobster!

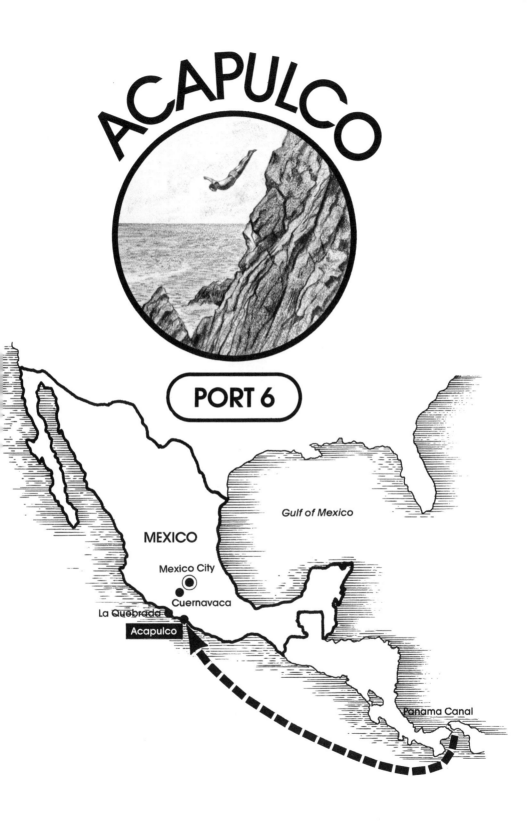

ACAPULCO

PORT 6

MEXICO

Gulf of Mexico

Mexico City

Cuernavaca

La Quebrada

Acapulco

Panama Canal

Acapulco—Mexico

ACAPULCO

Acapulco, Queen of the bays, was famous and settled and important in the sixteenth century—250 years before the idea of the United States was born. From its shores sailed the "Manila Galleon," the treasure ship to the Philippines. The journey took two months. It was the tradition that in June a trade fair assembled in Manila and the ship was loaded with the treasures of the Orient—silks, spices, porcelains. Six months later, the ship fought its perilous way against the trade winds back to Acapulco.

As Spain's power declined, the marauders, freebooters, and pirates became more brazen. They lay in wait along the coast of Baja California, then further south, until they were practically outside Acapulco harbor. Fewer and fewer ships got through. Finally, Mexico was cut off from the Old World by the Napoleonic Wars and through necessity it became a nation. Acapulco became a forgotten fishing village until the 1950s, when it was rediscovered as the center of the "Riviera of the Pacific" and sun-worshippers were soon jetting in from around the world.

So now it's all different—yet strangely the same.

The ships are now run by Air West, Western Airlines, and Aeronaves de Mexico. But the treasure still ends up here. This Port of Mexico, seaside city of 400,000, is willingly overwhelmed, not by freebooters or pirates, but by 4 million annual invaders, gilded groups of jet-setters who park their morals and uptight attire at the airport and speed off noisily in pink jeeps, looking like a flight of flamingos, thin and rosy pink against the brown-thatched poverty of an Indian hut.

Visitors bringing "it" with them, strangely wonder why they can't get away from it all. So you decide to leave it all behind as you come ashore in the early morning into this city of color and salt to observe the local flora and fauna.

The morning is sunny and fresh, not yet too hot, a good time to take a bus tour to explore on your own. You climb aboard. A dog jumps onto your bus but is hustled off by the driver.

You look out the window at the wildlife. Cormorants, snow egrets, herons, and a secretary from Des Moines swimming together at Launa de Coyuca, all wondering how the fishing will be today. Look at the mullet, snook, and catfish leap wantonly just beyond the shore. Be careful—a little further out a great white shark stirs his tail and sails off to look for breakfast.

It's a full day for those of us who have just "dropped in" for a day, but there is time enough for the beach...for the spectacular resort wonder of Las Brisas, carved into a hillside...for searching out fine Taxco silver at shops along Costera Aleman...for El Pueblito, the village market, and the Zocalo and the Flea Market ...for finding the resort wear and clothes that are a specialty of Acapulco's many good shops for men and women...even for Old Fort San Diego, a few blocks from the Zocalo, which dates back to the trading days...for the Princess Hotel and El Mirado, wonders of modern architecture and luxury.

It's late afternoon, a good time to rent a *calandria,* a horse-drawn carriage. The little horse daintily clatters its way along the Costera Miguel Aleman, waving its red balloons from the fashionable east to the working west side of town.

You see a couple riding horseback across the sand near the Princess Hotel. The sun goes down begrudgingly at Pie de la Cuesta, and huge white waves roll in. It's late afternoon—siesta time for the rich. There are sounds of the sea, leaves blowing in soft humid air, the first nighttime guitars, murmur of love words, in this humid, hedonistic, tingling town of a hundred hotels, stretched jewel-like around the throat of the Queen of Bays.

You must be back on the QE2 before seven, so you just

make it and climb to a high deck, looking back longingly at the crescent of lights as evening begins to sparkle. Evening is a special time in Acapulco. It's the time when gypsy-looking ladies will examine the hundred expensive garments in their sliding glass-mirrored wardrobes and wonder wistfully, "Who shall I be tonight?"

It's the time when the bars around the big hotels will grow active as volcanoes and great dinners of red snapper and lobster and giant camerones will be served in Paradiso, yes, and Taj Mahal. At eleven, at full moonshine and madness time, the divers at La Quebrada will hold flaming torches, illuminating the night like fireflies, as they plunge 150 feet into the sea below, and not even know that you have gone.

You draw away reluctantly, like a departing lover unwilling to leave so soon. The lights of the bay melt into inky darkness. Yours has been a brief liaison, but the memory lingers and that night you dream that you are riding the winds on a giant red and white parachute sailing over it all again.

SHORE EXCURSIONS

As the QE2 cruises northward along the Mexican coastline, there is speculation aboard about how some of your new shipmates are enjoying their three-and-a-half-day "Mexican Holiday" which is taking them from Acapulco to Taxco, Cuernavaca, and Mexico City before a jet flight to Los Angeles to rejoin the Queen.

The fifty-two-page "Shore Excursion" book developed by Thomas Cook, American Express, and Cunard for the QE2's world cruise becomes favorite reading for those looking ahead to touring each port.

Over 150 shore excursions are offered to the full-trip passenger on this cruise. Passengers who have elected to take only a segment of the cruise may also participate in any of the excursions that fall into their section of the journey. You see, as well as offering the full eighty-day cruise all the way around the world, *Cunard makes it possible for people who may not be able to spend all of the necessary time or money to take just a portion of the cruise.* Two-, three-, and four-week segments to the Caribbean, the Orient, the Middle East, the Mediterranean, the Black Sea, and Europe are offered.

The Cunard people are very jealous of their reputation and they carefully selected Thomas Cook Company and American Express Company to prepare and handle all shore arrangements along the entire route of the cruise. Each tour is spelled out in detail in the brochure, which specifies the time each tour leaves and returns to the ship, itineraries, and prices. Meals are provided on the tours, as well as first class hotel accommodations where necessary.

The tours are selected by passengers in advance, and all reservations are made long ahead for motor coaches, guides, hotels, restaurants, museums, railways, airlines, and nightclubs. The variety of tours ranges from half-day tours to places like the ruins of Pompeii, to a seven-day deluxe Gourmet's Tour through France. The variety of tours offers something for everyone at every port. The only problem might be in deciding which tour to take—they all sound so fabulous. With approximately 1400 full-cruise passengers and another 1000 or so people taking segments of the trip, Thomas Cook and American Express have to anticipate every kind of interest in their tour planning, and they have done a fantastic job.

A "shore program office" is located on board the QE2, with an experienced traveler and lecturer—in this case, Sheridan Garth—who offers lectures about the cities, people, and countries you are to visit next. Mr. Garth is an excellent lecturer, whose knowledge and experience can be counted on to add interest and excitement to your next stop. He is the author of a delightful book, *The Pageant of the Mediterranean.*

BENEFICIAL INACTIVITY

With two full days and nights of uninterrupted cruising before you reach Los Angeles, there is plenty of time to enjoy what you like to call "beneficial inactivity."

The daily paper, "The QE2," is put under your cabin door early each morning. It shows the Dow Jones averages and the prices of the leading stocks. You think of how beneficial inactivity can pay off, even in the stock market, like that time years ago when you bought a large block of a new stock issue that was coming out that morning. It came out nine dollars a share and soon went to eleven dollars. About this time you decided you needed a new pair of shoes, so you left and went to the shoe store on West Seventh Street. After the shoes were selected, tried on, and purchased, you decided to beat the noon rush and get a sandwich and a cup of coffee.

Thus it was that you didn't return to the stock broker's office until two or three hours later. Upon your return, you found that the stock purchased that morning was now up to twenty-four dollars per share! If you had stayed at the broker's office, the plan had been to sell out at twelve dollars.

From that day on, you called this "beneficial inactivity." On that occasion it was very beneficial indeed!

Main Street—Disneyland, Anaheim, California

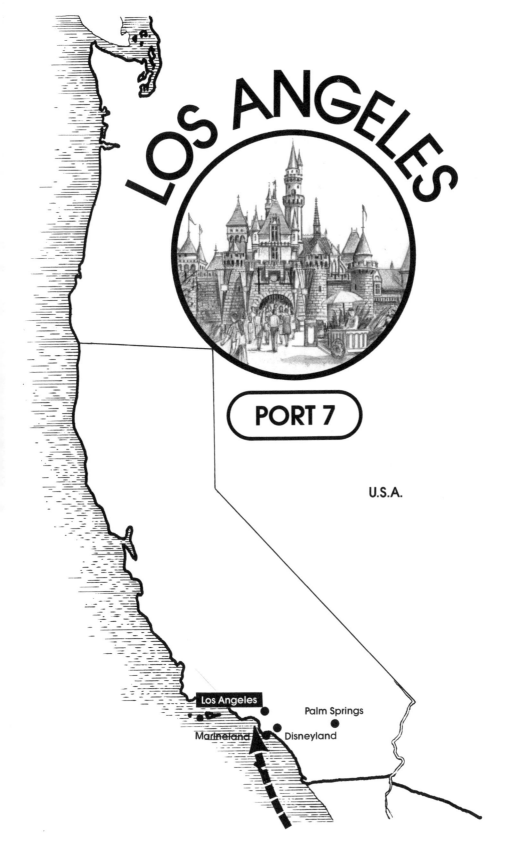

LOS ANGELES

PORT 7

U.S.A.

Los Angeles

Palm Springs

Marineland

Disneyland

LOS ANGELES

Lost among the comets, nebulae, galactic clusters... perched precariously on a troubled planet, hugging a continent strangely exposed to the great flames of the sun's corona, staring blankly out on the Pacific like a blind man, sits Los Angeles.

Four hundred sixty square miles of superlatives. Fastest growing. Most exciting and glamorous (Hollywood). Richest (Beverly Hills, Bel-Air). Most active (L.A. does what San Francisco talks about). Best police department (north of Watts). Kookiest (cults). Spaced out (North American, Hughes, Douglas, Northrup).

From the QE2's highest deck, one first sees the city spread out white and flat like glistening mayonnaise on a piece of hearty bread. A river of brown earth called the Los Angeles River seems to go nowhere, as does a huge suspension bridge near the dock. Freeway mobiles hang suspended. Sculpted mountains rise to where they are lost in smog. Crazy quilts of multi-colored land seem to stretch out to a monotonous infinity, all sewn together by streets and freeways, bisecting high-rises and paralleling shopping centers. The cars, like errant raisins, are everywhere, wandering in the yeast of suburbs like space travelers—a mass of 3000 pounds of gleaming metal per brain ambling up and down center dividers, looking for a parking space, their identities, or gas. Crouching, spreading, sprawling houses and people, seemingly all proud of different ideas and addresses from the mountains to the sea, are all one sees.

Beyond, in the once virginal Santa Monica Mountains, greedy land developers, armed with bulldozers, grind up the canyons finer than chopped liver into open-faced sandwiches, just big enough to build a house on. "A real steal," the developer says to the prospective purchaser. A year later, after the rains, it slides into home plate next door and its young owners are out.

Long lines of palms thrust their heads above the smog, looking down condescendingly on rings of houses set with ruby bougainvillaea as brown bodies dive into turquoise pools, and a thousand other acts glorious and ignoble repeat themselves in forty suburbs looking for a city.

You wonder why so many choose to live here in this city built on sunshine, oil, and oranges. The oranges are gone—moved south. The oil, too, is played out, except where it bubbles mischievously, obstinately, perversely under fine white beaches, Beverly Hills mansions, and skyscrapers along Wilshire, or threatens to swallow a bone or two of *homo sapiens* to add to all the rest at La Brea Tar Pits. Only the sun remains, or so they say—those who have seen it poke its head out behind the smog from time to time—the natives past forty who swear it's there. Still, so many people live here—there must be a reason—you decide it might be fun to try to find out what there is about it that makes the visitor stay.

TOURING LOS ANGELES

You have only one day in Los Angeles and, although the pre-planned Thomas Cook Tours are a bargain, you decide to rent a car and start out to explore the city on your own.

The glitter of Wilshire Boulevard joins the old and new, the downtown Civic Center and the ocean at Santa Monica. Near the downtown end is El Pueblo de Los Angeles, birthplace of the city, and Olvera Street, its oldest. You explore and suddenly are transported back in time. What you hear is the liquid music of a guitar, the slap of a potter's wheel, the cooing of a ring-necked dove. You approach a stand. There is a smiling brown face bending over a puestos, tortillas simmering in the noonday sun.

Little children run by, carrying earnest messages back and forth between people who think of themselves as all related, and black-eyed *señoritas* flash semaphore messages past their *dueñas'* watchful guard to their lovers in the park, and look straight ahead in the Plaza Church, pretending they do not see the hot replies.

Strangely moved, you get back into your car and drive on.

Beyond the mountains is Pasadena, the empty Rose Bowl waiting patiently for New Year's. But never fear, you're told, there's always action at the Coliseum, Dodger Stadium, or the Forum. And that's why its bronzed and beautiful inhabitants call Los Angeles the Sports Capital of the World.

Natives and visitors alike work eagerly to capture leisure at Universal Studios, where you can peek behind the scenes at the world's largest movie and TV studio…and find yourself part of the action on a special effects ride.

Then on to nearby Disneyland, the Magic Kingdom, where you can follow your dreams to Adventureland, Fantasyland, Main Street U.S.A., and all of the other attractions of this sixty-acre storybook park that has won a place in everyone's imagination, young or old.

Next, take the Santa Ana Freeway to Knott's Berry Farm, the popular Old West theme park with more than 100 rides and attractions, including best-you-can-buy jams and preserves, and one of the best chicken dinners this side of Sunday.

Being a film buff, you seek out Tinseltown. At the conflux of Hollywood and Vine is the mythical center of Hollywood, a place famous the world over for turning out pictures for kids from six to sixty—all the same. You walk on the stars along Hollywood Boulevard, embedded in concrete, measure their footprints at Grauman's Chinese Theater. Then watch the parade: Hare Krishnas and hairy apes, screwballs and losers of beauty contests, gigolos, nature addicts, Indian fakirs, shoe salesmen and other voyeurs, absconding bank cashiers, religious messiahs, unemployed actresses, and others—all do their thing on Hollywood Boulevard.

Lunch at your choice of twenty-seven different *al fresco* restaurants and kitchens at world-famous Farmer's Market, a unique and colorful setting for more than 160 different shops and stalls, where you can find goods and goodies from around the world, including spectacular displays of choice fruits and vegetables.

And for a real QE2 traveler's busman's holiday, take the tour to Marineland, with its aquatic shows, to picturesque Ports O' Call Village, with its shops and restaurants, and winding up on the bridge of the *Queen Mary* in Long Beach harbor.

Take a winter break for a day in sun-drenched Palm Springs, where the rich come to rest and the rest come to see.

The Sky Jump Parachute Drop—Knott's Berry Farm

LEAVING LOS ANGELES

It was a silvery moonlit night as the QE2 pulled away from Los Angeles Pier 93. At a signal from the captain, the ship's steam-powered whistles gave forth a mighty blast and the majestic ship began to glide slowly down the channel and past the breakwater.

As the tugs nosed us out into the main harbor channel, the lights from land reflecting on the water turned it into a pathway of gold—a thrilling portent of good. And as we passed the Ports O' Call Restaurant on shore, we knew that some friends were eating dinner there at that moment, having come especially to await our ship's departure. Of course, we couldn't see them, but we waved goodbye as we passed by the large picture windows of the restaurant.

Looking out upon the harbor, we had the feeling that the shore lines were loosed and we were sailing into the unknown, embarking on the adventure of a lifetime. Our hearts were full of emotion, trying to thank God for making it all possible.

Our course was set for Honolulu, about 2000 miles westward, away out there in the middle of the blue Pacific. The last time we had made this trip by steamer was in 1956, on the *S.S. Lurline*. Now, twenty-four years later, we were traveling at practically twice the speed and with the many luxurious comforts of our magnificent floating hotel, the QE2.

We thought of all the ports ahead of us on our journey around the world. Each port promised to be like a newly discovered pearl, and at journey's end what a beautiful string of thirty pearls we would have to treasure in memory!

When the QE2 is in port one dresses casually, but at sea formal dress is *de rigueur* for dinner. It provides the ladies with the fun of wearing a different dress each evening.

For this author, not much given to wearing tuxedos, it

required a lot of talking to get us reconciled to all this "fuss and bother." Yet there was undeniable pleasure in these festive evening affairs, a return to the elegance of another era.

That first evening out of Los Angeles, strolling the deck before dinner, we spied a crowd milling around in front of us. We joined them. Lo and behold, we found ourselves at the entrance of the Queen's Room, where stood the captain of the ship for this part of the journey, Captain Robert Arnott. An attendant asked us our names and presented us to the captain, who shook our hands and greeted us most cordially. There was even a ship's photographer there, who took our picture—another memory captured for our memory book.

Soon we entered the Columbia Dining Room for dinner. Our waiter, a young English lad of twenty years (all the waiters are young Englishmen in their early twenties), was Malcolm Russell, matching the diners' finery with his red jacket and black tuxedo-style slacks. Our head waiter's name was Jonathan Norton, also English. The culinary feast they assembled for us that evening was memorable: consommé, fresh trout, sweetbreads, cro-quettes, broiled chicken, salad, blanc mange, a cup of Kona coffee, and a piece of delicious macadamia nut coconut cream pie.

While we sat at dinner, the ship's orchestra was playing "Alice Blue Gown," a song our mother used to sing when we were young.

That man is twice blessed who has the memory of a good mother. Now that she is gone we remember and cherish all the beautiful songs she sang. "Let Me Call You Sweetheart" and "Moonlight and Roses" bring back a flood of memories, priceless treasures of youth. Sentimentality and nostalgia mix within us freely, shamelessly.

It is in man to sing. Melodies lift the heart. Music is for all to enjoy and cherish. Music washes away from the soul the dust of everyday life. It laughs, it is solemn, it cries. It sways the body or moves the feet. It challenges the deepest thought and it has a tone for every mood.

Music, once admitted to the soul, becomes a sort of spirit that occupies the memory. It touches the heart…for *music is the spirit voice, the voice of God in man!*

EN ROUTE TO HONOLULU

"It's a wee bit fresh outside."

These words of our steward, Len Knight, are a typical British understatement. It is, in fact, cold and windy weather that will hold for much of the four days and nights across the Pacific until we reach the warm shelter of Hawaii.

Peering out of the porthole, we could see nothing but sky and water, an immensity of ocean everywhere that flooded us with awe at God's handiwork.

It is chilly weather for being out on deck, but there is no shortage of things to do. We run across some people playing ping-pong. On the deck, some hardy souls are playing shuffleboard. In a cage, a man is driving golf balls. In the Casino, still others are getting their exercise pulling like mad on the slot machines. In the writing room, people are sitting at desks writing letters and post cards to friends and family. Then, we join the passengers sitting on deck and visit awhile before lunch.

These are quiet, restful days. Away from the jangle of the telephone, from city distractions and noises. It is wonderful to have the leisure to enjoy a favorite pastime…reading. Give attention to reading, and pay attention to *what you read.* Reading is the loom on which one's inner garments are woven. We can no more escape the thoughts which our reading imparts to us than we can escape the Law of Action and Reaction. What we allow to lodge in our own minds will mold us into its own image.

Books are the life blood of the leaders. They are the

transfusion which we need and must have to stimulate us for the climb to the rugged peaks of successful living and attainment. All things being equal, a well-furnished head pioneers the way for a noble heart.

Every person who knows how to read has it in his power to magnify himself, to multiply the ways in which he exists, to make his life full, significant, and interesting. When we read we may not only be kings and live in palaces, but what is far better, we may transport ourselves to the mountains or to the seashore, and visit the most beautiful places on earth—without fatigue, inconvenience, or expense. When we read the best books, we will have as guests of our minds the best thoughts of the best men.

MAN AND HIS POTENTIAL

You wonder secretly to yourself:

Am I living close to my full potential?

Do I underestimate my own value?

Do I know where I am now? (Besides being in the middle of the Pacific Ocean!)

Do I know where I am going? (Besides to Hawaii on the QE2!)

Am I living with positive expectations of tomorrow?

Am I open to good things happening to me right now? This minute?

You open your eyes and look out at the sea—at the timeless, limitless sea, stretching out to a seeming infinity beyond.

You realize that your eyes are just two tiny three-quarter-inch eyeballs, yet they can encompass miles and miles of sea and sky and more, during your voyage around the world. The more is what you're after. You don't want to just travel, you want to see the most beautiful things in the world as a poet or an artist sees them.

Gazing at the moon and stars at sea, we thought of the vastness and grandeur of the universe. Then we sat down and counted ourselves among the happiest individuals in it, blessed with the opportunity to take this adventurous journey.

After four days of sailing under overcast skies, we looked out the porthole and saw the sun shining brightly. The bright sunshine assured us that we had arrived for certain in Nature's Paradise.

We dressed quickly and went out onto the aft deck. Ah, warm, soft air! Traveling now at slow speed, our ship was passing Diamond Head. A feeling of familiar exultation filled us. It was no accident that the gray skies had vanished. We had come to our place in the sun...our beloved Hawaii!

Waikiki Beach—Honolulu

HONOLULU - HAWAII

PORT 8

KAUAI

Lihue

OAHU

Honolulu

Wailuku

MAUI

Hilo

HAWAII

HAWAII—THE SUNNY, ENCHANTED ISLES

Spend some time in *paradise*—where dreams come true. Go wading with a *wahine,* eat pig and poi at fabulous three-hour luaus. Go out to sea in a Polynesian outrigger, eat *mahi-mahi* until you can swim like a fish, get a golden tan, and you are eligible to become a bikini inspector on Waikiki. Stick a beautiful flower in your hair and be happy—you're in Hawaii!

As you walk down the gangplank, the air seems just a little cleaner, the sun a little brighter, the native girls with their leis just a little prettier than ever before.

When visitors arrive, the natives place leis, floral garlands, around their necks and greet them with a kiss. These leis are made of many-colored flowers of delightful fragrances, all strung together into long necklaces. Perfume is made from some of these native flowers, such as ginger and *pakaki.* What traveler is not made to feel instantly at home upon receiving a "big fat kiss upon the cheek" and a lei around his neck? You suddenly feel younger.

There's something about perpetual sunshine that is reassuring, a subtle stability in the eighty-degree temperature. You breathe deeply of what the Environmental Protection Agency unromantically calls "the cleanest air of all urban areas with a population over 200,000."

The gentle trade winds keep the air moving. Other places have winds, but Hawaii has only soft, refreshing breezes that act as a natural tranquilizer.

Towering mountains
Gleaming white beaches
Exotic shops and shapes
Restaurants of many cultures
Entertainment ... endless variety
Fishing
Golf
Awesome volcanoes
Majestic waterfalls
Beautiful gardens
Best of all
Happy, friendly people
To make one's stay truly
Unforgettable.

While the Hawaiian Islands contain 6450 square miles and are actually comprised of eight islands, about ninety percent of the visitors spend most of their stay on the few square miles of Waikiki on the island of Oahu. It has rightly earned the nickname of "gathering place."

The beach at Waikiki is perhaps the finest in the world, with its year-round swimming, surfboard riding, and surfside dining. But it has changed over the years, the inevitable result of becoming one of the world's prize tourist attractions. There are now over 300 tall buildings on Waikiki. The problem in the future is going to be where to build new buildings so that they will not block the views of the present hotels and apartments.

You don't need many clothes in Hawaii. Most of the time you're either in your swimsuit or shorts. Most women wear cool, flowing muu-muus. They say that when missionaries first came to these Isles of Paradise, the native girls knew as little about clothes as a horse knows about algebra. Their entire wardrobe consisted of a smile and a golden tan. The missionaries thereupon hastily invented the *holoku*, or muu-muu. The smiles and typical tans were never abolished…and, much later, the younger ones eschewed their mama's muu-muus in favor of bikinis and ginger perfume.

The Hawaiians call the ocean their breadbasket, and it is rightfully called the world's greatest supermarket, for it yields the major share of the islanders' daily bread.

The first thing you have when you get to Waikiki is a pineapple boatload. You never seem to get enough of the native fruit. Coconuts, mangos, and papayas are tropical fruits which originated in the lowlands of Central and South America and are island favorites. But the most famous of all, of course, is the pineapple. Fresh from the fields and grown in Hawaii's rich soil and warm sun, it is a favorite Hawaiian delicacy. For the tourist a visit to the Dole Pineapple Cannery is a "fruitful" sidelight. Here you can learn about the history, canning, and many uses of this fruit.

Strolling down the beach, you stop where a group of musicians are playing on the sand under a coconut tree.

Hawaiian music
Soft and sweetly charming
Makes you feel at home
In "Blue Hawaii."

INFLATION

I know everything is going up, but the soft, warm rain is still coming down. They haven't yet put a tax on sunshine or the beautiful red and gold sunrises or the magenta sunsets.

Everything is going up! But bird songs cost no more, no twenty percent luxury tax on the ferns and flowers and shrubs around my door, or on clouds that sail through turquoise skies like dream-ships putting out to sea. All this is free.

Now, you know everything is going up! But the price of real

joy is the same. It costs no more to work or sing, or to fan the ancient flame of love, while listening to the silence of overhanging stars and drifting clouds.

Man will cry that everything is going up! Now we get tired of what you say. The things that really matter cost just the same today. The beauty of the big, broad sea, the mountaintops, the sky. The beautiful girls on the beach at Waikiki; they are tax-exempt forever…oh, lucky you and me!

SIGHTSEEING IN HAWAII

There are so many things to see and do in Hawaii, and QE2 visitors can't possibly take them all in. But there are nearly two full days between disembarking and the time the ship lifts anchor the following afternoon, time enough to get a true taste of the islands' enchantment.

A number of prearranged Cook's tours are available for QE2 passengers as shore excursions: a tour of Honolulu and Waikiki beach, the house and gardens tour, the Circle Island and Polynesian Cultural Center tour, and the Pearl Harbor Cruise. These are all inexpensive and delightful introductions to the island of Oahu. Cook's tours are also planned for Kauai, Maui, and Hawaii, among the other islands. In addition, there are many short or full-day tours offered locally.

You decide to get a sky view of all of Hawaii. You get into the plane, buckle your seat belt, and away you go.

The flight is a montage of red-soiled pineapple and sugar-cane fields, lava beds, cattle ranches, coffee plantations, volcanoes, green valleys, white beaches, high cliffs, and magnificent rainbow-hued waterfalls. It's all you've ever heard about Hawaii, and more.

There are also some beautiful sights to see in the Waikiki area if you do not care to take the longer tours.

You start to walk along the beach in your bare feet—all the

way to Kapiolani Park, about two miles away. If you take this walk in the early morning, starting at the other end, at the four large historic rocks on the Diamond Head side of the Moana Hotel, you can stroll back along the beach with the warm morning sun at your back and see this world-famous beach come alive for the day.

You will pass many of the islands' most beautiful hotels— the Outrigger and Surfrider, the Royal Hawaiian, the Moana and Halekulani, each built with distinctive island architecture. Gray's Beach along the way takes its name from the Widow Gray, who once operated a boarding house here. Families caring for the royal beach houses resided along this beach a century ago, and it was here that kings and nobles came to relax and to party. Now it's your turn.

As you walk, or pause to rest in the shade of *hau* trees on the beach side of the Cinerama Reef and Waikiki Shores, you experience some of the true spell of Hawaii. The tides are soft and gentle and you wonder how long these tides have been coming in and going out.

You watch the surfers riding the gentle waves a hundred yards out. Balmy trade winds softly rustle leaves overhead. You feel in harmony with the joy and beauty all around, the best of natural surroundings. At such a moment, nothing from the lovely Isle of Capri to fascinating Noumea off the coast of New Guinea, no, nothing you have ever seen compares with these gentle islands.

FOSTER GARDENS

Another place you may enjoy visiting is a part of old Hawaii located in the heart of Honolulu named Foster Gardens, a tropical paradise, a world away from the congested concrete and asphalt jungle of streets and buildings in modern Honolulu.

It's a riot of flowers, lush green ferns, and tropical trees, hidden like a pearl in an oyster shell surrounded by thirty apartment buildings. Here in the stillness of this tropical oasis, you can feel and picture old Hawaii as it was a million yesterdays ago. Birds sing the same songs and, from trees hundreds of years old, native girls pick the same flowers to put in their hair. Just for a magic moment, time seems to stand still.

A reflective mood overtakes you, a sense of gratitude, too, as you consider that you have lived in the best of all centuries, have had the privilege of being a part of what is now a diminishing and soon-to-vanish generation whose life began at the turn of this century. We have spanned the age of the horse-and-buggy to the age of jumbo jets, space ships, and space craft hurtling at speeds faster than sound, not to mention all the terrors and blessings of nuclear energy.

The reader will have gathered by now that we have opinions formed out of firsthand experiences. They were shaped in a Christian home where we were taught to admire and revere and try to express all of the true, unchanging values and virtues of life: goodness, sound character, honesty, hard work, responsibility, discipline, kindness, love, decency, courage, loyalty. All of which, we have learned, yield for us true happiness and peace of mind.

Here in Foster Gardens, we found a world of beauty and sublime peace, a fitting testament to the woman who made it possible. Had it not been for the foresight and dedicated generosity of Mrs. Foster, this lovely Nature's Paradise would never have been donated to the city. But she made provisions for the upkeep and maintenance of this natural park. Otherwise, greedy subdividers would long since have changed it into another concrete and asphalt jungle, in their blind dedication to what is called "progress."

LUAUS

It is evening and you take a sunset sail as the winds blow you past Diamond Head. When you return, someone has

Throw Net Fishing—Hawaii

arranged a luau for you. This Hawaiian feast teaches stressful Americans from the mainland how to relax and live a little.

One of the finest is the luau at the Sheraton-Waikiki every Saturday evening at 6:00 P.M.

You're late. When you arrive, the others have already been eating under the stars for an hour. Your waiter reassures you with, "Don't worry, still two hours to go."

While you feast on delicious specialties, beautiful young women perform Hawaiian hulas. The dancers seem to become one with everything in nature. They bend, sway, and gesture, moving in countless ways to tell their countless stories. You know that behind these graceful, expressive, sometimes dignified and sometimes earthy dances lie years of study, meditation, and prayer. Their performance is enhanced by the pulsing rhythms of drums, the rattle of gourds, and the rustle of bamboo instruments. Your host explains that in ancient Hawaii there was no part of life, from birth to death, in which the hula did not play an expressive role. Hula was an integral part of the Hawaiian religion, and that religion bound together every ordinary and special activity of the people.

Later, handsome young men do the Samoan fire dance and silk-throated singers warble island love songs—all combining to make this a sensational night in paradise.

You agree with what you've been told—no visit to these islands would be complete without going to a luau.

The Royal Hawaiian has a similar luau every Sunday night, and others among the famous hotels and restaurants also set forth this feast of food and entertainment.

SHOPPING

Honolulu is truly a paradise for shoppers, with its multitude of boutiques and its fine department stores offering something for every age and every taste.

Ladies, if you would like to buy an elegant gift for yourself or your friends, and at the price of a waiter's tip, buy several beautiful polished kukui nut necklaces. The native kukui nut symbolizes affection and oneness with the spirit of the Hawaiian Islands.

Another island favorite is the macadamia nut. The Macadamia Nut Factory on Kalakaua Avenue in Waikiki has over 200 unique macadamia nut gifts. Mailed anywhere, these are a welcome taste of the islands for friends on the mainland.

ALOHA

Our visit to Hawaii was all too brief, as good times are, and we left Honolulu in the late afternoon under a piercingly blue sky bathed by a golden sun, with the fervent wish in our hearts—to return.

May wonderful things happen to you
When you, too, visit the Paradise Islands!
Till we meet, Aloha!

HAWAIIAN LEGACY

The next day, as we put on our colorful Hawaiian shirts, we suddenly discovered that we had carried away a legacy other than fond memories and souvenirs. Look in the mirror and pat your stomach. Is all that really you?

Next came the resolution. We made up our minds to lose weight. Our self-admonishments were firm. Discipline is what we need! We must exercise...and build up our health by discipline *and* exercise.

Therefore, we made straight for the gymnasium and located the steam bath. We eschewed the elevators, walked the stairways, began watching the bread and desserts...trying to rediscover the thin man that lives inside us somewhere...and rediscover the virtue of moderation.

Health is our biggest asset. It was perhaps the prime factor in our taking the QE2 around-the-world cruise, and we were not to be disappointed.

One of the reasons was a tremendously impressive man named Eric Mason, the QE2's Athletic Director. He is a rare man in that he is rich in practical experience and has an abundance of common sense—which isn't so common today.

The QE2 is the only cruise ship in the world to offer a comprehensive Health and Physical Fitness Program. It is under Eric Mason's supervision and guidance, as one of the world's best-known health and fitness consultants. During some phase of the eighty-day cruise, Eric Mason is also asked by his boss, Brian Price, the Cruise Director, to give one of his three lectures—Health Is Wealth, Fitness Is Fun, and How to Stop Smoking.

Here are Eric Mason's twelve rules for your good health:

1. *Don't weaken* once you have made up your mind to exercise daily and practice sound nutrition.
2. *Increase* your consumption of health-building protein foods.
3. *Ease off* those fattening refined sugar and starch foods.
4. *Try to be moderate* in all things you know are detrimental to good health.
5. *Eat lots of fresh fruit,* for this provides an abundance of natural sugar. Citrus fruits are rich in vitamin C, which fights infection.
6. *Exercise every day.*
7. *Eat slowly* to aid good digestion.
8. *Remember at all times*—You are what you eat.

9. *Call on your doctor* if you notice any irregular changes or are in any way uncertain about your health.

10. *Inhale and exhale deeply* when you first step out of doors each morning, and notice how much more confidently you face that crowded commuter.

11. *Spend at least* half an hour each day walking and deep breathing in the fresh air. Draw that stomach in and stand up straight and really feel alive.

12. *Enter each new month* by missing two consecutive meals. Drink lots of water during this miniature fast and give your poor overworked digestive system a complete rest.

Eric told us that lack of exercise is probably public health enemy number one. Physical inactivity causes muscle laxity and lets the entire organism go soft and slack. The circulatory system, lungs, muscles, and mental alertness are quickly exhausted by the slightest effort. The unconditioned, sedentary individual can only mobilize half of his actual capacity.

Regular activity, involving as many muscles as possible, helps increase vitality and prevents muscle laxity. Swimming, walking, playing basketball or handball, and other exercises keep us physically and mentally fresh and youthful, endowing us with endurance and well-conditioned bodies.

Your pulse tells you how fast your heart is beating, showing you by its behavior during exertion or stress just how fit you are, what kind of shape you're in. A person in shape has a lower pulse rate and is in better condition, with heart, lungs, and circulatory system capable of handling greater loads and being able to cope with the stresses of everyday life.

You become a believer and next morning you are among the many jogging and exercise enthusiasts assembled on the boat deck at 10:00 A.M. The first activity is a jogging class, scientifically planned for people of all age groups. It starts with a brisk walk, one lap of the boat deck (which is a fifth of a mile), gently easing class members, some grossly out of shape, into this important cardiovascular exercise. The second lap is half-walk, half-jog, with the third lap jogging all the way (for those who are in shape for it). Three-fifths of a mile might not sound like very far, but the QE2's speed causes headwinds, so the exercise is really like jogging up a steep hill.

Huffing and puffing, you make it back to a deck chair. Eric pulls you up, pats you on the back, and then spends a half-hour teaching you exercises based on the natural principle of stretching. The wisdom and value of these exercises have already been published in his book, *Stretch and Relax to Health and Fitness.*

The rest of Eric Mason's morning is taken up with his class for beginning swimmers, followed by instructing people in how to use the equipment in the complete gymnasium on the QE2. He also offers advice and guidance on anything to do with health and fitness, which can include advice for an older person suffering from arthritis, or a young person getting in shape for a particular sport.

Waikiki Beach with Diamond Head

EN ROUTE TO YOKOHAMA

This was the longest uninterrupted time at sea. For seven days, from Honolulu to Yokohama, the vast Pacific glided beneath our keel, giving us time to catch up on our thinking.

A century ago, as we have observed before, the man who achieved a journey around the globe was called a hero. Today, he merely earns the name of globe-trotter. It is nearly 500 years since the brave Portuguese discoverer, Ferdinand Magellan, first sailed around the world. Since then, the broad Atlantic and Pacific have dwindled to the proportions of a rapid ocean ferry system. But, despite the speed with which we now sail from continent to continent, the actual distance is still there, as we were reminded during seven days of sea vistas.

What a ready-made, seven-day opportunity to review some lifelong daydreams of visiting faraway places on this good earth!

Travel broadens one's outlook on life in a way nothing else can. Travel can be as purposeful or relaxed as you choose. If you have hobbies, you can collect things to bring home. If you have a special cultural interest, you can broaden it. If you have a special educational bent, you can learn what others are doing in your field in other countries. You can take your work with you, consult with businessmen about your product or profession, make contacts as you go.

Shopping tours of unusual and quaint shops are a highlight of any trip. If you have items you collect, special clothes you would like to have, or special gifts you desire for friends, make a list and use it as a guide in the stores you visit. We are all travelers on the highway of learning. By experience and observation we learn the fine art of living.

But dreams of what lies ahead and what you can possess don't take up all your time. There is also time to reflect on the past.

When you look back on your lifetime, you do not remember dates. You remember events, and you often trace your life back through a series of happy events, or a few sorrowful occasions. Each day of your life is an adventure, a new piece of road to be traveled. You must ask God for direction.

Our years have taught us that there is a Higher Power throughout the entire universe. When one is in correspondence with this Higher Power, one feels the Presence that satisfies the soul. A strength and a power and a feeling of confidence floods our being. We are thankful for that Presence lighting up our pathway into the forever.

DIVERSIONS AT SEA

"Excuse me, it is four-thirty. I have to go up to the Double Down Room and play Bingo. I won thirty-seven dollars yesterday. I feel lucky today…"

"Sir, would you care to guess how many miles the QE2 will have traveled from noon yesterday until noon today?"

You invariably reach into your pocket. Though you come close several times, you don't win the pot. Still, your very human nature keeps you guessing. Each day you think, "Perhaps tomorrow I will win the jackpot!"

Adjacent to the entrance to the Columbia Dining Room is a wide hall containing a large table. Here every day are passengers engaged in putting together jigsaw puzzles. Some of these puzzles are as large as three by four feet. Everyone passing is welcome to add any pieces to the pictures. The larger ones sometimes take two or three days and several hundred man-hours (person-hours?) to complete.

It is interesting to watch the pieces begin to fit together. And these elaborate puzzles are more than just a way to pass the time. Fitting the right pieces together seems to be what life is really all about.

R$_x$ FOR STRESS

Things we are enjoying:

• The luxury of leisure
• Our good health
• The clean and invigorating ocean air
• And, best of all, peace of mind

Napoleon said, "The best cure for the body is a quiet mind."

Life is full of irritations. Our tensions mount, and first thing we know we are loaded with stress. Stress has the power to destroy our enjoyment of life. It is the response of the body to any demands upon it.

Stress is dangerous. It triggers certain glands to function in the body and create hypertension. Too much of that is not natural. So, your own thoughts can start the deterioration of your own body. The relationship of the stress mechanism to car-diovascular disease is well-documented.

When you're the guy at the top of a large company with many employees and several union contracts, the pressure is never off. You had open heart surgery two years ago and you just wanted to pull out. Sometimes you can't pull out; then it is just a matter of time until they carry you out.

Trying to keep calm inside in this world of turmoil and change is a monumental job. But each of us has to work on it twenty-four hours a day, for this is the seat and root cause of our main diseases. Emotions cause stress and tension. Relax and hang loose!

People puncture you—even telephone calls can upset you and cause physical discomfort and pain. Then there are the common hazards of life to cope with.

When you have emotional strain, it increases your desire for food or drink. Eating gives satisfaction and a pleasant feeling, and must be kept under control.

Tension starts with the brain issuing commands to contract muscle bundles throughout the body. Anxieties can afflict people at crucial moments. Choking is simply a matter of too much tension.

Dr. Irving Page says, "Our blood cholesterol goes up and down with our emotions. Most people get a few knots tied in their stomachs due to the daily stress of today's modern living."

Science has proven that stress is a killer. We live in an age of anxiety. And because we are confronted with more and more situations that produce stress, increasing numbers of Americans at younger ages are suffering from high blood pressure, heart attacks, and strokes. *Furthermore, each of us must deal with our own emotional upset and tension caused by the everyday pressures of living.*

STORM AT SEA

In the air they call it "turbulence." On the sea it's "inclement weather." Whatever it's called, we had a taste of it when the Pacific showed us some of its awesome power on the way to Yokohama. The wind blows a gale, whipping up whitecaps and waves, and the sea is very rough. We were told that this storm stretched out from Japan to Los Angeles. No breakfast, no lunch, as your thoughts turn from meditation to medication.

For a small sum, one of the ship's doctors gave us a shot for "motion sickness," the same malady, we presume, that our seagoing ancestors called seasickness. The shot worked. The motion sickness was taken away, leaving us a little drowsy.

Some passengers told us that they're only happy when they're on the water. This was hard to believe on a stormy day at sea. But the QE2 rode it out like a duck on a wave. As "blood will tell" in a man when and how he meets trials and dangers, so does the lineage of the QE2 reveal itself. This magnificent ship was built by men with not only common sense, but a deep knowledge of the elements, seamanship, and expert naval architecture. We did not meet any forty-foot waves in our storm, but the natural Law of Buoyancy will always keep this vessel afloat and give her the leadership in speed which she holds.

The QE2 is probably the safest and fastest passenger ship afloat. The structure was built throughout from incombustible materials with complete automatic sprinkler systems.

THE HIDDEN FORCE

What makes the waters rough?
What makes the heavy swells?
What makes the whitecaps on the ocean?

It is the force of the wind.

When there is no wind the sea is smooth.
A gale is when the sea is rough.
We call it a storm.
A hurricane.
A typhoon is rain and wind.

THE INTERNATIONAL DATE LINE

The day which passed most quickly for us on this voyage was the one we deliberately dropped from the calendar between Hawaii and Japan on crossing the International Date Line, designated on the 180th meridian, just halfway around the world from Greenwich, near London, England.

At each time change on our journey we often heard the same questions: How come this three-hour difference in time? How come we lose a whole day way out here in the middle of the Pacific Ocean?

The answer is that the world has been arbitrarily divided into twenty-four-hour time zones of one hour each fifteen degrees.

(See the Time Zone Chart on page 119.) The zones are based on the rate of travel of the sun's passage from east to west over the continents and seas of the earth's surface. The International Date Line is an imaginary line that coincides with the 180th degree of longitude, there being 360 degrees designating the circumference of the entire earth. The International Time Zone is reckoned from a similarly imaginary line, called the prime meridian, which marks zero degrees placed at the Observatory at Greenwich, England.

The sun seems to travel over fifteen degrees of the earth's surface each hour. For each fifteen degrees east of Greenwich, the time is advanced one hour. For each fifteen degrees west of Greenwich, the time is set back one hour. At longitude 180 degrees East, the time is twelve hours more advanced than Greenwich time. When it is noon Saturday in Greenwich, Saturday is just beginning on the eastern side of the date line, and just ending on the western side. Therefore, there is a twenty-four-hour time difference between the two sides of the 180th meridian in the Pacific Ocean between Hawaii and Japan.

Upon crossing the hypothetical place of the International Date Line in the QE2, you receive a handsome certificate commemorating the event, to add to the ones received for crossing the equator and traversing the Panama Canal. Your certificates, signed by Captain Robert Arnott, are not only to impress your friends. They attest to the fact that you have something in common with the real pioneers who charted the earth before you.

TIME ZONES AROUND THE WORLD

The world's 24 time zones often follow geographical and political boundaries. In general, each zone's time is one hour earlier than that in the zone east of it. The base zone's time is called *Greenwich time*. Zones west of it are numbered + 1 to + 11. Their times are from 1 to 11 hours earlier than Greenwich's. Zones east of Greenwich are numbered − 1 to − 11. Their times are from 1 to 11 hours later than Greenwich's. The *International Date Line* lies in a zone designated ± 12. In this zone, points east and west of the line differ in time by 24 hours. The table below lists the zones of 45 cities and the time in each at noon Greenwich time. The table may be used to find out corresponding times in the cities. For example, it shows that when it is 1 P.M. in London, it is 6 A.M. in Chicago. Tokyo's time is 14 hours later than New York's time (7 A.M. to 9 P.M.). When it is 8 P.M. Sunday in New York, it is 10 A.M. Monday in Tokyo.

City	Zone	Time	City	Zone	Time
Berlin	− 1	1:00 P.M.	New York	+ 5	7:00 A.M.
Budapest	− 1	1:00 P.M.	Nome	+ 11	1:00 A.M.
Buenos Aires	+ 4	8:00 A.M.	Oslo	− 1	1:00 P.M.
Cairo	− 2	2:00 P.M.	Ottawa	+ 5	7:00 A.M.
Chicago	+ 6	6:00 A.M.	Paris	− 1	1:00 P.M.
Copenhagen	− 1	1:00 P.M.	Philadelphia	+ 5	7:00 A.M.
Denver	+ 7	5:00 A.M.	Quebec	+ 5	7:00 A.M.
Detroit	+ 5	7:00 A.M.	Rio de Janeiro	+ 3	9:00 A.M.
Edmonton	+ 7	5:00 A.M.	Rome	− 1	1:00 P.M.
Fairbanks	+ 10	2:00 A.M.	Saigon	− 8	8:00 P.M.
Glasgow	− 1	1:00 P.M.	Santiago	+ 4	8:00 A.M.
Havana	+ 5	7:00 A.M.	São Paulo	+ 3	9:00 A.M.
Honolulu	+ 10	2:00 A.M.	Shanghai	− 8	8:00 P.M.
Istanbul	− 2	2:00 P.M.	Stockholm	− 1	1:00 P.M.
Leningrad	− 3	3:00 P.M.	Sydney	− 10	10:00 P.M.
London	− 1	1:00 P.M.	Toronto	+ 5	7:00 A.M.
Los Angeles	+ 8	4:00 A.M.	Tokyo	− 9	9:00 P.M.
Madrid	− 1	1:00 P.M.	Vancouver	+ 8	4:00 A.M.
Manila	− 8	8:00 P.M.	Vienna	− 1	1:00 P.M.
Mexico City	+ 6	6:00 A.M.	Washington, D.C.	+ 5	7:00 A.M.
Montreal	+ 5	7:00 A.M.	Wellington	− 12	midnight
Moscow	− 3	3:00 P.M.	Winnipeg	+ 6	6:00 A.M.
Naples	− 1	1:00 P.M.			

YOKOHAMA—A WELCOME SIGHT

Through the week at sea, seven days with vistas of nothing but water, water, and more water, a refrain from an old familiar song plays through your head, a stirring call to adventure...

On the road to Mandalay
Where the flying fishes play
And the dawn comes up like thunder
Out of China, 'cross the bay...

Visiting the Orient, West meeting East, was for us a truly exciting adventure. Standing out clearly in our recollection of the first glimpse of the Orient, after days of ocean travel, suddenly emerging from the waves, was the changelessly welcome sight that seems to symbolize both New and Old Japan—Mount Fuji, which rose before us in full view in all its timeless fame and splendor.

As the QE2 maneuvered gently in toward the landing pier at Yokohama, we looked out from the deck at the spectacle and color of the Orient. Never in marble or in bronze have we seen finer specimens of limbs and muscles than those displayed by the compact, muscular, copper-colored boatmen of Japan.

They laughingly called out: *"O-hai-O! O-hai-O!"* That's Japanese for "Good morning."

It was an auspicious welcome to the Orient, and we forgot the vast stretches of ocean behind, suddenly eager to meet whatever lay ahead.

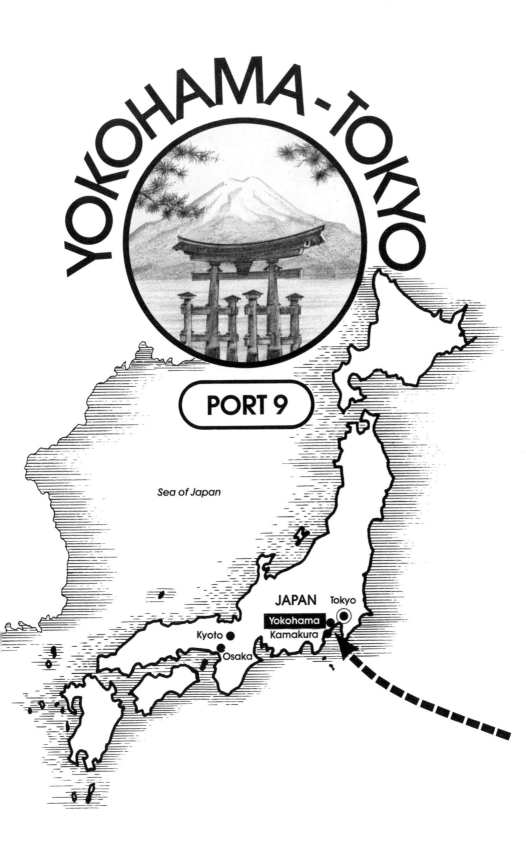

YOKOHAMA

We arrived in the port of Yokohama early in the morning. The sun was shining beautifully—a good clear day. Apparently this is no more common in Yokohama than in Los Angeles and many other great cities, for Japan also has a serious problem with air pollution. The industrialized seacoast is under an almost perpetual blanket of smog, and you're lucky if you can see Mount Fuji for an hour or two in the morning. As the QE2 came to rest, it was nice to feel the ship completely still and motionless after our week at sea.

An announcement over the loudspeaker the previous evening had informed us that before any passengers would be permitted to leave the ship, the Japanese authorities were to see each person. A special bulletin was also issued about the quarantine inspection. We rose early, about 5:30 A.M., dressed, and were down in the Queen's Room waiting in line when the Japanese police boarded the ship at 6:30 A.M. They inspected each passenger's disembarkation pass. The formalities were brief and courteous but, with over 2000 passengers to be checked, it was some time before all had passed inspection. (This was the first time we had experienced such an inspection during the cruise.)

But soon it was over, and a six-piece band dressed in red uniforms serenaded us as we set foot on Japanese soil for the first time. A variety of tours had been prearranged, and our tour bus was waiting.

Yokohama is a bustling, industrialized city, home of more than 2,700,000 people. Its colorful seafront promenade has many shops as well as warehouses and miles of wharfs. An exotic port city of long standing, Yokohama was almost totally destroyed by air bombardment during World War II, but it has been completely rebuilt.

Among our first impressions, we were struck by the fact that there seemed to be not an inch of vacant land. All land had some kind of building on it. The streets were narrow, so narrow that it was a wonder how any two cars could pass. We saw every kind of architecture—old, new, and in between—reflecting the varied industries and activities of this industrial port city. The exception was that there were few tall buildings, testament to the fact that Japan is subject to rather frequent earthquakes.

Here one finds many of the same souvenirs and gifts that can be found in Tokyo and other Japanese cities—electrical goods, watches, cameras, prints, antiques, silks, handmade dolls, china tea and sake sets, kimonos, miniature bonsai trees, ceramics, bamboo ware, and much more. In many stores record-of-purchase forms are attached to passports to save from ten to thirty percent in taxes.

Local foods include *sushi* (raw fish in vinegared rice with hot mustard), *okaribayaki* (barbecued chicken with vegetables cooked at your table), *kobe* steaks, *tempura, yukatori,* and *sukiyaki* dishes.

Our tour guide was a young Japanese woman named Suzuki. She told us that Yokohama is the second largest city of Japan, that it covers an area of 164 square miles, and that it is the largest seaport in Japan, supplying a capacity for fifty-four vessels.

Our guide described a place everyone ought to visit—the Silk Center. The use of silk can be traced back to ancient times in Japan, where silk weaving techniques were developed to a high art, as witnessed by the elaborate Nichijin silk textile which has been in vogue since the fifteenth century. Silk became a principal export item during the nineteenth century after the opening of the port of Yokohama in 1859. Although the industry has faced stiff competition from synthetic fibers in the postwar period, in recent years the special and unique qualities of traditional silk textiles have once again played a leading part in fashion throughout the world.

As we explored the city, we had a glimpse of Yokohama Stadium, used largely for baseball, which is as popular in Japan as it is in the United States. Behind us, while we toured this clean city (noting how someone was always picking up any papers or debris), entire families of Yokohamans were going down to the pier to see the QE2. For 500 yen (about two dollars in the U.S.), they could go out into the harbor in a sightseeing boat to sail around the magnificent ship.

But then, too soon, we were on our way again, speeding past miles and miles of rice fields in the open country, toward our next stop…Tokyo, approximately twenty miles away…

SIGHTSEEING IN TOKYO

Our first impression of Tokyo, Japan's capital and the world's largest city with over 12 million people, was of people— and traffic! We had already been warned by Suzuki about Tokyo's notoriously heavy traffic, and we knew of its huge population, but like so many things in life it must be experienced to be fully comprehended.

We drove by ancient temples and modern office buildings while we soaked up some of the atmosphere of the city. Later, when we had a chance to walk around, we were glad we had bundled up well, for the temperature was around forty degrees and made our cheeks tingle. We saw many people wearing gauze masks over their faces, and wondered if the cold weather had brought on an epidemic of colds.

Here, as always, we enjoyed rubbing shoulders with the people of places strange and new to us. We saw many small babies being carried on their mothers' backs. The Japanese mother's coat has a pouch fastened on the back, with a hood that can be turned up to completely cover the baby. We were struck by the beauty of the Japanese children we saw.

The old and the new mingled everywhere. Traditional kimonos and some modified ones are still worn in the streets by many women, but girls and women under thirty years of age wear Western clothing—even blue jeans!

When you're out walking in Tokyo—and you'll do a lot of it—be sure to keep in mind, when you step off the curb at a street crossing, that vehicle traffic moves on the lefthand side, not the right, as we are accustomed to. So, be sure to keep your presence of mind when you cross the streets in Japan! By the way, believe it or not, Japan now produces more automobiles than the United States, and automobile production is supposed to be the leading industry of the U.S. economy.

GETTING AROUND IN TOKYO AND JAPAN

Suzuki had told us that if you're in a hurry in Tokyo, don't take a taxi. You could get hung up in a traffic jam and run up a $100 bill on the meter!

If you do take a cab, remember one thing about tipping: Pay only the amount ticked up on the meter. Most cab drivers do not speak English, so it's a good idea to have your destination written out beforehand in Japanese. Carrying a map is also a good idea. If you are visiting friends or going to a destination in a little-known area, your Tokyo cab driver may have trouble finding it if all you have is a street number. Numbering of houses within districts is done by *date built* in some areas, not the location.

Mass transportation, on the other hand, is fast, fabulous, and inexpensive—if you can avoid the rush hours. Eight subway lines now crisscross Tokyo and there is also an electric train system. Fares on both are nominal and the service is excellent. You can ride for a whole day for $2.50 on a special ticket offered by the Japanese National Railways. The trains whisk you between points of interest at surprising speed, as do the various subway combinations and transportation skyliners. "Japan's Bullet Train," of course, is world-famous, a must for long-range touring.

DINING OUT IN TOKYO

You'll get along fine in large Japanese cities even if you don't like Japanese food, because many American chain restaurants are handy wherever you go—including doughnut and coffee shops, McDonald's, Dairy Queen, Kentucky Fried Chicken, and Wimpy fast-food places.

But why eat where you can eat any day at home? In Tokyo you can enjoy snacking from the sidewalk vendors, usually set up in the evenings, especially in university areas. They serve tasty and inexpensive Japanese snacks of roasted sweet potatoes, noodles in broth, and charcoal broiled chicken wrap.

For inexpensive dining, many large companies have cafeterias open to the public, and major office buildings also have good eating places generally open for lunch and on through the evening dinner hours. Just don't try to get into one between noon and one o'clock. In the various shopping centers, if you can time your appetite, you can even get an egg, toast, and coffee breakfast for as little as $2.50—a real bargain in Japan. There are no less than seventy-seven such eating places in the main Tokyo Railroad Station of the Uaesu Underground Center. If you're not hungry but want to rest your feet, for about $1.75 you can have tea or coffee with music.

"A picture is worth a thousand words," and that's certainly true if you don't know much about Japanese food. Restaurant managers in Tokyo know this, and they recognize the dilemma tourists are in much of the time when looking at a Japanese menu, so many restaurants have window displays of their dishes. They are really colored wax dishes showing both the menu items and their prices, but you may decide that if the mock-up looks that good, the real thing must be delicious.

We were in luck our first day in Tokyo, for our tour had scheduled us for luncheon at the beautiful Chinzanso Garden Restaurant. Here, in a gracious setting, six of us were seated at each of the many square tables that had a hot grill about two and a half feet square in the center. We were served a delicious lunch, cooked before our eyes on a burning grill. On the grill were placed *sukiyaki* meat, thin slices of beef, pork, chicken, and veal. Along with these were slices of raw carrots, green pepper, some fresh corn, and parsnips. These were fried and then dipped in a *soya* oil which gave them a delicious flavor. A bowl of rice with *soya* sauce came with the meal. It was all so good that, inevitably, we ate too much!

MORE TOURING

After lunch we stopped briefly at the Imperial Palace Gardens, a beautifully unique setting in the center of Tokyo. Tourists are not permitted in the Gardens themselves, but one can see quite well from the outside. A large water moat surrounds the Gardens and in the center of the Gardens is the Imperial Palace.

Next was an elbow-rubbing, flashing light stroll through the Asakusa, one of the city's busiest and noisiest amusement centers. Then, suddenly, we were in the quiet of the Asakusa Goddess of Mercy Temple. *The Japanese are an innately religious people.* About sixty percent are of the Shinto faith, about thirty-nine percent are Buddhist, and only about one percent are Christian. There are temples everywhere, and many of the old customs are still practiced in their religious worship.

The burning of incense is always part of the ritual. At the Goddess of Mercy Temple it is burned in a large censer in the center of the Temple Square. We saw the people rub their arms, faces, and shoulders with smoke from the burning incense. There is a belief that if they can get the incense smoke on any part of the body which is afflicted, it will be healed.

Our tour guide, Suzuki, told us more about Shintoism and Buddhism. Shintoism is a native religion of old Japan, primarily a system of nature and ancestor worship. Buddhism occupies an important place in Japan's religious life. It has exerted a profound influence on the fine arts, social institutions, and thought of Japan. Many Japanese still consider themselves members of one of the major Buddhist sects, while some observe both Buddhist and Shinto rituals, the former for funerals and the latter for births and marriages.

In Shintoism there is no concrete thing worshipped as containing the concept of God, such as the veneration shown the statue of the Buddha in a Buddhist temple. In Shintoism, God is in the Somewhere all around you, and there are therefore many, many designated gods: God of Water, God of Air, and others. So, in the main hall of a Shinto shrine, before you pray you should clap your hands twice to get the attention of the god. If you forget to clap your hands, the god doesn't hear your wish. This practice does not apply in a Buddhist temple, where prayers are directed to the concrete statue of the Buddha.

ETIQUETTE WHEN PRAYING AT A SHRINE

1. See to it that you are dressed appropriately for the occasion. Pass under the *torii* and walk through the *sando,* or approach to the shrine.

2. Go the hand-washing stone basin and cleanse your hands thoroughly. With a dipper, pour water into your cupped hand and then bring the water to your mouth and gargle. (Do not bring the dipper directly to your mouth.)

3. Advance before the god enshrined. Then throw some money (either paper currency or coins) into the offertory.

4. Bow deeply two times.

5. After that, clap your hands twice.

6. Then, make a deep bow once more.

KAMAKURA: THE GREAT BUDDHA STATUE

A drive thirty-two miles southwest of Tokyo brought us to Kamakura, the former governmental seat and now a most pleasant summer resort. The main attraction here is the colossal bronze image of the Buddha, the *Daibutsu*. It weighs 103 tons, was cast in the year 1252, and is one of the largest works in bronze that man has ever made.

The statue of the Great Buddha is fifty feet in height. Within it is a chapel with room for 100 worshippers. The face alone is eighteen feet in length. Underneath its drooping eyelids are eyes of pure gold. The circumference of the thumb is three feet.

There are more statistics, but the unique feature that sets this statue apart is its Sphinx-like calm, its look of immovable superiority to all the evils of the earth, its dreamlike contemplation of the Eternal Infinite which embraces all that lives—past, present, future.

Upon a huge stone pedestal, in the form of a lotus flower 100 feet in circumference, this gigantic figure has been seated in solemn contemplation for over 700 years.

THE SACRED LOTUS FLOWER

The lotus, which blooms during the month of August, has long been deemed sacred in the Orient because, growing from muddy, stagnant slime, it holds up to heaven flowers of exquisite purity and beauty. Thus, it symbolizes immortality—how the

Great Buddha—Kamakura, Japan

aspiring soul, fed by the Light of Heaven, unfolds into a certain and gloriously fulfilled beauty.

In Buddhist writings it is said, "Though thou be born in a hovel, if thou hast virtue, thou art like the lotus growing from the slime." Accordingly, the lotus is associated with the mysteries of death and immortality. We saw bronze vases filled with lotus flowers made of metal standing on many Buddhist altars, and statues of the Buddha, like the Great Statue of Kamakura, have, as an appropriate pedestal, a smooth lotus leaf in stone or bronze.

KYOTO

Cherry blossom time in Japan is deservedly famous, and we regretted not being there for its full beauty. One of the principal pleasure resorts of Tokyo is Ueno Park. It is especially beautiful in the month of April when all its cherry trees are blossomed out in full glory. Usually pink in color, cherry blossoms have been lauded by the poets of Japan for centuries. In their delicate beauty they are to Japan what roses are to Western nations.

Kyoto was the classical capital of Japan for over 1000 years. While we did not have time for this visit, many of our friends on the QE2 took the tour which included Kyoto, so we got many an eye-witness description of the city.

Kyoto is reached by way of the "Bullet Train" out of Tokyo Central Railway Station—a three-hour, 120 miles-per-hour ride from Tokyo. In Japan's fifth largest city, a sightseeing tour begins with a visit to the Imperial Capital itself. Then you visit Kinkakuji Temple (the Golden Pavilion) and Nijo Castle with its famous "nightingale" floors.

Time should be allowed to appreciate the serenity of the Heian Shrine with its beautiful inner garden, and time to stroll about in Kyoto's handcraft center for some "tax-free" shopping, since Kyoto is noted for its fine silks, embroideries, porcelain, and lacquer wares. Kyoto is a city of some 250 Shinto shrines and 1500 Buddhist temples. It is a truly wonderful place, from all accounts, for the visitor who enjoys walking trips and do-it-yourself exploring.

JAPANESE INFLATION

When visiting Japan, be prepared for the difference in value of the dollar as compared to the yen. That means being set to meet unexpected costs of food, cab fares, living, movies, and other purchases. The cost of living in Tokyo is now the highest in the world, according to a recent price survey of 130 countries made by the United Nations. Travelers come back with shocked tales of five-dollar cups of coffee, hundred-dollar cab rides, thirteen dollars to see a movie, and two hundred dollars a night for a hotel room. That is why you are glad to return to the QE2 for your stay overnight.

But don't be dismayed. If you do decide to stay ashore, it is possible to find modest overnight sleeping accommodations within easy walking distance of shopping and sightseeing areas. One thing you can bank on, even if you must choose a place to lodge that has no frills, is cleanliness. Everything is always immaculate. You'll leave your shoes outside the entrance of a *ryokan,* with its sliding screens and a comfortable mattress on the floor. It is still possible to find such inviting accommodations for a night, plus two meals, for as little as fifty dollars.

ANOTHER JAPANESE MIRACLE

We drove by the buildings of the famous Imperial University, which cover fifteen acres of campus and include admirable classrooms, dormitories, laboratories, a hospital, and faculty residences.

Shinto Temple—Japan

The Japanese educational system is no less a miracle than its industrial development. In other nations the educational systems have ripened slowly, rooted in centuries of experience. But seventy years ago Japan had practically nothing of the kind. She sent her best and brightest out to gather knowledge in the Western world. Some were sent to England, some to Germany, others to France, and many to America. They brought their lessons home. Today Japan provides public schooling for all children through six years of elementary school and three years of junior high. Most students go on to three-year senior high schools, and those able to pass the difficult entrance exams enter four-year universities. Today Japan enjoys one of the world's highest literacy rates and enviable ranks of scholars, engineers, and scientists.

DEPARTURE FROM YOKOHAMA

After two days in Japan, we were scheduled to depart at 5:00 P.M. We went up onto the Boat Deck at around 4:30 to hear the thirty-three-piece band play, and we were astonished at the mass of people below. Thousands of Japanese families were there to see the QE2 leave Yokohama. The pier, which was about a half-mile long, was packed solidly with humanity from one end to the other. It was cold up there on the Boat Deck, but we enjoyed hearing the band play "Missouri Waltz" and many other familiar American and British tunes, and we were moved by the spectacle on the pier. It was as if the whole city of Yokohama had come to see us off.

When we pulled away from the pier, the red sun was setting in the west. Our feelings were mixed, happy but sad. It reminded us of life itself, how the time for departure comes for each of us …those thousands of hands waving at us as we pulled farther and farther away into the sunset. We had an image of life as in a Japanese painting. As a brook starts from a small spring trickling from beneath a rock…meandering down through smooth places, sometimes rocky, sometimes sunny places, sometimes dark…but ever flowing on, hopefully trying to do some good along the way…until finally it reaches the sea…the sea of eternity.

A whole new crowd of people had come aboard the ship at Yokohama, in addition to the cruise passengers who were already on board. There were many Chinese, Japanese, South Americans, and Europeans among them. Many, we learned, were going to Hong Kong to buy goods of many kinds, for Hong Kong is the marketplace of the Orient.

For us, however, the Philippines was first in mind, with Manila as our next Port of Call…

EN ROUTE TO MANILA

With new passengers on board, the fire and lifeboat drills were repeated for their benefit. With that under their belts (or should we say lifejackets), the newcomers did not seem satisfied to wait for Hong Kong to do their shopping, but beat a hasty path to the QE2's own shopping arcade. There are many fine shops clustered together in what looks at first glance like the Rue de la Paix, New Bond Street, or Madison Avenue—one exclusively for jewelry, watches, and fine arts; another for Waterford crystal and China; another for souvenirs; another for clothes; one for perfumes and colognes; and another a drugstore, with books for sale.

All of the ship's stores, bars, and casinos, by the way, close up tight whenever the QE2 ties up at any port. When the ship leaves port, conversely, they all open up for business while on the open sea. (And no sales tax is charged for any goods or spirits.)

LINGERING THOUGHTS OF JAPAN

That first evening out of Yokohama, one of the pleasant memories that stayed with us was of the veneration given in Japan, as in other Eastern countries, for age.

In Japan, a man of sixty-five is just entering the age of wisdom. A man in his eighties is regarded as having attained the age of wisdom and high stature—not as someone to be discarded or made an object of pity or humor. This veneration of age and respect for the accumulated knowledge of a long lifetime is something we occidentals could wisely adopt.

The shelving of a valuable employee upon his reaching the age of sixty-five frequently results in a company's needing to hire two or three or more younger, inexperienced employees to cover the range of work the "old-timer" did so expertly and single-handedly. Failing to recognize the continuing contributions of old people is a modern blunder that is costly in every way.

CAPTAIN AND CREW

On our last night out of Manila, we were invited for cocktails in the Captain's suite at 7:15. Our host was Captain Robert Arnott, a pleasant and most friendly man who sets the tone for the entire crew. We also had the pleasure of meeting his lovely wife, who assisted him in greeting the guests.

At the party we also met Captain Ian C. Borland, a fine Scottish gentleman who has spent the best part of his life with Cunard, thirty-four years at sea. He is in charge of port arrangements and marine equipment. Our talk touched on the escalating costs of operating the giant ship and the need for such seemingly small cost-cutting moves as reducing the size of the QE2 newspaper from six to two pages. Inflation, it seems, follows us around the world!

Besides appreciating the fast, efficient service of our room steward, Len Knight, and stewardess, Barbara Ward, who somehow managed to keep our room immaculate without ever disturbing our routine, working only when we were out of our room, we felt always in good hands with the Cunard crew. We enjoyed hearing the English accents of the ship's personnel. In all the shops and facilities, the crew was exceptionally polite, clean, and well-mannered, and it was always a pleasure to speak with them.

Later that night, in the small hours before dawn, we lay listening to the stillness. Everyone was asleep and the ship was quiet. You could barely hear the hum of the exhaust fan, and the room was full of hush. This ship, we thought, does not even creak. She is truly a queen in every way.

This quiet time is a very good time to think and to concentrate on the past day and the new day ahead. Our last thought before drifting off to sleep once more was of the good spirit aboard this ship…this competent and friendly ship which was carrying us around the world…realizing for us the dream of a lifetime.

Pleasant dreams….

Coconut Grove—Manila, Philippines

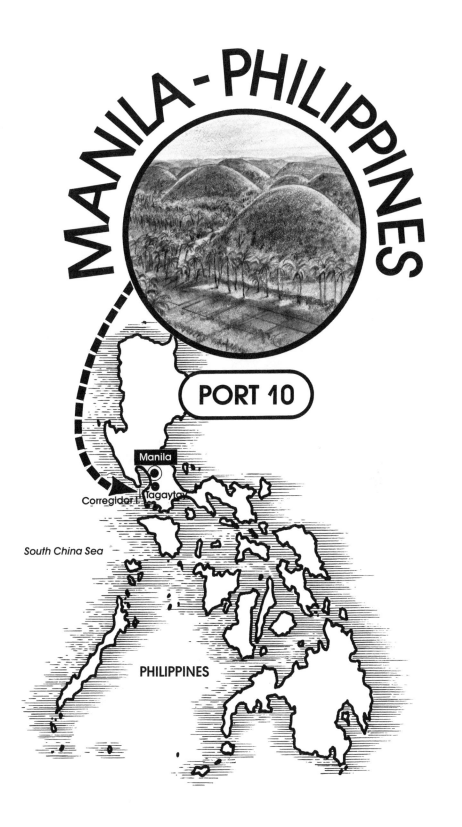

MANILA - PHILIPPINES

PORT 10

Manila
Corregidor I. Tagaytay

South China Sea

PHILIPPINES

MANILA

Luzon, where Manila is located, is the largest of all the Philippine Islands. The city was established back in 1573, and it is the political, educational, and economic center of the country. The capital of the Philippines itself is just outside Manila, in Quezon City, where the government offices are housed. Manila itself is densely populated, with about 360 people per square mile, and a total metropolitan population of about 4.5 million.

The Philippines consist of some 7100 islands, the second largest being Mindanao, about the size of Indiana in the United States. The climate throughout the islands is tropical, in the lowlands averaging eighty degrees. The wet season is from June to November and it is *wet!* Rainfall on Luzon averages between 35 and over 200 inches per year, with the average for Manila at 82 inches. The Philippines lie right in the typhoon cyclone belt, so they endure no less than fifteen devastating storms in an average year. The islands also have a number of active volcanoes, and they are not exempt from destructive earthquakes.

Our tour guide, Jean, briefly told us of the three phases of the history of these islands: the pre-Spanish period, the arrival of the Spanish under Magellan in 1521, and the American influence, which began in 1898 when the United States under Admiral Dewey ended the Spanish-American War.

The Filipino people are mostly of Malay stock, descendants of the Indonesians and Malays who migrated to the islands long before the Christian era. Intermarriage with the Chinese began as far back as the ninth century when they came to the islands to trade. Consequently, Chinese ancestry prevails in most Filipinos. Under each rulership there was naturally an influx of immigrants, from the Malays themselves to the Spanish, Chinese, Arabs, and Americans. Each introduced their respective customs, religions, and languages.

In religion, eighty-three percent of the people are Roman Catholic, nine percent are Protestant, and about five percent are Muslim. As for languages, there are *some eighty-seven native dialects spoken!* Even today there are many "lost tribes" living in the remoter islands, each separate unto itself and preserving its own tongue. Since 1939, however, the native language taught in government schools has been Filipino, with nearly half the population also learning English. There are over 39,000 public schools, by the way, giving the Philippines the highest literacy rate in the entire Pacific area.

On July 4, 1946, the Philippine Islands became an independent republic, with a President as head of state, elected for a six-year term; a Prime Minister who appoints the Cabinet; and Supreme Court Justices, appointed by the President, who hold office until age 65.

TOURING MANILA

We drove through the main part of the city, a mass of humanity and cars. Traffic through the heart of town is bumper to bumper. Passing through the new business section of Manila, we observed fine modern buildings with lawns, all very well designed. Along one street we saw displayed at least fifteen or twenty roasted pigs, for sale by the slice or by the whole pig.

We didn't buy a pig, but we did purchase two nice blue embroidered shirts, plus a set of beautiful embroidered tablecloths and mats. The famous embroidered shirt of the Philippines is called a *barong tagalog.* The long-sleeved style is worn out over the trousers as a jacket substitute even at formal affairs. The shirts are available everywhere and cost from twenty to twenty-five dollars. A must for any visitor!

Our first stop was Fort Santiago, adjacent to the river. Here, many American and Filipino prisoners died in the prison during World War II when the area was occupied by the Japanese. The scene of the Bataan death march nearby was pointed out to us. Our guide took us through the dungeon of the old fortress, giving a most harrowing description of man's inhumanity to man, telling of how hundreds of prisoners were suffocated or drowned in the six small underground cells.

We also visited the Manila American Military Cemetery and Memorial, burial place of more than 17,000 Americans who died in World War II. Each of the 17,000 graves is marked with a marble cross bearing the name of the soldier and his date of death.

Jean called our attention to part of the old walled original city which still remains. Built long ago by the Spanish, but largely destroyed in World War II, it is called *Intramuros,* which means "within the walls."

Enclosed within Intramuros is one of the first churches built by the Spanish in 1586, Saint Augustine's Cathedral. Its beautiful cloister, gardens, chandeliers, and elaborate carvings are well worth seeing. Also within Intramuros is the Manila Cathedral, a magnificent structure that was rebuilt several times, the most recent being in 1959.

Near the Pasig River is Malacanang Palace, the official home of the President. It is open to the public and has displays of Philippine art and exhibits from the Spanish colonial period. Lovely gardens surround the palace and its many elaborately beautiful rooms. Malacanang was General MacArthur's wartime headquarters.

From Intramuros, we drove through Escolta and along Rizal Avenue, while Jean told us about the Philippines' national hero, José Rizal, for whom the main street is named. Rizal was incarcerated in Fort Santiago during the nineteenth century, and there is a museum containing his memorabilia inside the fort.

Rizal was executed by the Spanish in a nearby park that now bears his monument.

José Rizal was obviously hundreds of years ahead of his time, and his progressive ideas brought about his downfall. He was misinterpreted and alienated, and at age 25 he was martyred. He was the author of two books written in Spanish, which chronicle his progressive ideas and versatility as a sculptor, painter, and writer.

Other notable highlights of a visit to Manila are Makati, the modern section with its fine shops and attractive homes; Forbes Park, which is informally called "Millionaire's Row" after its luxurious homes; and the colorful Chinatown district, which has many popular shops and restaurants.

OUTSIDE MANILA

Outside Manila, the countryside is tropical and pictur-esque—miles and miles of rice fields, small villages of thatched huts on stilts, lush native greenery.

The Bamboo Organ in the Las Pinas church, about a half-hour drive from Manila, is something tourists should see. Father Cera, an Augustinian friar, wanted an organ, but having no other material to build one, decided to use the bamboo which grew around the church. He took many lengths of bamboo—950 of them—and covered them with sand while they were drying to protect them from harmful insects. Then he worked on the organ for three years, by which time an organ with 718 bamboo shoots played the hymns for his delighted congregation. Some-one is always around to play it for you, and it is more than an organ. Its poignant notes proclaim a tribute to man's ingenuity and the power of his hands and spirit unified in quest of "impossible" ends.

The national shrine of Corregidor Island lies across Manila Bay. All manner of war relics may still be viewed there, grim reminders of its fall in World War II after long occupation by American forces. Boats operate for sightseers who want to see the Malinta Tunnel and the remains of the barracks. One of the Cook shore excursions from the QE2 includes a trip by hovercraft to the Corregidor Island.

SHOOTING THE RAPIDS OF PAGSANJAN ON YOUR OWN—THE THRILL YOU WILL NEVER FORGET

Two hours south of Manila is Pagsanjan Falls…shooting the rapids of Pagsanjan is quite an exciting experience. Strangely, your trip begins from the Pagsanjan boathouse on the river below the rapids. Each couple is assigned to a canoe with two highly-skilled boatmen, one boatman in front and one in the rear of the canoe. The first part of the trip will take you up the river and up the rapids.

Getting safely into the canoe, which is hand-hewn from a native tree, and setting low in the water, is only the first challenge of an exciting adventure.

You are told to keep your hands inside the canoe at all times and are soon pushed upstream through the dense Philippine jungle and up the rapids. The rapids are a stream of rapid white water constantly twisting its way through a maze of large boulders.

The boatmen navigate the canoe up the rapids by jumping out onto the ever-present rocks, one pushing from the rear and one guiding the canoe from the front.

Your tiny canoe, traveling upstream, finally arrives at its first destination. You find yourself on a small lake setting at the base of the Pagsanjan Falls.

After a short visit ashore, the return trip down the river and *into the rapids* begins. Daylight fades as your canoe enters the narrow gorge. You look up from within the deepening shadows of the moss-covered cliffs. Hundreds of feet above you, the bright green jungle glistens in the sunlight. You pass by a symphony of small waterfalls, blossoming out into a soft mist as they fall. The unspoiled and breathtaking beauty overcomes you. The thought comes to you, "What am I doing here, halfway around the world, deep in the heart of a tropical jungle, rushing down a river in a small canoe? So far from the protective custody of my beautiful ship that I have begun to call home?"

As you enter the rapids there is no longer time for concern. *You find yourself screaming as the canoe races downward, twisting, turning, and slamming off the sides of large boulders.* Your feet are under water, but you don't notice it till later. Through it all, the boatmen shouting to each other, never seeming to lose their composure, finally slip the canoe into calmer waters.

Climbing carefully out of your canoe and onto the dock, you think back…You vaguely remember passing a canoe, broken in half, its occupants struggling for shore, one man with his camera held high above him.

We all shipped some water. I'm sure there wasn't a dry seat on any of the eight canoes. As the natives said, "We were lucky to catch the increased force of the rapids after a rainstorm." We questioned this reasoning before fully noticing the exhilaration and excitement among the fellow travelers. Two elderly ladies said it best by exclaiming, *"This is really living!"*

Back in our stateroom, we had dinner sent in and relaxed with a cooling and refreshing drink. We went to bed thinking about the interesting sights and sounds and smells of a country we had never known before, and all that we had seen and done that day.

Yesterday, the Philippines, Manila, and Corregidor were just names…now they were a part of us…forever.

We heard the engines start, the anchor being pulled up. The ship eased forward. We couldn't stand not to say goodbye properly. So we got up and looked out of the porthole just in time to see the last lights of Manila Bay twinkle off in the distance. Destination: Hong Kong!

EN ROUTE TO HONG KONG

We were looking forward to visiting China. Here is a country with an area twice as large as the United States. *Just imagine: One billion people live in China!*

China was once what the United States is now—the birthplace of inventions. Paper was manufactured there in the third century. Tea was produced a century later. Gunpowder was first invented in China. This same astonishing race produced the

Mariner's Compass in the fourth century, porcelain in the third, chess and playing cards in the twelfth, and silk embroideries in almost prehistoric times.

Such facts are a good reminder that life never stays the same, and the lead is always changing hands. So it is in today's world…

Drastic and dramatic changes are taking place *now*—a new era of shortages, scarcity, controls, higher prices. This is the kind of thinking you have to engage in—figure out what's going to happen in the future, and figure out how you can participate in it.

Remember, too, that *achievements are the accomplishments of persistent individuals.*

EXTRA CARE

One "extra care" service provided by the *Queen Elizabeth 2* is the security of safety deposit boxes and banks. If you travel around the world this way, you don't need a money belt to safeguard your money. The QE2 provides safety deposit boxes for your money and your jewelry, too, and the Queen is a great place to wear it.

There are also two Barclay's Banks on board that will change money of all denominations and cash traveler's checks. They will not accept any deposits, however…but then you don't go on a world cruise to save money!

One of the most popular places on the ship between ports of call is the Photo Shop, located on the Upper Deck adjacent to the Casino. Here they will develop your film and make all the prints you want in any size.

Here also are the candid pictures of the activities on the ship, taken by the ship's photographers. Hundreds of photos are displayed on the walls and in racks on the deck so you can pick out your favorites and take them home to bring back pleasant memories. Even if you don't know a shutter from a satrap, you can come home with hundreds of great photographs of you and your cruise.

TRUE LIVING

On Sunday morning, on our way to Hong Kong, we followed our usual practice of attending morning church services conducted by the Captain. At home or away, one always feels better by going to church. This "way of life" teaches man to rule his passions and impulses by reason and right. By so doing he safeguards himself and the society of which he is a part.

Life, the Captain tells you, consists of much more than mere existence ... more than breathing, eating, wearing a few clothes, and taking up space. The most important thing has not been learned: how to conduct ourselves so that we may truly live. True living is to enjoy each day. Happiness depends, not on the things around us, but on our *attitude. It is not how much you do, or what you do, it is HOW you do it. Your attitude rules the "HOW." You can make it difficult or you can make it a breeze.* Here is the crux, the core of life: *"As a man thinketh, so is he."* So simple, but how true, how profound! How few understand and practice this natural law!

True living means self-development; the first and most important thing in this world for every individual to understand is *himself.* This is the greatest problem in life. Knowledge of self requires study. The greatest responsibility given to every person is the development of self, which means the *equal* development of our *physical, mental,* and *spiritual* faculties.

True living means doing our best every day, being a blessing to others as well as to ourselves. *"My first business is to so live that at least a few will thank God that I lived, when my little day is done."* You are living only when you are useful, constructive, and accomplishing worthwhile things. Accomplishment brings happiness.

True living means *thinking, observing,* and *learning.* It recognizes the difference between *truth* and *trash,* and that *quality* of life is more important than life itself. Our *bodies* must be fed, but much more important, so must our *minds* and *souls.* For to build a *man* is life's greatest project…for each of us!

True living is life lived quietly, *confidently,* and in prayerful fellowship with God in the fields and the valleys, the mountains, the ocean, and the sunshine. Living such a life is the end of the rainbow, where is hidden the pot of gold of which we are all in search.

QE2 in Hong Kong Harbor

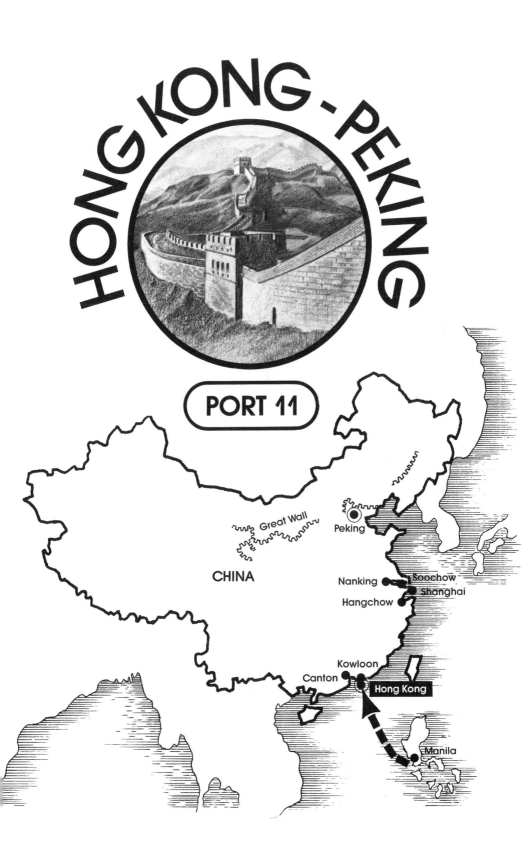

HONG KONG - PEKING

PORT 11

CHINA

Great Wall

Peking

Nanking   Soochow
Shanghai

Hangchow

Kowloon
Canton   Hong Kong

Manila

ARRIVING AT HONG KONG

Early on Monday morning, we arrived in Hong Kong. We hurried out on deck to gaze out upon the glorious sight of Hong Kong Harbor, one of the most beautiful in the world. A hundred ships lay at anchor here, displaying flags of every country on the globe. Although the day had hardly dawned, these waters teemed with activity. Steam launches, covered with awnings, darted to and fro like flying fish. Innumerable smaller boats, called *sampans,* propelled by the muscle power of Chinese men and women, surrounded each incoming steamer like porpoises clustering around a whale.

These sampans would be one of our most vivid memories of Hong Kong. Thousands of Chinese live in these little boats. Whole families are born, live, and die without ever leaving their sampans, and as many as three and four generations will live in the same manner. Some of the younger generation, however, are said to be becoming accustomed to Western ways, and they are leaving the little boats to live their own lives on land.

The QE2 docked next to the Star Ferry at Ocean Terminal on Kowloon Peninsula, about a mile across the harbor from Hong Kong Island. One can enjoy a profitable visit to Hong Kong without ever leaving this huge oceanfront pier. On the pier is a four-story building, about two blocks long and a block wide, with over 200 shops of all kinds. Here you will find low prices on hundreds of items—Japanese cameras, Swiss watches, Japenese lacquer, wood carvings, silks, perfumes, sapphires, diamonds, ivory sculpture, jade, silver, and gold.

But we hadn't come to Hong Kong to stay in one place.

There are four exciting days of sightseeing and discovery ahead for us!

HONG KONG

Hong Kong is a British Crown Colony with a population of 4.7 million people within its 400 square miles. The Colony is divided into three parts: the Kowloon Peninsula, the New Territories, and Hong Kong itself. We had docked on Kowloon Peninsula. Adjoining it to the west are the New Territories, consisting of 365 square miles of Mainland China and some 235 nearby islands. The importance of the New Territories lies in the fact that it borders the People's Republic of China, and that it provides the necessary farm acreage to grow the food supply for Hong Kong's millions.

"Kowloon" means "nine dragons," and it is a peninsula jutting out directly across the harbor. Here are the huge piers for ships from the four corners of the globe, and here is the terminus of the railroad connecting Hong Kong with China proper. (The city of Canton in China is about ninety-two miles westward.) Whereas the Hong Kong Island part of the Colony is more English and is the seat of government, the Kowloon side is more crowded, more Chinese.

Hong Kong is not only one of the most beautiful places in the world but it is also one of the busiest. It encompasses sixteen square miles with an altitude of up to 3140 feet. The name "Hong Kong" means "fragrant harbor," and it is actually the name of the principal island ceded to England by China in 1842.

The main island is eleven miles long, mountainous, mostly occupied by the city of Victoria, the administrative, financial, and cultural center of the Colony. It has a population of about 1.5 million people. In climate it is in the tropical zone, with an average annual rainfall of eighty-five inches and seventy to eighty-five degrees humidity. Even so, a topcoat is occasionally required in the winter season of December through February.

Overall View of Hong Kong and Kowloon

GETTING FROM HERE TO THERE

It is easy to get back and forth between Kowloon Peninsula and Hong Kong. Just catch the Star Ferry. It will take you across Victoria Harbor for thirty cents if you sit on the upper deck, only twenty cents on the lower deck, and it runs every five minutes.

The other way, which our tour bus would take, is the Harbor Tunnel. Seventy feet below sea level, it is about one and a quarter miles long. Opened in 1972, it cost about $320 million to build. The capacity of the passages every day is around 17,000, which is why the tunnel got back all the money it cost to build in its first four years of use!

SOME PERSONAL IMPRESSIONS

Almost before we left the ship, a crew of Chinese painters had started painting the outside of the QE2. It would be completely repainted in the four days that we were there. The men stood on a plank held by ropes hanging from the top rail. They balanced themselves on that swaying plank with seemingly sure-footed ease, dipping their long-poled rollers into the pails of paint and then rolling the paint on. No one ever fell—talk about being agile and having good balance! No circus ever put on a better demonstration of balancing, juggling, and tightrope walking than these Chinese painters.

Construction and building were taking place everywhere—high-rises, complexes, freeways, bustling development. We observed some differences in building in the Chinese use of bamboo instead of lumber, which is scarce. Bamboo is so durable that it is used for scaffolding on new buildings, scaffolding for painting, stepladders, clotheslines, brooms, and baskets.

The refugee shack settlements of a few years back are all gone, replaced by hundreds of huge apartment complexes, about twenty stories high. The buildings are a colorful sight, as their entire faces are aflutter with family washing. Each apartment seems to have bamboo poles extending from the windows or porches, and the washing is hung on these. No clothespins required—just poke the poles through the armholes or necks of clothing, the best kind of fasteners.

The Chinese are certainly not a lazy people. The struggle for existence demands that they keep active. By our standards they can live on almost nothing. A local merchant told us that one of his coolies, after twenty-five years of service, had recently had his salary raised to thirty dollars a month. "Now," the coolie exclaimed, "I intend to marry another wife. For years I have longed to have two wives, but have never been able to afford it. Now, with thirty dollars a month, I can indulge in luxuries!"

The women do the work of loading and unloading cargo, often with a baby fastened in a pouch on their backs. The older Chinese people, both men and women, wear the type of dress you see in pictures—black trousers and a long tunic topped with a high collar. The younger generation, those under thirty, dress in Western style, in denim jeans and mini-skirts.

CHINESE NEW YEAR

We were lucky in the timing of our arrival at Hong Kong, for the day we docked was the Chinese New Year. Days before the holiday, colorful flower stalls appear in front of the Municipal Council Building. Everywhere festive throngs prepare for the New Year celebrations, with shops and stalls selling flowers, goods, toys, and lots of religious articles.

Not until 1912 did the Chinese adopt the Gregorian calendar used by the peoples of the Occident. They counted a year as beginning from the first new moon after the sun entered the sign of Aquarius, in late January or early February. They reckoned twelve months to the year, with each year in a cycle of twelve years having a reigning animal—the Year of the Tiger, the Year of the Dragon, and so on. This year was the Year of the Monkey.

Everything was closed in observance of the Chinese New Year. The following day we were treated to a nine-course dinner on a floating Chinese restaurant, and everything was lit up especially for the New Year. One scene we shall never forget was the flaming sunset as we cruised the harbor on the Harbor Dinner Cruise Ship, toasting the New Year.

TOURING HONG KONG

We drove through the Harbor Tunnel from Kowloon to Hong Kong Island, emerging in sight of the Tidewater Shelter and Hong Kong Yacht Club. There is a lot of money in Hong Kong, both on the water and on land. Besides all the beautiful yachts, we learned that there are 450 Rolls Royces in Hong Kong, the largest concentration of these luxury automobiles in the world.

Tiger Balm Gardens was our first stop, built by a wealthy Chinese man whose wife and daughter still live in the Gardens. This wealthy Chinaman, now deceased, made his money in pure gum rubber and an ointment called Tiger Balm Ointment. This seems to be good for everything from a headache to a mosquito bite. There are many strange figures depicting Chinese mythology in the Gardens, and there is a vast array of articles on sale.

Continuing on our way, we passed the Royal Hong Kong Jockey Club. There is racing twice a week during the dry season, from October to June. Betting on the horses is the only legal gambling allowed in Hong Kong. If you want to gamble you have to go to the island of Macao, about fourteen miles away by jetfoil or ferry, where casinos are open twenty-four hours a day.

We passed through what our tour guide, Shirley, called the "Suzie Wong" district, notable for banquets and gaiety of all kinds. Red banners are used outside the restaurants. Made of paper flowers, they are lettered with descriptions of the kind of celebration going on—a wedding, a birthday, a newborn baby, a month-old baby. The writing on the banner also gives the last name of the wedding host. And who pays for everything in the wedding celebration? Why, the groom, of course!

The dramatic sound of a Chinese gong was used to introduce our second guide, John Morliss, who filled us in on the story of the tram that goes up and down Victoria Mountain to the Peak. The tramway has been in operation since 1880 without an accident of any kind. The car will stop within eight feet on the steepest part of the mountainside, but a demonstration was not insisted upon.

"Living on the Peak" is a measure of social status in Hong Kong; the higher up the Peak you live, the higher your status. At the higher levels a house would cost about a million U. S. dollars. In addition to its status, the basic attraction is that it's about seven degrees cooler up there, rising to 1300 feet above sea level. For the tourist, however, the big attraction is the marvelous view of the harbor and the islands.

At the lower terminus of Victoria Peak Tram, a short walk up Garden Road, is the Botanic Garden. Here you get a clear view of Government House, the home of Hong Kong Colony governors. The Garden provides a brilliant display of azaleas, ferns, and flowering plants. In the small zoo and aviary nearby, you can observe the lovely old Chinese custom of the bird-loving Chinese out "walking" their birds—in their cages! Both old and young take part in giving the caged birds an airing.

As we drove on, we were treated to the colorful array of sights and sounds of this fascinating city...passing by Repulse Bay and Deep Water Bay...Ocean Park with its Oceanarium and the striking Sea Horse on a hillside, made of 3700 dwarf banyan trees...the Royal Hong Kong Golf Club and the police training institute...the low cove industrial area...and much more.

We visited two of the city's renowned bargain centers. Thieves' Market and the Cat Street shops are where Hong Kong housewives go for bargains in jars, cooking pots, plastic ware, radios, records, yard goods, ornately carved furniture, and jewelry.

Even more interesting is famed Ladder Street, where you climb up a ladder for many, many stories to shop, finding better buys at each higher level! We learned that whole families live out their lives on the steps leading from Hollywood Road to Queens Road Central. Their tiny shops double as shop and home. Babies nap on chopping blocks. Over all is the constant sing-song of voices selling rat traps, cricket cages, soft drinks, and much more.

And at last we came to Aberdeen, the old Chinese fishing community—so colorful that it deserves a description all by itself!

ABERDEEN

Aberdeen, on the ocean side of Hong Kong Island, is famed for the boat people with the famous "floating restaurants" nearby. They are called "boat people" because they spend their lives on their boats.

In the old days, the water people believed superstitiously that if they left the water and went ashore they would die or get sick. In ancient Imperial China they were actually forbidden to live ashore. They have their own customs passed on from generation to generation, and they even have their own dialect.

About 60,000 people live like this. At first glance the poverty and dirt seem appalling, but oddly enough, we learned that these are among the hardiest and happiest of the many ethnic groups that populate Hong Kong. They have plenty of water for bathing, and the sea is generous with food. You would be hard put to find skinny, undernourished children.

The boat people do not have to pay rent for shelter. They can move in any time they like, on a first-come, first-served basis.

They do need two fishing licenses, however, one for fishing in China and the other for fishing in Hong Kong.

The water people of Aberdeen are sometimes called "Tanka," which in English means "egg family." They were so named because in the old days they were so poor that they didn't have any money for paying taxes, and they paid their fees in eggs. Today, many of these people are no longer really poor. The big fishing boats cost at least 25,000 Hong Kong dollars, and some cost much more.

Aberdeen is the site of the original Hong Kong, a small village. Sailors later applied the name to the whole island. When the present capital was built it was named Victoria, which is still its official name, but the original name of Hong Kong was too deeply entrenched, so the island is still known everywhere today as Hong Kong.

The name means "fragrant harbor," and it was applied to the settlement because most of its people were fishermen who also helped to support themselves by making a kind of incense, very pleasant-smelling, which they had for sale. Today, the incense is no longer to be found, and Aberdeen smells fishy rather than fragrant, but it is still a most fascinating place.

RELIGION IN HONG KONG

Every religion is represented in the metropolitan population of Hong Kong, but Buddhism predominates, along with Taoism and its deep devotion to ancestor worship. Belief in evil spirits is common, which makes certain stones, rocks, pools, and trees sacred to various people. Many deities of nature are given reverence. Confucianism has a wide following in the Colony, with its emphasis upon the importance of mental acuity and intelligence, and upon devotion to parents and old people.

The Anglican Church was named Church of State when Hong Kong became a British Colony. The Roman Catholic

Church plays a major role, as do many other denominations. There are synagogues and mosques and many Protestant churches. Percentage-wise, most of the population is Buddhist. About sixty-five percent of the Chinese are Buddhists, the other thirty-five percent being either Christians or Moslems.

In modern Hong Kong, you can find temples where incense is burned to the powers-that-be, and bells ring to attract the attention of deities. Two of the most famous temples are the Man Mo Miu (*Miu* means temple) in the West District, and the Tin Hau Temple at Causeway Bay. *Tin Hau* is Queen of Heaven, and the protectress of mariners and fishermen. Man Mo Temple is a very old edifice at the head of the famous Ladder Street.

FROM OUR HONG KONG JOURNAL

When in Hong Kong, do as they do...

In conversation, it is not good manners to change the subject abruptly. A good Chinese enjoys thorough exploration of a topic.

When dining with the Chinese, sip tea and other drinks slowly. Gulping signifies low breeding. Drink only when others are drinking.

When bargaining, stay friendly with shopkeepers, who usually expect you to pay about two-thirds of the asking price. If you fail to bargain, you lose face. If you argue too much, they may not sell at all.

Be tolerant toward a Chinese coolie who seems cross and rude. Remember that rarely do these men ever get enough sleep. Usually, a minimum of twelve of them live in a room or are crowded into a hut or cave.

When entering a Buddhist or Taoist temple, you do not have to remove your shoes.

Discourage beggars. Professionals exploit children to sit and beg for them.

Use both hands when you accept your bowl of tea. If cakes come with it, *eat them very slowly.* Never act hungry, which is very rude.

When dining out, admire each dish as it is served. Tea is served last, a signal that the party is over; time to go after a single sip. Refuse your host's pleas to stay longer; he is simply being polite.

Finish all of one bowl of rice but never ask for a second. It implies that you don't like the other dishes and are trying to fill up on rice.

Carry visiting cards. It is courteous, after formal introduction, to exchange visiting cards.

It is the Chinese custom to *list the family name first,* then generation name, then given name. Example: Wong Kee Foy would be called Mr. Wong.

SHOPPING IN HONG KONG

Hong Kong is the greatest shopping bazaar in the world, but to make the most of it you need four main things: *time, good humor, know-how,* and *money.* No matter what the tourist-shopper seeks, he'll find it in Hong Kong, and at a price he can't resist, *if* he understands how to *bargain with courtesy.*

Do you want Japanese cultured pearls? Here they are priced lower than in Japan. Cameras are a third less than in the United States. Some of the world's best watches sell for fifty percent less than anywhere in the States. Be careful in buying furniture, though. Often it has been crafted hurriedly, and the inlaid and carved pieces will shrink and crack in dry climates. You should know what to look for in furniture.

Most of the big hotels have elaborate shopping arcades, and all major department stores are located on the main streets, along Queens Road Central and around the Pedder Street district. If you don't enjoy price haggling, go to the department stores where prices are set, but you will pay more than in smaller, individual shops.

Three prices are aimed at three categories of buyers: 1) lowest for the Chinese, 2) next for British and other Western residents, and 3) highest for American tourists. This practice, however, has been generally nipped in the bud by the Hong Kong Tourist Association, which encourages "one-price stores," meaning 1) no bargaining, 2) tourists and residents are charged the same, and 3) all items carry price tags.

Visit a Hong Kong bazaar, especially the one called Cost Plus, located in Sea Terminal. It houses perhaps the best collection anywhere of the most unusual merchandise from all over the world at low prices.

Hong Kong tailoring can still be good value, but be careful here as with furniture. It's not as great a bargain as it used to be. You can still have a suit or a dress tailored from fine fabrics, but go to recommended shops. Don't listen to a "tout" urging you to go to a particular tailor.

Ship packages home through the Railway Express Agency, which is said to take full responsibility for arrival of goods.

LEAVING HONG KONG

It was evening when the QE2 prepared to put out to sea from the pier at Kowloon. Thousands of people lined the pier to see the ship off, and two bands were playing. As the gangplank was hauled up, the native Chinese brass band on the pier played "Amazing Grace," stirring the emotions.

The two huge iron doors closed, and a crew of several men cinched up all the bolts tightly. Then, with a scarcely perceptible stirring, the great ship was under way.

A pilot had boarded the ship, and it was he who would guide us safely out of the harbor. The music and the moment were both vivid reminders to us of all the pitfalls and hidden

The Great Wall of China

boobytraps we must face during our lifetime. He who thinks he is self-sufficient is a fool. There is no such thing as self-sufficiency. Man needs to be in close correspondence with the Higher Power in order to live in safety the life he is designed to live.

We moved out into the colorful harbor—a place you can never forget, once having seen its multitude of ships coming and going—liners, freighters, oil barges, ferry boats, junks both motorized and under sail, sampans, lighters, tugs, patrol boats... all busy about their business. Now, in the distance, we could faintly hear the music of the Hong Kong Band playing "Auld Lang Syne." We were out in the middle of the channel and big tugs churned the water with might and main, pushing us around so we could pull out of the harbor.

Cruising down the harbor was like passing through a fairyland. The colored lights from the tall buildings of the city, with the dark hills in the background, shone on us from both sides. After four never-to-be-forgotten days, it was a parting that was indeed "sweet sorrow."

Sampans in the Harbor—Singapore

SINGAPORE - MALAYSIA

PORT 12

South China Sea

MALAYSIA

Singapore

EN ROUTE TO SINGAPORE

The next lap of our journey carried us along the full length of Vietnam all the way to the tip of Malaysia. Rough waters are not unknown in the South China Sea, and we experienced some on our way to Singapore, five full days out of Hong Kong. But the sea finally became calmer and the air got warmer as we went sailing south toward the equator.

TIME OUT TO REST...AND THINK

Summer and winter vacations are not luxuries. They are necessities if a person is to keep at peak efficiency, strenuous year after strenuous year!

William James, the renowned American psychologist, admonished: "Beware of those absurd feelings of hurry and having no time, that breathlessness and tension, that lack of inner harmony and ease."

The danger sign is the hurry habit. Whenever you catch yourself "pressing too hard," watch out! Hurry has a habit of becoming chronic. Hurry, worry, and tension age a person fast. They can even bring on a heart attack, a stroke, or even death.

A world cruise on the QE2—or any cruise—is a great relaxer, a way to take time out to rest and think. Remember, *the environment you fashion out of your thoughts, your beliefs, your ideals, your philosophy, is the only one you will ever live in.*

When you are relaxed and carefree, happy ideas come to your mind without effort as inspiration. Relaxed attitudes are the means of obtaining the greatest happiness as well as the greatest efficiency in life.

Life is turbulent and inclement like the sea, never at rest, untamed, perilous. The secret of its everlasting interest lies precisely here, in the fact that you cannot explain it and never know what is going to happen next. A famous doctor wrote, "Since you are not going to get out of this world alive, you might as well learn how to live in it as long as you can."

THE VANISHING JINRICKSHA

Have you ever been taken for a ride? Well, we have—in more ways than one. On our 10th Anniversary Cruise around the world, we did not see a single *jinricksha* in operation. They have disappeared like the trolley car.

Two dozen years ago, when John Gunther wrote *Inside Africa,* he told of the South African town of Durban, "where tourists come to bathe in the warm waters and to be hauled about in 'rickshas drawn by picturesquely clad Zulus who wear horns and feathers." The "rickshas," a native told Gunther, "are made in only one place in the world, a town in New Jersey."

What Gunther heard was close to the truth. All of Durban's jinrickshas were made in the James J. Birch carriage factory in Burlington, New Jersey. If there were other makes of the "Oriental" vehicle elsewhere in the world, none equalled Birch in output or quality.

Jinrickshas rolled out of Burlington to Africa, Japan, Korea, China, Burma, India, Ceylon, the Philippines, and any other place where the familiar two-wheeled, man-powered vehicle carried passengers.

James Birch didn't invent the jinricksha, but the ones he started to make in his buggy factory in the 1880s were lighter and faster than any others. By 1900, he was king of the ricksha makers, turning out so many that it is said Henry Ford visited the Birch plant to observe his "assembly line."

When Ford's "popular fad" spread, the Birch factory's wagons and carriages gradually went out of production, but the jinrickshas outlasted them all. Time caught up with the rickshas, too, however, though it was not the well-made little carriages that expired. Rather, it was a growing sense around the world that hauling jinrickshas degraded the human who supplied the power.

Saigon outlawed jinrickshas in 1946, Singapore the next year, and the Philippines two years later. Pakistan did away with them in 1956, and Japan's rickshas eventually gave way to Japanese automobiles. These picturesque vehicles are now about as obsolete as bustles.

SINGAPORE

On Sunday morning, February 24, we docked at the East Lagoon Wharf in the busy harbor of Singapore.

Singapore occupies very little space on the map, but it plays a very large role as the "Crossroads of the Orient." It is an island of 225 square miles at the tip of the Malay Peninsula, the southernmost point of Asia, and it is the midway point on the historic trade route between India and China. Long wasted by wars, it was reestablished as a British trading station in 1819 by Sir Stamford Raffles. As British as British could be for over a century, it spent the long years of World War II under Japanese rule, but emerged a free and sovereign independent city-state.

Its thriving industry and commerce are one of the success stories of modern times. Its telephones work, its tap water is drinkable, its streets are safe and as clean as a whistle. Tourists flock here even though there are no special tourist attractions.

The population is largely Chinese, with some Malay and a smattering of Indian, Pakistani, Indonesian, Ceylonese, and others, including several thousand U. S. businessmen and their families to give it flavor.

Singapore's racial mix is only one reason why the island has been called "instant Asia." The color and vitality of an enormous region are concentrated here. Free-port bargain hunting is matched by some of the best girl watching to be found anywhere. The city's Golden Mile is a solid line of luxury hotels, banks, and shopping centers where you'll find the best of Asian goods on sale alongside such familiar names as Gucci, Dunhill, and Louis Vuitton. Then there is the food—Chinese chicken and fish, Malay satay kebabs, Indian curries, Javanese rijsttafel, and many other Eastern dishes.

Singapore has come a long way since Raffles established his trading station. Today the "City of the Lion"—the Sanskrit meaning of "Singapore"—is the third largest port in the world, a modern city of sampans and gin slings, high-rise apartments and harbor lights, a true meeting place of East and West.

TOURING SINGAPORE CITY

The pier is located in the harbor area with many warehouses and ship repair firms, three miles from the nearest store. So the city tour offered us a good chance to see the layout of the city.

Our bus took us to the top of Mount Faber, the highest point on the island at 385 feet. Here we enjoyed a panoramic view of the city itself, the harbor, and the Indonesian archipelago.

The view of the harbor was spectacular. It is divided into three sections: the West Walk, mostly houses and dry docks; the Main Walk, where passenger liners and cargo vessels berth; and the East Walk, also called the container port. Singapore is the port for ships of more than 150 shipping lines flying the flags of eighty-four countries. There are no less than 200 ships in port every day, and a ship leaves or enters the waters every thirteen minutes.

Signs of the city's modernization are everywhere, especially in housing. Thousands of high-rise apartments are being built. Here a family of five, who once lived in a cubicle no larger than a one-car garage, now feel close to paradise.

In Chinatown, too, the old is being demolished to make way for the new. But there are still many ancient structures, housing stores and restaurants, shops and lodgings, in this one square mile of 80,000 souls, ninety-five percent of whom are Chinese.

Our first stop was at the National Museum to view the famous Jade collection. From here it's only a short distance to Orchard Road, the emerging tourist center of Singapore. Here are the modern hostelries—the Mandarin, the Hilton, Holiday Inn, Hyatt, and Malaysian—all offering fine lodging, shops, and restaurants. At the Cultural Theater nearby, there is a presentation of old Singapore, a forty-five-minute show repeated several times each evening. Adjoining is the Rasa Singapura Food Center, which has the best of the city's traditional food stalls where you can try some of the local dishes.

At the Botanic Gardens, the main park of Singapore, we were forcibly reminded that we were in the tropics. Singapore is just eighty-five miles north of the equator and it's one of those places where you can fry a 1000-year-old egg on the sidewalk. (Better here than many places, the sidewalks are so clean!)

Sir Stamford Raffles started clearing the land and planting these gardens back in the 1850s, but it wasn't until 1875 that it was officially opened as the Botanic Gardens. It has inviting picnic grounds set amidst a lush display of tropical flowers, trees, and shrubs. Some seeds for rubber trees were planted in 1877, flourished, and from them the whole rubber industry in southeast Asia began. Here, too, is one of the most exotic orchid displays in the world.

One of the highlights of any visit to Singapore, for those who know it only from stories and movies, is the grand old colonial-style Raffles Hotel. The architecture is classified as French Renaissance, with huge rooms and high ceilings. The rooms now have air conditioners, but the dining rooms still feature the traditional ceiling fans and the bar still serves the famous Singapore Sling.

There is much more to be seen in Singapore. Buddhist and Hindu temples are sprinkled throughout the city. On Race Course Road there is the Temple of a Thousand Lights, with a fifty-two-foot-tall Buddha. The Sultan Mosque Moslem Temple is also famous. (Remember to wash your hands before entering.)

For bird watchers, a must is Jurong Bird Park, the world's largest aviary, containing over 7000 species from all over the world. The birds are kept in huge cages, most resembling their native habitat. The park also features the world's highest man-made waterfall, and the entire park can be seen while riding a delightful miniature train.

Tiger Balm Gardens (the twin of the one in Hong Kong) is another attraction with its fantastic mythological figures from ancient Chinese folklore. Nearby, the Pasir Panjang Paradise Cultural Show features performances each morning by East Indian, Chinese, and Malay dancers.

SHOPPING IN SINGAPORE

In this multi-racial, multi-cultural city, shopping can be a refreshing experience, not only because of the variety of goods but also the overall cleanliness of the shops and the city in general. Most sales clerks in the better stores speak English—it is, in fact, the medium of instruction in ninety percent of the schools.

But, before buying anything, practice "comparison shopping"! There are the usual Japanese cameras, Swiss watches, chinaware, electric shavers, radios and tape recorders, record players, and French perfumes. Other specialty shops handle fine Chinese merchandise and still others feature exotic Thai silk, Indonesian batik cloth, crocodile-skin items such as shoes, tailored goods, and sari material of silks and prints.

Thieves' Market on Arab Street is loaded with East Indian and Indonesian items. C. K. Tang is a good major department store. Raffles Place in the center of Singapore has many fine shops, banks, and businesses. Nearby is a major tourist attraction, Change Alley, the lively bazaar area where you can window shop or buy goods from all over the world, mixed in with the islanders' own relaxed life-style.

Peer into an average apothecary shop, a native drugstore, and you will see jars upon jars of native Chinese medicines, tiger bones, fossil teeth, crushed pearls, rhinoceros horns, innumerable herbs, and even tonic wines in huge glass jars with corpses of snakes coiled inside.

There are also markets where you can have the dubious pleasure of seeing pythons, freshly killed to order, dressed six-foot lizards, skinned civet cats, turtles, bats and monkeys hanging upside-down in their cages, and toads, either to be consumed as food or ground up into the latest medicinal brew cocktail.

After one look at this, you can't wait to get back to Raffles for that Singapore Sling.

FOOD AND DRINK

Singapore is noted for fine food, from its elegant continental restaurants to the popular food stalls in Peoples' Park Market, or the Chinese food of Glutton Square, Albert, and Bigis Hokkien Streets. It is a microcosm of foods from all over the world—France, Italy, Germany, India, Japan, Korea, all with just a touch of Malaysia thrown in for seasoning.

HOTELS

As you might expect in a city known as the "Crossroads of the Far East," Singapore has many fine hotels.

Among the better ones, the Singapore Hilton is certainly located close to business, shopping, and entertainment centers. It offers a full range of business services, including multi-lingual secretarial facilities. Hin's Heavenly Cookhouse has a rooftop swimming pool and serves fine local dishes. The Holiday Inn and the Equatorial both have air-conditioned rooms and good restaurants.

Among budget hotels, the Station Hotel and the Hotel Southeast Asia (air-conditioned) are worth considering.

Singapore's night life is mild rather than wild, and the best attractions can be found in some of the hotels, such as the Tiara Lounge in the Shangri-la, the Marco Polo Lounge in the Marco Polo, the Sky Room in the Sea View Hotel, and La Roulette in the Cockpit Hotel.

NATIVE CUSTOMS

One of the most rewarding aspects of travel is the chance to observe the different customs and traditions of other lands. Some we can live without. If you get invited to dine with native Singaporeans, for instance, you might find yourself confronting chicken feet or fish baked whole, innards and all.

A most deeply embedded custom among the Chinese is that one must never show grief publicly. The father and mother don't go to the funeral of their child, for example. They cry at home, not in public. A native funeral also tells you if the man was wealthy or poor. The custom is to burn all that the deceased will need in the spirit world—if he was rich, the real thing can be burned, otherwise paper dummies are used.

THE END OF THE DAY

Our one day in Singapore was over too soon, but our short stay left us with many thoughts and impressions.

No matter how meager the conditions of life in this far part of the world, though their lot be dirt and squalor, the people seem to be always happy and satisfied. Proof, perhaps, that "what we don't have and don't know, we do not miss."

You know you're in the tropics when you take off your damp clothes at night and they are still as damp as ever in the morning. So, it was a relief to return to the air-conditioned comfort of our luxurious stateroom on the QE2, our home now for more than a month.

EN ROUTE TO COLOMBO

For two days the bow cuts the water of the warm, gentle Indian Ocean, on its way, according to ancient tradition, toward an outpost of heaven, the island of Sri Lanka (the ancient name for Ceylon). Now is a good time to relax, to touch bases by letter with those you've left behind on the far side of the world, to reflect on all you've seen and all that still lies ahead.

In many ways a great journey is best seen in memory. So it is with life. *Life is woven like an Oriental rug. All the weaver sees is the back of the rug where each day he ties thousands of knots. He doesn't see the full design until it is all finished and trimmed.*

THE ACTIVE MIND

You will stay younger longer by keeping your mind active. Man has three divine dimensions: physical, mental, and spiritual. Each one of these must be constantly looked after, whether you are in your twenties or seventies, at home or away.

Use it or lose it is Nature's dictum.

You can be just as productive at eighty as you were at twenty, provided you keep your mind active, and you have not had any disease that affects your mentality.

If you do not exercise physically, you get muscle laxity. The same applies to your mental ability. Stretch your mind and you will keep in good mental condition. Keep your mind alert and young and happy!

Nurture your mind with good, wholesome thoughts. Read worthwhile books, and you will find that intelligence actually increases as one grows older.

Still, with all the tribute paid to the words "young" and "youth," there are still a few areas where "old" is best:

Old books…old wine…old friends…

Ideas that stand the test of time.

KEEPING IN TOUCH WITH *QE2 TIMES*

The *QE2 Times* is an early morning newspaper delivered free to everyone's cabin at 7:00 each morning.

It features highlights of world events, the daily weather report in twenty leading cities, the New York Stock Market showing the ten most active stocks, a crossword puzzle, and the solution to the prior day's puzzle.

Various information about the ship is reported, including the names of its crew, from the Captain to the galley; details of all religious services; the ship's position with course, speed, and temperature of air and sea; general information about the ship's shops; ship's notices; lost and found office; Barclay Bank locations and hours; and Thomas Cook Tour Office hours and reports.

Lists of winners of the daily raffle, requirements for obtaining visitor's passes and limits of two guests per passenger, information about the next port coming up, information about telephone calls and telegrams, announcements of special sales at several of the ship's shops, birthday announcements, special meetings of Masons, lectures by rabbis, Bible study, wedding anniversaries, Alcoholics Anonymous meetings, and ads for stores in ports coming up are all given in the *Times.*

You can also read the results of sporting events, including the scores of major events of sports in season.

The *QE2 Times* gives explanations of how to make telephone calls and send telegrams to any part of the world right from your cabin. Passengers wishing to make ship-to-shore telephone calls are advised that in addition to the conventional radio link, a satellite link is also available on the QE2.

Working Buffalo—Ceylon

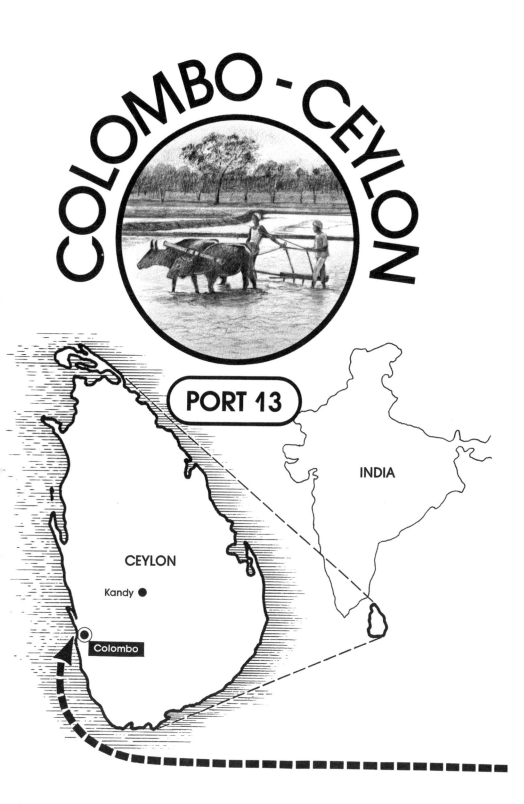

COLOMBO - CEYLON

PORT 13

INDIA

CEYLON

Kandy ●

◉
Colombo

COLOMBO

Early on the morning of February 17, we docked in the world's largest man-made harbor at Colombo. It was a warm, sunny day, the water was swarming with small ships, and the wharf was crowded with women in gaily-colored saris, the men in white flowing cloth wrapped around their hips and coming down to their ankles. The native people were an instant attraction, as we were to them. Most of the people are very dark-skinned with sharp noses and black eyes and hair. The minute you step onto the street, hordes of children gather quickly around you, begging for coins. If you give one a coin, it's the signal to be literally mobbed by them, so you have to beat a hasty retreat and dispense your coins only from a distance.

Sri Lanka, or Ceylon as it used to be called, is a paradise of lush vegetation, rice paddies, and coconut and banana plantations. Its landscape ranges from high mountains and the highland areas of the great tea estates, to thick jungles and tropical beaches at the seashore.

Sri Lanka's history goes back to a thousand years before Christ. A people from northern India, the Singhalese, settled and called it "Lanka," meaning "resplendent." Like most trade crossroads, it has a long history of internal wars and bloodshed. In the sixteenth century Sri Lanka was discovered by the Portuguese, and in succeeding centuries it was a Dutch and then an English colony, before obtaining its independence in 1948.

The island knows but two seasons in the year, the rainy monsoon-typhoon season from April to October, and the dry season from November to March. From what we heard of the monsoon winds and the torrential rains, we decided that we had come at the best time!

TOURING COLOMBO

We selected the Cook's morning tour of Colombo, and it was to prove one of our most fascinating tours. The city is one of beautiful homes and wide paved streets with tropical trees in rich bloom, including many coconut trees—this was our first glimpse of a lovely yellow coconut.

As we drove through the streets of the city, there were flags flying everywhere, honoring a visit from the King of Nepal. Soldiers and other officials were standing at attention outside the State Building where the King was staying as a motor coach procession formed to take him on his tour. You feel like yelling, "Come along with us, for every Queen's tour is fit for a king!" Then you remember that they're called Cook's Tours and decide against it.

Soon we are navigating the narrow downtown streets, lined on either side with native vendors hawking handmade articles, fruits, and vegetables. Natives go by carrying huge baskets of bananas, coconuts, oranges, everything imaginable, on top of their heads. This, we are told, accounts for their admirably straight and erect posture. A minor traffic jam grinds us to a stop as an ox-drawn cart filled with bags, bundles, and boxes of merchandise blocks our way. Everywhere you look people are wearing gold earrings and bracelets. Gold, the guide explains, has never let them down. Like a faithless lover, paper money promises much but only gold delivers.

The tour included many religious shrines and temples— Saint Lucia's Cathedral, Hindu and Buddhist temples, and Wolfendhal Church, dating back to the days of Dutch rule. Most people of Sri Lanka are religious, with Buddhism predominating, and they attend the temples regularly to meditate and pray. There are special observances all over the country at full moon.

We had a good view of the domed Town Hall across from Victoria Peak. Following Galle Face Road through a better section of the city, we drove past a tiny island nestled close to the shore, now a bird sanctuary. Our tour took us through the business district, called the Fort, the native trading center of Pettah, and then out farther into the fashionable area known as the Cinnamon Gardens.

Continuing on through picturesque rural areas, we saw many native houses built of sun-dried mud, solidified with bamboo plaiting, with neither windows nor chimneys—all exceedingly primitive. We observed that some of the inhabitants of these structures wore the costume of Eden. But the adults, considering the climate, were tolerably clothed. Yet, if it ever comes to a choice between a garment and a piece of jewelry, the native always takes the gold or silver. A child, if his or her parents can afford it, will be adorned with bangles, anklets, and medallions before getting a shirt or a petticoat.

One of the drawbacks to happiness in Sri Lanka is the multitude of land leeches and other bloodsucking pests which seem to drop from nowhere onto the unwary pedestrian. We were told how every morning, especially during the wet summer months, one's shoes must be "well shaken before taken," on account of scorpions. And one should not be overcome at turning down the bedsheets and finding a coiled cobra for a bedfellow.

Driving inland, we were quickly surrounded by fat, moist plants thrusting their heads out of green water, and birds calling to each other from the trees. It was a living jungle just waiting for man to turn his back so it could grow across the road and set the world right again.

About 600 years ago, this jungle was the site of the once proud capital city of the island, now visible in the ruins of Polonnaruwa. Here, vast Buddhas are carved from solid rock. A dramatic sight is Sigiriya, a rock fortress over 600 feet high with giant, topless Amazons painted on the rock overhangs.

Our guide, Bertie, pointed out prominent carvings along "the way of the lion." The lion carvings are traceable way back to around 500 B.C., when the island was invaded by "the Lion People" from India, and they honor a legendary ruler named Lion Arm.

We also saw the sacred Boddhi tree, where a statue of the Lord Gautama Buddha marks the spot where the Buddha received enlightenment as he sat meditating, about 2500 years ago.

At the end of our tour, Bertie gave us a most gracious chanted blessing in her native tongue and a warm "God bless you!"

ON OUR OWN

In addition to our wonderfully conducted Cook's tour, there was much of interest to see on our own. Out among the people, we found that Sri Lanka is more than a city. It's an exploding world teeming with life—markets, shops, carnivals, bazaars, young mothers hardly more than babies themselves suckling their young, an army of baby beggars, taught from toddler size to beg as a way of life.

A hotel alongside the beach served tea and sandwiches. The manager explained that the motion picture *The Bridge on the River Kwai* was made nearby.

Coming back into the bazaar, there's a hair-raising moment when you take a picture of a snake charmer with snakes coiled around his neck. You bend close to see, and as you do so he softly plays his flute and taps a basket. You decide you must have a close-up. Suddenly, the snake inside springs out at your lens. You click the shutter and then drop the camera and run screaming into the crowd, hoping you haven't scared the poor man too much.

Though no one had captured the snake on film, you're sure there are at least a dozen pictures of you running away.

Working Elephant—Ceylon

ELEPHANTS IN CEYLON

There is many wild animals on the island, including leopards, crocodiles, antelope, bear, and many birds, as well as an abundance of fish, both in the sea and in fresh water. There are also some 2000 wild elephants roaming freely in the jungles, and, more importantly, about 2000 domesticated work elephants.

Elephant power is used in Ceylon's jungles, since machines cannot operate through miles of tangled swamplands. And the elephants of Ceylon adapt as work beasts much better than the wilder, larger African elephants. There are also sacred temple elephants, and these great animals play a vital role in the life of the island.

There is a humorous saying here: "If you want to do something big, wash an elephant." The keepers of the work elephants prove this daily when they take them down to the river for a daily scrub. First, the elephants are made to kneel in the water. They are swept by a huge broom and then told to "rinse." At the command, they raise their trunks like fire hoses and shoot water over their scrubbed workmates for a rinse-off.

RELIGION AND SUPERSTITION

Today's customs on Sri Lanka are still influenced by a deep-rooted mixture of religious superstition, with witchcraft and magic rites to exorcise evil spirits. There is a popular Lime Ceremony to appease the gods, which uses seven limes, signifying purification. The juice of the limes is squeezed over the head of a person who is believed to be sick because of evil spirits. If the witch doctor mispronounces even one word, the whole ceremony is null and void.

Inland from Colombo it is an eighty-mile drive to the historic stronghold of Kandy, famous for its "Temple of the Tooth." Faithful pilgrimages are made here because it is the venerated resting place of the sacred tooth of the Lord Buddha. It lies in a golden casket beneath seven other caskets, well hidden and sheltered by bulletproof glass. Only high dignitaries are permitted to view the tooth itself.

The edifice is grimy with age, yet kings of Burma and Thailand send yearly contributions for its maintenance. And even in faraway Japan, Buddhist priests speak of it with the utmost reverence. The relic is said to be the eye-tooth of Gautama Buddha, taken from the ashes of his funeral pyre 2500 years ago. But, though it has been revered for centuries, it is well known that no human mouth could ever have contained it, for it is two inches long and an inch in thickness, being apparently a piece of ivory from an elephant's tusk. Still, every year in the month of July, a grand procession takes place here in honor of this tooth, revered by a third of the human race.

Another fascinating legend linked with religion is that of a mammoth footprint on Adam's Peak in the mountains of Ceylon. The mammoth print is claimed individually by each religion. The Buddhists claim that Buddha visited Ceylon three times and left his everlasting mark on the highest mountainside. The Hindus claim that it was made by the god Siva. Moslems say that Adam himself stood on that peak. Christians give the apostle Thomas credit for somehow making the footprint. So, there is an almost continuous pilgrimage trailing up Adam's Peak, a most treacherous ascent because high winds sweep its cliffs, often hurling pilgrims down into the valley, while prowling wild beasts lurk in the dense forests, threatening those who attempt the pilgrimage.

FLORA AND FAUNA

In addition to its famous temple, founded in 1371, Kandy is famous for its Botanical Gardens, filled with orchids and spices. A vast area of 150 acres, it contains some of the most rare and interesting trees in the world. Bamboo grows 100 feet high and is nearly a foot in diameter. It has actually been measured in its growing season and clocked at about a half-inch an hour, or a foot a day, which seems to be a lot faster than some of the native waiters.

Breadfruit, a melon-shaped staple, is one of the mainstays of food for some families. They weigh about three pounds each and are produced nine months out of the year. Five or six trees can provide nourishment for a whole family.

The spectacular mimosa plant grows in these tropics. It seems almost impossible not to attribute feeling and intelligence to this famed "sensitive plant," since, at the slightest touch of any part of it, the entire shrub contracts and shrinks from intrusion like a terrified child.

One of the loveliest palms on the earth, the Palmyra Palm, also grows here. And another, called the Talipat Palm, blooms but once after preparing for the event for up to eighty years. Then, having gained the object of its whole existence, it gradually dies, thus resembling some human hearts who, after one glorious climax, are content to die after fulfilling the zenith of life.

And, of course, there is one of the island's finest products, pure gum rubber, now almost a rarity in our synthetic age.

BACK ON BOARD

Putting the capstone on a wonderful visit to Sri Lanka was a marvelous exhibition by about thirty native dancers, given in the Up-Down Room on shipboard. Dressed in colorful native costumes, they presented a fantastic performance of their Mask Dance, Drum Dance, and Spinning Dance, finishing with spectacular somersaults in the Kandy Dance.

It was a rewarding end to a fabulous day. But, even as we relaxed, filled with thoughts of Sri Lanka's beauty, we were already thinking of another dream of a lifetime about to be fulfilled—India, and seeing the Taj Mahal by moonlight, and again in the first light of sunrise.

This is the most exciting time of my life. I enjoy so much more, I see so much more beauty. The best is yet to come. My dreams are getting better all the time. I am enjoying life, and with the experience of many years I am wiser, and can live better and do better work than ever.

If you expect the best, then the best comes to you. It is a natural law, called *the Power of Expectancy.* We draw to us the things we expect. *Expect a victory* in advance…Have the *attitude* of Positive Expectancy. *Faith* is *believing* before receiving. *Think* and *act* like a *winner. Expect the best. Desire and persistence* are the Driving Power. *Dynamic Expectancy…the victorious way of life.*

EN ROUTE TO BOMBAY

Leaving Colombo and the island of Sri Lanka, the QE2 plied its westerly course around the southern tip of India. We continued to follow the coastline northward toward Bombay.

All the passengers were talking now of India, "The Pearl of the East," a country as large as Germany, Austria, France, and Spain rolled into one, but containing fourteen percent of the world's population, *over 650 million people.*

The numbers are mind-boggling. A little research told us that eighty-four percent of the Indian people are Hindu, ten percent are Muslims—but that ten percent numbers 65 million!

Nature has done much to shape India's course. It is cut off from the rest of Asia to the north by the highest mountain range in the world, the Himalayas. Here, Mount Everest juts skyward 29,141 feet, the highest measured peak in the world. For hundreds of years the Indian peninsula was kept a world unto itself by the Indian Ocean to the south. The small ships of earlier centuries could not navigate the fierce and frequent storms of the Indian Ocean.

Geography also determines India's climate. The intense

heat is due largely to the fact that the cooling Siberian breezes from the north are cut off by the high Himalayas, thus depriving the entire peninsula of its natural air-cooling system.

How happy all the passengers are to have the security of the huge air-conditioning system on the QE2!

For rough seas, there are stabilizers. For hot weather, there is air-conditioned luxury and cool drinks served on the top deck. As the British know full well, once you have gone to all the trouble of building a civilization, the only sensible thing to do is take it with you to the four corners of the globe.

THE CHOICE IS YOURS

After the pages of the calendar have been torn off in sufficient number so that one has reached the age of sixty-five, it is necessary for each of us to make a soul-searching analysis in order to make no mistake about our future course.

The first question is, "Should one retire and enjoy the fruits of a lifetime of labor, or should one continue to enjoy the work which one has enjoyed over the years—daily employment?" The answer may be different for each of us.

But one thing is certain: A person must keep active. Those who don't are headed for the psychiatrist's couch. A person must have goals. To live fully and enjoy a long life, one must be creative, useful, active, and constructive. The quality of your life is more important than life itself.

One of the choices that comes to us with time is travel. For the young, travel is a part of education. For the elderly, it is a part of experience and an investment in health and well-being.

CHOICE

Nothing ranks people so quickly as their skill in selecting things that are really worthwhile. Every day brings the necessity of keen discrimination. Not always is it a choice between GOOD and BAD, but often it is between GOOD and THE BEST.

DECISIONS

Run everything through your own mill.
    If you are wrong...
Be wrong with your own decisions—
    Not someone else's.

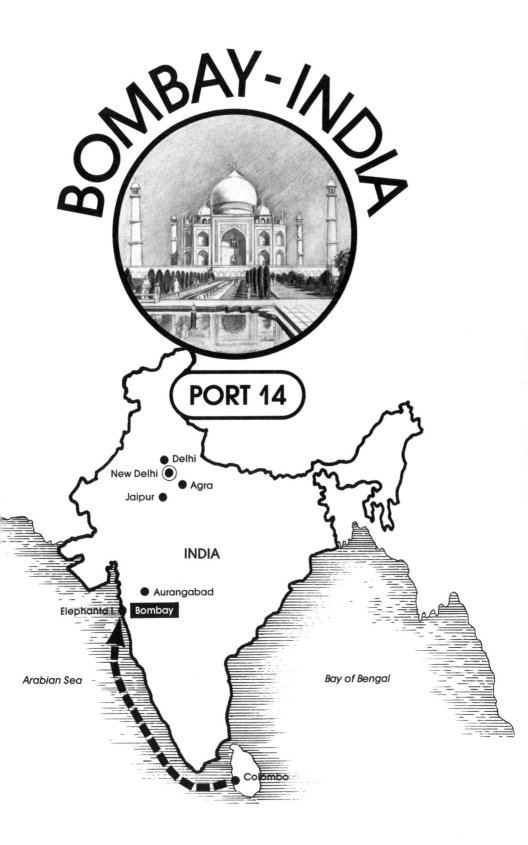

BOMBAY-INDIA

PORT 14

● Delhi
New Delhi ◉
● Agra
Jaipur ●

INDIA

● Aurangabad

Elephanta ▪ Bombay

Arabian Sea

Bay of Bengal

● Colombo

Sacred Cow on the Street—India

BOMBAY

The first thing you see is the magnificent Gateway of India Monument at Apollo Bunder overlooking the waterfront of the ships in the harbor. The city itself is on a chain of islands hugging the coastline.

Our bus ride took us through Bombay shortly after noon, and we had our first clear impression of India's great population. It almost has to be experienced to be believed—there are crowds literally everywhere you look—people living in all kinds of structures, many of them shacks and hovels made up of whatever can be put together, though there are a scattering of fine residential areas and luxurious apartment buildings. Through one of the nicest sections, Malabar Hill, a drive up a hill brought us to the famous and lovely Hanging Gardens, the best place for a panoramic view of the city below.

As we came down and drove toward the airport, we saw the commuter trains coming into Bombay, literally bulging with people. Many ride on top or hold onto the backs of the cars. More cling to the outside, using anything for a hand-hold.

Soon we arrived at Bombay Airport, where we boarded what turned out to be a comfortable, smooth-riding jet plane of the Indian Airlines. We departed at 1:30 P.M., and after flying mostly over agricultural lands all green and cultivated, a little over three hours later we touched ground again at our next stop, Delhi.

DELHI

There was a good view of Delhi from the air, of the hustling city of 6 million people, with squalor and riches intermingled.

The plane dips low over the plains to give you a panoramic view of the ruins of ancient cities of splendor built by the sultans of the region to sustain their luxurious living, proving that insecurity and devastation were the lot of the people of the land when usurpers came and took over, then as now.

Delhi is actually two cities: Old Delhi, with its thousand-year history, and New Delhi, created after the capital was moved here by the British in 1911. The real design and planning of the new city did not begin until after World War I, and rapid expansion came after India's independence in 1947.

Delhi is the most famous of India's old cities because, for centuries, the mightiest monarchs in India reigned here. Still bearing silent testimony to the days of grandeur is the wondrous Peacock Throne. Set with thousands of rare gemstones, its worth immeasurable, it was literally the seat of government until a conqueror came and carted the great throne away in 1739.

It has been returned since then and is, as before, housed in the Red Fort, a mammoth red sandstone edifice that was built in the seventeenth century. Today it's still a thrill to explore its marble corridors, the Painted Palace, and luxurious baths.

We boarded the bus for Agra and passed the government buildings and fine residential sections on the outskirts of New Delhi on our way out of town into the fascinating rural countryside.

DELHI TO AGRA: PICTURES OF INDIA

The bus ride from Delhi to Agra took about five hours. The road was rough, but that did not deter the bus driver, who had a "lead foot" all the way. Whether on the open road or dodging vehicles on busy village streets, the thought never occurred to him to slow down. Pedestrians, seemingly unconcerned, leaped nonchalantly out of the way at the last minute—all except one bicycler who hesitated a second too long and was knocked down. The driver slammed on his brakes, jumped out of the bus, and bawled out the poor victim as if it was the cyclist's fault for getting in the way. Then the driver hopped back into the bus and drove off, leaving the stunned victim on the ground.

Aman, our guide, supplied intriguing facts on India's multi-faceted religious customs. Once we saw a gentleman walking toward us by the side of the road, his hair red with artificial color. The color is used for a "holy day," like the Christian Sunday. Dry color is sprinkled on. (It is actually used like water colors when wet.) The hair is also dyed at festivals or changes of seasons, such as the festival of spring. In some religions, besides using hair colors, the people throw animal dung on each other's faces when they pray to the good spirits. You decide not to ask what they do when they pray to the bad spirits.

Along the road we saw all kinds of animals: a dancing bear, a mongoose, cobras, vultures, cranes, storks, buzzards, many herds of goats and some of sheep, and many herds of water buffalo. Wagons and oxcarts crammed with people or produce rumbled along the road, pushing their way through a sea of cyclists...bicycles by the thousands, perhaps more than in any place in the world.

The whole trip is a giant kaleidoscope of exotic vistas and sights: a camel caravan in the desert...elephants rolling logs... snake charmers charming their snakes on crowded sidewalks... the glint of green parakeets' wings in tropical sunshine...the sight of screaming monkeys leaping from tree to tree.

A pall of smoke hung over the cities we passed through. Some of it came from industrial smokestacks, but most was from the thousands of outdoor campfires used by the people to cook and keep warm in chilly weather. Cow dung is used for fuel, and the straw makes the dung cakes smoke profusely. Formed into round cakes, eight inches or so in diameter and about one inch thick, they constitute the poor man's oil, coal, and wood. Riding throughout the countryside, you see cow dung cakes drying everywhere—stacked up in piles about four feet high, on riverbanks, on the tops of roofs and buildings, and you decide never to complain about smog again.

We passed an old wrinkled man sitting cross-legged in the street, chewing a straw and occasionally reaching up with the thumb of his left hand to scratch his head. It is a matter of speculation whether he scratched because he was figuring out how much we were going to pay him to take his picture, or because he was lousy.

Considered almost sacred, a water well is a source of life in India. All through the land, you see water bullocks walking around in thirty-foot circles, turning the arms of giant water pumps. The water, pumped into a big storage tank, is used for drinking as well as watering plants, animals, and trees.

Some 70 million bullocks provide nearly sixty-four percent of all the energy used in India's agriculture. This compares with seventy-six percent human labor and ten percent mechanized. A bullock cart carries over 1500 pounds of cargo and lumbers along at about five miles per hour.

Bullock beasts of burden and sacred cows have long been closely involved with both the livelihood and the philosophy of India, ancient and modern. An ancient question put to strangers has always been, "Have you come for cattle or philosophy?"

NIGHT IN AGRA

At 10:30 in the evening, we finally reached Agra, weary and aching from our long, jostling ride. We were taken to our hotel, the Mughal, a most beautiful place made mostly of marble, with large, modernly-furnished rooms.

But a special treat had been arranged for us. After a half-hour to freshen up, we boarded a bus again and drove for about fifteen minutes…to see the Taj Mahal by moonlight. It was a beautiful night, the moon was full, and the air was a balmy seventy degrees.

As we stepped out of our bus, a stillness fell over the group as if we were about to partake of a spiritual experience. We walked silently through the huge Moorish archway, and then knew that it was true as we saw in the distance the lovely white dome and minarets of the Taj Mahal shimmering in the moonlight. It was breathtaking. We all stood motionless, partaking each in our own way of the Eucharist of *one man's love for his woman.*

We proceeded up the walkway, laid out in an intricate and loving pattern of stones and green paths. A long, clear lagoon in the center reflected the tall cedar trees growing on either side.

The sacred place was closed at this hour, so after an hour of almost silent meditation on the glory, beauty, and high purpose of which man is capable, we walked back to the entranceway where our buses waited to take us to our hotel…and sleep.

THE TAJ MAHAL

We were up before dawn, and after a delicious breakfast we once again headed back to the Taj Mahal. There had been a thunder shower during the night, making the whole countryside a fresh, vibrant green. Soon we were passing through the archway gate and there, reflected in the stillness of the lovely lagoon, even more magnificent by day, was one of the Wonders of the World, *the world's most beautiful monument to human love:* the Taj Mahal.

"Taj" is a Persian noun meaning "crown" or "diadem." The white marble mausoleum named the Taj Mahal means "Crown of Buildings." The story behind it is a 400-year-old love story that never loses its appeal. Each telling adds another piece of mosaic to its beauty.

The building is a monument to love, erected by the emperor of the ruling Mogula, Shah Jehan, to the memory of his beloved Empress Mumtaz Mahal, who died in 1631 after bearing their fourteenth child. More than 25,000 artisans labored for twenty-two years. All of the Orient furnished its materials: the

pure white marble from one province in India, jasper from the
Punjab, sapphires and lapis lazuli from Ceylon, and agate, onyx,
turquoise, and carnelians from Tibet, Persia, and Arabia. Diamonds, sapphires, amethysts, and turquoises are carved into
flowers adorning its walls.

How can one describe the indescribable? Someone has
said that the Taj Mahal looks like a massive structure, yet without
weight, as if made of an ethereal substance. It has also been
called "purely rational and yet purely decorative."

As we came nearer, we did not want to speak a word, only to
stand in silence, absorbing the breathtaking effect of the pure
white marble structure. We climbed the steps and were in-
structed to take off our shoes and walk in our stockinged feet, or
to put on the cloth overshoes that were provided so that our
shoes would not scratch or mar the marble flooring. Anticipating
that the marble would be cold, we put the coverings over our
shoes...and entered.

To run your fingers over the white marble, to examine
closely the intricate, inspired designs, is an unforgettable experience. Some of the marble is sculptured in delicate latticework
resembling fine lace. Everywhere is pure, hard, white marble, the
slabs carved in floral designs and inset with thousands of
precious jewels. On the walls are sculptures of an infinite variety,
many featuring the lotus flower.

We lingered here for what seemed a timeless period (about
two hours, we later found), overjoyed to be seeing what has been
called the one completely faultless edifice that man has ever
created. Can anything be more beautiful than this? We wondered
...the most perfect structure in the world, dedicated to the
memory of a beloved companion and wife, and in its realization
capturing some part of the essence of love.

To stand before the Taj Mahal in the early morning hours,
gazing on its miracle of beauty...to see the sun gild the slender
minarets till they appear like beautiful wax tapers lighting this
abode of peace...and then to behold the Taj itself, a glorified

The Taj Mahal—A Witness of Man's Love

expression of immortal genius, seemed to all of us like a dream too wonderful to be real.

It is, in truth, a dream in marble and, sweetest of all dreams, a dream of love.

Shah Jehan's body lies near that of his beloved under the great dome. He had not intended it to be so, for he had built a smaller, black marble tomb for himself directly across the River Jumna. But his son Shad, who had deposed and imprisoned his father—so that the Shah Jehan spent his last years gazing at his beloved Taj from the window of his prison cell—had him entombed beside his most loved wife, Mumtaz.

Ironically, the deposed Shah was never permitted to enter the Taj Mahal when it was completed, his wish being denied by the son of the woman he so adored.

RETURN TO THE SEA

The long day saw us return by bus from Agra to Delhi, through the endlessly varied landscape now colored for us by the wonder of the morning's vision. Still silenced by this vision, we flew again from Delhi to Bombay.

It was just about sunset when we reached Bombay, and it was beautiful to see the sun tinting the entire city in its red glory. It was the time of day when the people began to come out and stroll up and down the narrow, crowded streets, the milling crowds filling the colorful bazaars with noise and confusion.

The QE2 had anchored about a mile off shore, and a half-dozen small tenders, ferry-type boats, waited to take us out to the ship. How lovely it looked, waiting for us there in the distance, ablaze with lights! And how good to feel the deck once more beneath our feet, to freshen up and dress, to dine on superb (and safe) cuisine, and at last to retire to our stateroom.

Our visit to India was over, but it was ours forever, the most memorable adventure that we had yet known on this most memorable of journeys.

THE POET'S SORROW

About this time you pick up a brochure on the deck chair beside you. The name of the brochure is "The Poet's Sorrow." Intrigued by the title, you begin to read it, page by page, until you come to the end. Finally, in the last paragraph and the last few lines, the writer reveals what is the poet's sorrow: "The poet's sorrow is that *he dreams more, and feels more, than he ever succeeds in putting on paper, or into words.*"

Having read this, you think that this sorrow is not peculiar to the poet. It is common to all of us. Who has realized his best dream? Who hasn't dreamed more than has ever come to pass?

What does it prove? Simply this: The reach must exceed the grasp. Why else would there be the abstract concepts of Heaven, Hell, God, and Beauty; things that man can know by touch but are too far above him to grasp and precisely define? It might just mean that fulfillment takes time...more time than we can possibly have on earth. We weren't built for fifty or seventy or a hundred years. We were built for seventy-times-seventy-million years, for it would certainly take that long to fulfill *all* of our dreams.

It is said of man that "God has set eternity in his heart." This means that it will require the eternal years to unravel you down to what you really are. That is the way you are built, so vast that only eternal years can unravel you. What we are trying to say is that you are built on so vast a scale that you cannot live it in seventy years. Time won't answer the hunger of your heart. And your sorrow is that you can't find anything here that will give you abiding satisfaction. Every businessman feels it, every musician feels it, every writer feels it. There is more inside you than you ever succeed in getting out.

What does this mean? It means that we must find adjustment for what we were built for. There is a more powerful force than the human being, a higher power, and somehow this force is working through you as it works through all human beings. We have seen supreme happiness and joy in lives within which the God-nature has awakened. This love of God may be experienced in the heart of us.

This *is* important. It is not important for a day, for a month, for a year, nor for time. It is *eternally* important to us. Grant that none of us will ever rest or be deeply satisfied this side of our hearts experiencing that for which we were made.

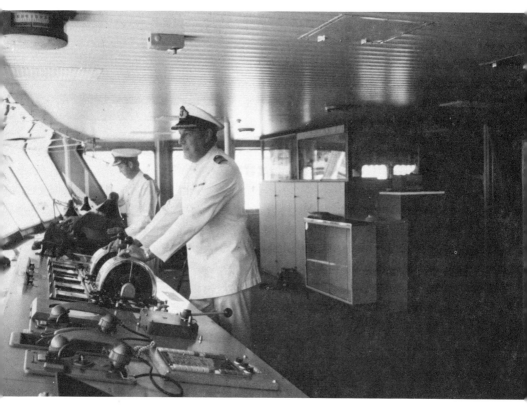

Bridge of the QE2

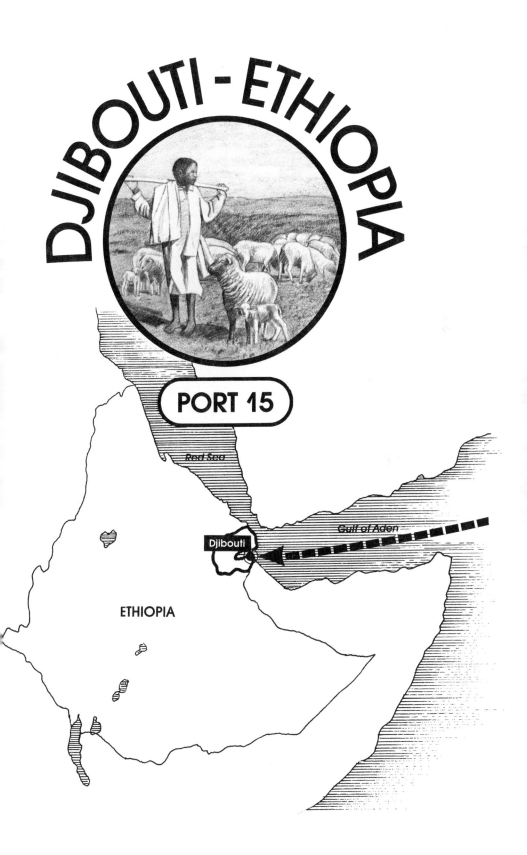

DJIBOUTI - ETHIOPIA

PORT 15

Red Sea

Gulf of Aden

Djibouti

ETHIOPIA

Working Elephant—Djibouti

DJIBOUTI

Colonization of that portion of the East African coast bordering the Gulf of Aden and the Indian Ocean took place in the 1860s for a very good reason: protection of the Suez Canal which was then under construction to the north. The French signed treaties with tribal chiefs that created French Somaliland. Larger colonies to the south became British Somaliland and Italian Somaliland, areas now combined into the Somali Republic.

But the tiny, sun-blistered French colony retained its own identity, achieving independence from France in 1977 as the Republic of Djibouti.

The city of Djibouti, where most of the people live, is an oasis of flowers and palm trees, white buildings and mosques, behind which lies one of Africa's most barren deserts, an area that has been called "too hot for the devil." Although the community has existed for 2000 years, it owes its modern importance to its strategic location on the Gulf of Aden at the opening to the Red Sea. Djibouti has a natural deep-water harbor. It has for centuries been the trading outlet for caravans coming down from Addis Ababa, the capital of mountainous Ethiopia. The caravans largely gave way to the rail line from Addis Ababa to Djibouti, which was completed at around the turn of the century.

Although Djibouti is independent today, its strong links with France continue, including several thousand French troops still garrisoned here.

DAY IN DJIBOUTI

No organized formal shore excursion from the QE2 was planned for Djibouti, even though this port provides direct access by rail inland to the spectacular scenery and ancient history of Ethiopia. The chief reason, we learned, was the recent Communist takeover in Ethiopia, aided by Cuban troops and Russian tanks. The country was still in turmoil, and with guerrilla street fighting still a danger, it was not a safe place for tourists.

But Djibouti itself was at peace, and we could not miss our first opportunity to set foot on African soil. While the QE2 was taking on massive quantities of oil (one reason why many ships stop here), we went ashore.

It was an exciting day for this sunny port city, for this was the QE2's maiden visit, and the entire city seemed primed to welcome our ship's passengers. Everywhere we saw how shopkeepers had spread out their wares over half the sidewalks for display. Djibouti is a duty-free port, and there were colorful bargains in Persian carpets, elaborately ornamented knives, daggers, brass-studded chests, vividly dyed African fabrics, wood carvings, and hand-tooled leather goods.

Most of the buildings in the city are a dazzling white. Everyone, it seemed, had a herd of goats. We felt the French influence when we stopped at a charming sidewalk café, where we enjoyed a cup of the famous Yemen coffee, which is shipped across the straits to Djibouti from the Arabian peninsula.

It's a day for picture-taking. Our friendly taxi driver spoke English and told us proudly about his family and his three children. He insisted on posing alongside his cab, of which he was equally proud.

At a supermarket we learned one lesson about taking pictures in foreign lands. One of the ship's passengers was taking a snapshot of a native shopping in the market. He failed to pay the native for taking his picture, so…the man picked up a bottle and threw it at the cameraman. *Take warning: As any member of the Actor's Guild will tell you, you should pay people for taking their picture—preferably in advance.*

Djibouti is one of the hottest places on earth, and it is one of the trade crossroads of the world. We happened to arrive there in the winter season, which was in February, and the weather was warm but comfortable. We tied up to the pier, adjacent to the French ship *Jacques Cousteau.*

EN ROUTE TO THE SUEZ

As the QE2 sails through the Red Sea, journeying toward the Fertile Crescent, the Cradle of Civilization, you sit out on deck thinking about things that have made this trip possible, and that naturally means money and investments.

As one becomes older, one's experience is his working capital. But no amount of experience can compare with having a hefty portfolio of well-chosen stocks. While you are cruising the Seven Seas, taking a vacation, your money is hard at work producing dividends, interest, and appreciation. And you appreciate it.

Of course, we are all unique individuals and have different life-styles. Your *life-style* is your style of living, what your goals are, what you want from life, what makes you feel good, happy, and content. It is developing your full potential, to live rich and die rich, learning to measure your wealth, not only in terms of money but of culture and goodness. Money may be the yardstick for *success,* but not for satisfaction. *Wealth is an external. Satisfaction comes from within.*

One of the first lessons for all of us to learn is *the real cost.* The real cost of anything is the amount of your life you spend to obtain it. This applies to everything—your home, your car, your boat, your furniture, your clothes, your life-style, and all of your appetites. What we do with our money is essentially what we do with our lives.

It's fashionable nowadays to belittle wealth, but assuming you worked hard and didn't inherit it, then you traded part of your life for every dollar and you damned well deserve to enjoy it.

Seen in this way, whenever anyone criticizes or makes fun of your wealth, they are criticizing or making fun of you.

There's nothing to be ashamed of in having money. Like a good friend, money has a place in everyone's life. And, make no mistake about it, as you get older your money can be a very good friend—one of the best.

A famous businessman was asked, *"What do you want out of life?"* He answered, *"I want everything life has to offer, right until my last moment on earth."*

Life has much to offer, but *you* have to grow and have the capacity to choose the best life has to offer.

Well, here's Malcolm with our tea and biscuits, crackers and Swiss cheese...and the great Arabian Desert lies ahead. At dawn tomorrow we will see the realization of another man's dream and a lot of men's money: the Suez Canal.

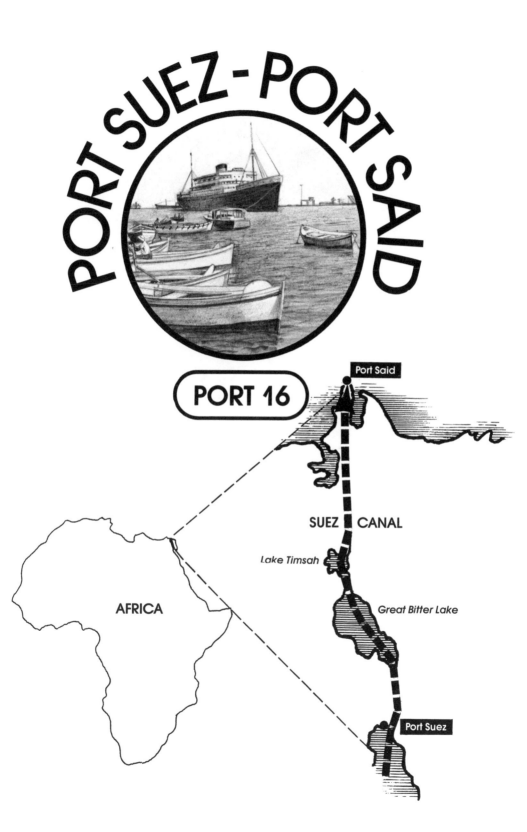

PORT SUEZ - PORT SAID

PORT 16

Port Said

SUEZ CANAL

Lake Timsah

Great Bitter Lake

AFRICA

Port Suez

Custom House and Port Said—Egypt

FERDINAND DE LESSEPS

The Suez Canal is an ancient dream. The historian Herodotus records that at around 600 B.C., more than 100,000 slaves died in a massive effort to dig a system of canals inland to the Red Sea. One reason given for abandoning the project was an oracle's warning that the canal might be an unwelcome aid to Asiatic invaders! Another fear was that salt water from the Red Sea would flood the Nile Valley, which would have meant the end of crops grown in the Nile's rich silt.

Over the centuries the dream never completely died. In 1789, Napoleon explored the possibility, but gave up the idea when his French surveyors concluded—mistakenly—that the Red Sea was thirty-three feet higher than the Mediterranean. Although an English survey team later corrected this error, it remained for a French diplomat who was not even an engineer, Ferdinand de Lesseps, to achieve what others had dreamed of.

De Lesseps first came to Alexandria as French vice-consul at the age of 27, and in 1835 became consul general. During his time in Egypt, he became interested in the canal project, studying all of the previous efforts. He also became friendly with influential Egyptians, including Mohammed Said, son of the Viceroy Mohammed Ali.

When Said became Viceroy in 1854, de Lesseps was assured of the active help and friendship of Mohammed Said to realize his dream. De Lesseps was commissioned to form a company whose purpose would be to pierce the Isthmus of Suez by a navigable canal, to exploit the waterway when constructed, and to build two ports at its two terminals.

Getting the commission was only part of the enormous problems de Lesseps would face. One—which would plague him for all ten years of construction work—was financing. Another was British opposition. Fearing French pretensions in Egypt, Britain was not disposed to help de Lesseps. But eventually blocks of shares were made available to all the great powers desiring to participate. Neither Great Britain nor the United States bought any, so France took up more than half of the shares and the Egyptian government subscribed heavily for the balance. (Eventually, Benjamin Disraeli, as Prime Minister, would purchase Egypt's shares and gain control of the canal for England, a control which would last until Egyptian independence after World War II.)

De Lesseps himself turned the first spadeful of sand in 1859, at the place where the town of Port Said would be built as a supply site for the project. The canal itself was dug in three stages: the first long channel from the Mediterranean inland through shifting desert sands to the dried-up bed of Lake Timsah, then a connection from Lake Timsah to the Bitter Lakes, and finally a channel piercing the desert from the Bitter Lakes to the Gulf of Suez.

The first stage was literally dug by men, 80,000 of them at one stage or another, using picks and shovels. Especially built dredgers were used in the later stages. A sweet-water canal also had to be dug just to supply water for the army of workers.

Against all manner of obstacles, de Lesseps forged ahead, and after ten years of work the Suez Canal was opened to traffic on November 17, 1869, with great pomp and splendor. Kings, princes, ambassadors, and delegations were there. Official ceremonies and receptions were held. The great composer Verdi was commissioned to write an opera to celebrate the opening. So when you hear the trumpets playing in *Aida,* picture yourself at the opening of the Suez Canal and listening to the opera Verdi composed for the occasion. De Lesseps was received in London by Queen Victoria, who conferred upon him the insignia of Knight Grand Commander of the Star of India.

Both de Lesseps and the Suez Canal would see turbulent times in later years. De Lesseps went on to attempt to build the Panama Canal, but was defeated by malaria and a hard rock isthmus he had not faced in the sands of Egypt's desert. But his great achievement in the Suez earned him his place in world history.

The world's longest canal, 104.5 miles long, shortened the earth's sea lanes by thousands of miles, in contrast to the old route around Africa's Cape Horn. It saved shipping time and money and brought huge growth and prosperity to Mediterranean ports. It realized de Lesseps's dream of bringing Europe, the Middle East, and Asia closer together, and at the same time helped create an interdependence that still makes the area of vital importance today.

THROUGH THE SUEZ CANAL

We arrived at the mouth of the Suez Canal in the early morning hours. There we anchored, for it seemed like a hundred ships were all waiting their turns to make the passage. It was still dark, cold with the deep chill of night in the desert—and it was impressive to see all the ships lit up like cities in the dark.

Port Suez is a refueling and waiting point for ships passing through the canal, unlike Port Said at the northern end which is a busy international marketplace. But the town of Suez, rebuilt in the seventies, has a population approaching 400,000. All we could see in the morning darkness, however, were a few horses and some people moving along the shore, trees growing, and the lights defining streets and dwellings.

It was 10:00 A.M. when the QE2 started on her maiden passage through the Suez Canal. There were flags on buoys along the way, marking the pathway through which the QE2 was to travel. Unlike the Panama Canal—through which ships are pulled by powerful engines that guide the vessels through the narrow cuttings—ships can sail under their own steam through the Suez Canal. It is also on one level, so the enormous engineering marvel of raising and lowering the great ship through the locks of the Panama Canal is not necessary in the Suez.

Throughout the morning, all we could see on either side were endless vistas of sand and more sand. The water was a greenish color, flowing like a ribbon through the center of this barren desert. To our right was the Sinai Desert and to our left was Egypt. We saw tanks and trucks and armed soldiers on both sides of the canal, but otherwise the Sinai side was uniformly bleak and desolate. On the Egyptian side, however, we often saw greenery, palm trees, many roadways, radio towers, and oil stations, along with some tents and military dwellings.

The canal is not entirely straight on each side, some places being wide and wavy, others becoming very narrow. Although the canal averages 198 feet in width, it opens out at times into broad lakes or contracts into channels with only a few feet of room to spare for the QE2, the largest passenger ship ever to make this passage. The Queen, we knew, had been built to traverse the canal at its narrowest points, and the ship moved along at a fast clip.

Thus, our passage through the great "ditch" proceeded uneventfully through the full day it took to reach Port Said and the Mediterranean. But it was not a day without excitement, for we thought often of the prodigious effort needed to build this waterway, in accordance with the Suez Canal Convention of 1888, "always to be free and open, in time of war as in time of peace, to every vessel of commerce or war, without distinction of flag." (It has not always been so, for ships were targets at one time during World War II and the canal was briefly closed. It was also shut down from 1967 to 1975, as a result of the war between Egypt and Israel, when fifteen ships were trapped in the lakes.)

And there was another, deeper mood of anticipation that rode with us that day. For tomorrow, we knew, we would dock at Alexandria, and then on to Cairo and the Great Pyramids, built before the time of Christ, one of the world's ancient wonders which we had waited all our lives to see!

TIPS FOR THE QE2 TRAVELER

Cash: There is no need to carry cash while on board the QE2. You can have everything charged to the Hotel Central Account System. Once a week, payments for all charges can be made at the Cashier's office with all major credit cards.

Tipping: It is customary on a long cruise to give gratuities on a two-weekly basis.

Cameras and binoculars: Various ports forbid the use of cameras and binoculars in the military areas of their ports.

Postage: Do not count on getting stamps on board at each port where the ship docks. This does vary.

Tax-free purchases: Cruise away and let your tax-free purchases arrive home by post. Merchandise is purchased direct from the manufacturers, and prices show extensive savings over normal U.S. shop prices. Even with a nominal customs duty, your savings are very worthwhile.

Land tours: These can sometimes be tiring, and often when we returned to the ship, rather than dress and go to the dining room for dinner, we would eat in our room. The room stewards kept fresh fruit in the room—apples, oranges, bananas, and grapes. We also enjoyed delicious cheeses, and occasionally a superb rice pudding with raisins.

EN ROUTE TO ALEXANDRIA

I'm sitting in the Reading Room of the QE2 and, believe me, it is quiet in here. Not a soul in sight, not even a mouse.

I'm trying to think of how I can *simplify* my life when I get home. It seems there are a thousand things to do, and I'm contemplating the things I might eliminate and those that are not the most important.

I think of Thoreau, who went to the woods where it was quiet and where he could think and be close to nature. Life is not complex. We are complex. Life is simple and the simple thing is the right thing.

Life is what we make it. Life can be simple if we will set it up with simplicity as a goal. It will take courage to cut away from the thousand and one hindrances that make life complex. But it can be done.

Abraham Lincoln was a man who cut through the smoke and baloney and got quickly and briefly to the core. We don't have to know ten million things, just the right thing. That's the secret of the farmer who has wisdom, the secret of anybody who really has wisdom. We don't need to know everything, just to know certain things well. That is what I call *essential knowledge,* meaning indispensable truth. I can live and die very successfully without knowing plenty.

This business that there are all kinds of things in the world that can't be understood is a lot of nonsense. Anything that can't be understood doesn't exist. Instead of being complex, sometimes it is in simplicity that we understand them. Some people, including the government, would call this view simplistic because they have a word for everything. Consequently, they will confuse us with a hundred different issues.

The older I grow, the more I value the simple things, such as honor, honesty, simplicity, sincerity, dependability, pride, and discipline. For these qualities in you I am grateful. I ever seek to develop these qualities in myself to a higher and higher degree. For these are the qualities which will finally make us great and useful.

Oh, my goodness, it's almost 3:30 P.M., time to go down to the cabin, put on my light Bally shoes, and then take my dancing lesson. See you at the next port!

The Pyramids—Cairo

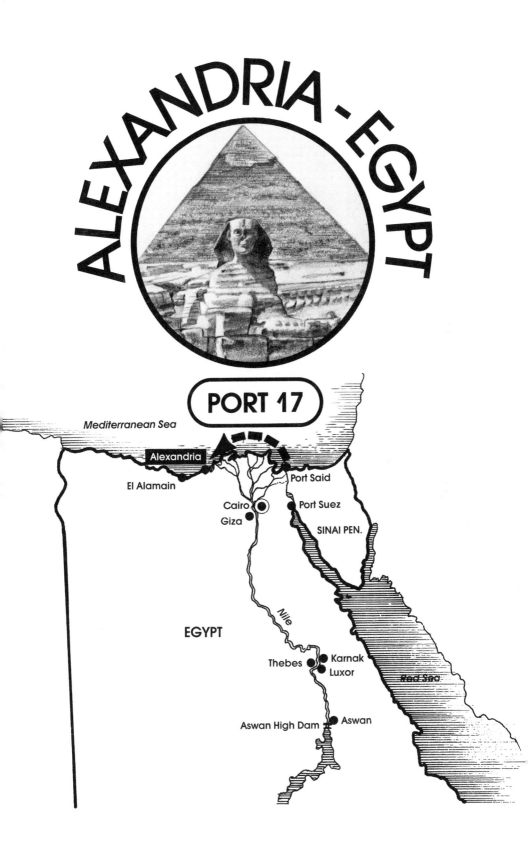

ALEXANDRIA · EGYPT

PORT 17

Mediterranean Sea

Alexandria

El Alamain

Port Said

Cairo

Giza

Port Suez

SINAI PEN.

Nile

EGYPT

Thebes

Karnak

Luxor

Red Sea

Aswan High Dam

Aswan

ALEXANDRIA

The next day we steamed into the Mediterranean on our way to the seaport of Alexandria, named for Alexander the Great, who founded this second capital of Egypt in 331 B.C.

The entire Mediterranean area is rich in history, for it touches all of the ancient world. This is the Cradle of Civilization, the beginning of recorded history. It became the maritime crossroads for the development of the continents of Europe, Asia, and Africa, and it was the world's busiest sea lane until the discovery of the New World in 1492. Into this sea flows the River Nile, the world's longest waterway of some 4000 miles. Today the Mediterranean area is a mixture of many races, its cultures having been passed along from one people to another.

Early Sunday morning, the ship berthed alongside the main wharf. There is a sense of history almost in the very stones beneath your feet. Here to Alexandria, Caesar came, and later Cleopatra fell in love with Antony. Archimedes and Euclid studied in Alexandria's great libraries. Napoleon landed here in 1798 and marched on Cairo. The French withdrew after a three-year siege, only to be replaced by English and Turkish troops, and thus it was for this beleaguered country until its full independence was finally achieved in 1946.

But that's recent history. For us, Alexandria is the gateway to all that we have heard and read of Egypt since we were children ...the mosques of Cairo...the three major pyramids on the Giza Plateau...the great Sphinx...the temples and tombs of Luxor further up the Nile...Memphis, ancient capital of Egypt where the huge statue of Ramses II is found...the famous Steppe

Pyramid at Sakkara...the Valley of the Kings where the tomb of King Tutankhamen is located.

Our bus is waiting...Cairo is only three hours away!

CAIRO

They have all come and gone: sultans, ambassadors, distinguished visitors, and travelers. In the hills nearby, in the first century, persecuted Christians found refuge, some among them said to be direct disciples of Saint Mark. Some several hundred years later, Mohammed was born, founder of the Moslem religion. Today, as then, chants of his devotees are heard: "Great is Allah! Allah be praised!" The first and oldest mosque is thought to be in Cairo, city of a thousand minarets.

Originally, Cairo was a vast fortress, its high brick walls protecting the Caliph's palace and military quarters. His descendants, the Fatimites, constructed superb palaces and schools, and Cairo became the spiritual center of the Islamic world.

But Cairo also knew, in the middle of the twelfth century, the devastation and ravages of the bloody Crusades...the inroads of the Mongols...and, on the morning of August 8, 1303, the awful cataclysm when, at the hour of prayer, the Nile overflowed its banks, the earth shook, and the heavens darkened, opened, and fell, engulfing both innocent and guilty by the thousands.

Time brought again, however, the elegance of sultans seated on couches inlaid with gold and mosaics, when there was sumptuous feasting for days with illustrious visitors from far away. As we look into history, we always see it repeating itself— extreme poverty huddling close beside extreme luxury and wealth, great achievements juxtaposed with bloody conflicts. Times have not changed...in Egypt, nor anywhere else on planet Earth.

But none of this seemed to matter in timeless Egypt. That evening we were taken to view the pyramids at sunset and attended a sound and light reenactment of history at the desert's edge.

You find yourself sitting in the dark on the warm Egyptian desert, nine miles from Cairo. Here on the Giza stands *the mightiest of human achievements…the Pyramids.*

The lights slowly come on. Before you is the Great Pyramid of Cheops, 455 feet high.

Multi-colored floodlights weave a texture of deep antiquity and mystery as they illuminate the Sphinx and the Pyramids, while recorded voices narrate, sounding as though they come from within the Sphinx itself. This display, a beautiful and memorable experience, is presented nightly and is conducted in English, French, German, and Arabic on a rotating schedule.

It makes you forget the moment and feel part of something bigger than yourself. It makes you realize what you've always suspected was true—4000 years isn't so long after all.

SIGHTS OF EGYPT TODAY

As if by command, the sun rose at exactly 6:00 A.M., clear and beautiful, striking the window of our luxurious room in the Heliopolis Sheraton Hotel in Cairo. Breakfast consisted of orange juice and rolled oats with fresh milk—the best rolled oats we ever had, sweetened with honey from local beehives.

About those beehives: At first we couldn't believe our eyes. Beehives on top of the houses! We were surprised to see them perched up there, but on second thought it seemed a right and bright solution to keep the bees safe above the level of mortals' traffic.

And such traffic! Crowds are everywhere, hundreds seem to wait at street corners to board the buses. No one waits for anyone. When pedestrians want to cross a busy street, they simply lurch out into the traffic and thread their way across. Whoever gets an edge on the street corner or avenue entrance swiftly jets in ahead. There seem to be no traffic rules, yet somehow no one gets hit and we did not even observe any scratched fenders, though cars and buses squeaked past each other so closely that a sheet of paper wouldn't fit between them.

Horses and donkeys were common, hauling things in carts and wagons over cobblestoned streets. Right in the middle of one crowded street were two little donkeys hauling a heavy load of stone. They appeared to be not the least bit skittish, even with the din of traffic and such a snarl of wheels pressing around them.

In addition to the beehives on the rooftops, around many of the rural houses—which appeared to be made mostly of mud and stone with turf roofs—we saw chickens, ducks, pigs, cows, donkeys, and camels. We passed many herds of goats grazing and many herds of cows contentedly consuming lush green grass.

The land is very rich and fertile, producing four crops a year. Lots of alfalfa and beans are grown, using irrigation by canals from the Nile. Annually, the delta area between Alexandria and Cairo floods. When the water recedes, it leaves a fertile silt to grow the rice crops and long-fibered Egyptian cotton—the world's best. And you health-minded readers can thank the Nile for the tons of chamomile tea produced here every year.

On the morning of our second day in Cairo, we visited the famed Museum of Antiquities, where we viewed the priceless collection of artifacts taken from King Tut's tomb, the richest find among the relics of the great dynasties on display at the museum.

A short distance from the museum is Anwar Sadat's house and the 100-year-old Botanical Garden. On the way we passed an "Egyptian Cadillac," which is the name given to a horse-drawn cart with what appeared to be at least twenty people crammed into it. The roads, fortunately for all aboard, were generally smooth and good.

After a peek at the house and gardens, we were off to new experiences... our first camel ride and our second glimpse of the Pyramids.

It was a beautiful and memorable experience to have seen the Pyramids and the Sphinx by moonlight, and now we would visit these ancient wonders by day. There was time for lunch at the Mena House Oberia Hotel, in the very shadow of the Pyramids, and soon we would touch those massive stones with our own hands.

HERE HISTORY BEGAN—
THE PYRAMIDS

There are in all some eighty pyramids in Egypt, but the three at Giza, nine miles west of Cairo, are the best known. And of these, the Great Pyramid of Cheops is the most awesome.

This is the tomb of Cheops, Pharaoh of the fourth dynasty, 5000 years ago. Here is the great pyramid which he built to defend himself against death. It is the greatest of the ancient world's Seven Wonders, and the only one remaining.

The Great Pyramid is the largest stone structure in the world and the oldest man-made structure on earth. At its base it covers thirteen acres, or four city blocks, and it is higher than a forty-story building. It is built of some 2,300,000 enormous stone blocks, each averaging two and a half tons in weight. Yet, these giant stones were skillfully assembled by a now-lost engineering skill which has yet to be discovered.

Originally, the Pyramid was thought to be hollow. Of course, when scientists and engineers investigated, they found that it was of solid construction and built of huge sandstone blocks. When finished, it was encased in glistening white limestone.

For centuries it was a sealed building. They could not find an entrance. Though there was an entrance, the builder of the Pyramid did not put it where you would naturally look for it. It is fifty feet from the ground and 286 pyramid inches east of the center on the north side. The builders seemingly did everything to hide it. Man, as you know him, has his story written in the Bible and in the Pyramid. No traveler, king, merchant, or poet has stood on these sands and not gasped in awe.

The Pyramid of Khephren is adjacent to Cheops. It is 445 feet high. A third monumental tomb adjacent to Khephren is the Pyramid of Mykerinos. Great and powerful were the pharaohs who built these tombs for *eternity.*

The Pyramids stand for man's dream of immortality. In the course of time, human achievements crumble and fall, but the spirit which conceived these monuments cannot perish! The Spirit of Man commemorates the greatest victory of all, the victory of the Spirit over death.

The Greeks rightly said of the Egyptians that they looked upon their earthly dwellings as a kind of inn, but saw their graves as their eternal home. This accounts, in part, for their making far more elaborate preparations for death than for life.

The palaces and lavish capitals of Egypt's kings have almost vanished from the earth. Their stupendous rock-hewn tombs with the Pyramids remain, emphasizing the triumph of the eternal over the temporal.

The Pyramids are the most perfect tombs, "the strongest tents," down whose great stone sides each rising sun streams in a peculiar, measured radiance, at angles over which science puzzles.

Inside the Pyramids, the secrecy of the tombs concealed the mummified bodies of royalty and pharaohs. They were placed there in the belief that the soul needs to occupy the body in order to travel forth on its Longer Journey. And what lost formula did the Egyptians have for their herbs, oils, and spices used for embalming, that their scent still lingers after thousands upon thousands of years?

The great Pyramids still hide many of their secrets.

Sphinx and Pyramids—Cairo

THE SPHINX

Many names have been given to the Sphinx as it has stood stoically facing the rising sun each day for thousands of years. It crouches in a sandy hollow, a 240-foot-long, lion-shaped body with a human head and royal headdress, symbolic of strength and wisdom. The Greek historian Herodotus gave it the name which it merits. The enigmatic Sphinx represents life's unanswerable dualities and complexities.

The Sphinx stands on the Plateau of Giza, near the Nile River, where it has withstood the ravages of weather and the hacking pickaxes of vandals for 5000 years or longer. The changeless Sphinx has watched the passing glory of earth's greatest mortals: Antony and Cleopatra, Alexander the Great, the Caesars, Napoleon.

Could the Sphinx speak, it would echo the Arabic slogan given it: *"The world fears time, but time fears the Pyramids and the Sphinx."*

THE ROSETTA STONE

It was in 1799, near Rosetta, a town in northern Egypt, that one of Napoleon's officers discovered a stone that was to become the cornerstone of Egyptology. It was a monolith bearing parallel inscriptions in Greek and in Egyptian. *From these hieroglyphics, deciphering of the ancient Egyptian writings became possible.* Then, meaning came to the inscriptions in the Pyramids of the lotus flower, fishes, hares, drakes. And, today, scholars read the 5000-year-old tales of the glory that was Egypt almost as easily as they read Chaucer.

We saw the original Rosetta Stone in London when we visited the British Museum.

There are many interpretations, but all are based upon the eternal premise that the plans of men never wholly succeed.

Only that which God, in His ancient wisdom, has ordained remains unchanged through the ages, for all peoples and religions. *Do not answer good by evil ... Justice comes before strength.* So say the many voices of ancient Egypt. And they are understood, then as now, echoing down through Greece and Rome—to the modern world today.

Traveling around the world cements our individual understanding of what the Sphinx and the Great Pyramids symbolize, that human achievements may crumble but the Immortal Spirit which conceived these stone monuments cannot perish.

It seems that every generation forgets the lessons from history. Most of our troubles and miseries today are caused by our spiritual inadequacy.

THE NILE

Does it not seem natural for the great stone pillars of the ages, the Pyramids and the Sphinx, to have been placed near the giver of land and life to Egypt, the River Nile?

For thousands of years civilization flourished by the great river, which overflowed annually and faithfully so that life was maintained by those who tilled its banks. The ancient Egyptians believed that the annual overflow in July was caused by the compassionate tears of their ruling deities, Isis and Osiris.

The river's rising tide swept out of the flat tablelands on either side and then receded, leaving behind a life-giving treasure of fertile silt. The three crops a year on which the early Egyptians survived were made possible by the annual rebirth of the life-giving waters, presided over by the love of a compassionate Creator, whatever name the Giver of Life was given.

TWO PHARAOHS

The reigns of the great Pharaohs of Egypt have long since ended, but the memory of one stands out: Akhenaton, the greatest of the royal house of Amenhotep. Perhaps, however, Akhenaton is more easily identified when his lovely wife, Nefertiti, is mentioned. Her radiant beauty has been immortalized by centuries of the world's greatest sculptors and artists.

But the greatest contribution of Akhenaton was his open declaration to his people of the One Supreme Heavenly Deity, whom he called Aton. This is one of the immortal prayers offered to the One God: "O Living Aton: You are the Maker and Giver of all things, and men live by your grace; living and life-giving for ever and ever."

Akhenaton had an illustrious successor whose name is better known in modern times, though he was a minor pharaoh whose brief reign of six years ended before he reached the age of twenty. His name was Tutankhamen, and his enduring fame rests on the fact that in the 3000 years since his body was entombed in an unfinished tomb in the Valley of the Kings, the treasures buried with him remained undespoiled and untarnished, waiting for their astonishing discovery by Howard Carter on November 26, 1922. Hundreds of thousands have now viewed part of that glittering treasure on its tour.

EGYPT IN THE BIBLE

In all of Egypt's thousands of years of history, where does the modern Judeo-Christian religion fit in? Not much mention is made in today's secular history of the importance of the Biblical records which tell how Egypt repeatedly held out the helping hand of asylum to key figures in the Holy Bible.

First, there was Abraham, father of many nations, who, after his migration to Canaan, sought and found livelihood for himself and his family in Egypt. Years later, when he came up out of Egypt, he was a very wealthy cattle owner.

Then, one of Abraham's favorite grandsons, Joseph, was sold as a slave into Egypt, and he also "struck it rich" there. Through exercising his talents and God-given abilities, Joseph found himself promoted to the second highest position in the nation, that of prime minister. Then he looked after the needs of his aged father, Jacob, and all of his brothers and their families, giving them asylum in Egypt from the periodic devastating droughts.

Generations later, Moses was born. By then the Hebrews had so multiplied as to become a threat to Egypt. It was in the vicinity of Giza where Moses was said to have been found in the bulrushes on the River Nile by the Pharaoh's daughter. What long-range vision God displays when He places in the right spot a key person whose potentials He needs to carry out His divine plan among mortals! Moses became "learned in all the knowledge and wisdom of the Egyptians." To that great leader, all the Hebraic-Christian world is eternally indebted for his obedient recording of God's sacred, unchanging Laws of Life.

And there was another Joseph, "in the days of Herod the King," who fled with the young child Jesus and His mother Mary to Egypt. There, it is said, they lived in the seclusion and shelter of a cave under an old Coptic Orthodox church. Thus, Egypt cradled the Holy Family through three critical, dangerous years, until it was safe for them to return to Joseph's homeland, Nazareth in Galilee.

EGYPTIAN WATER POTS

You've heard many stories about the ancient secrets of the Egyptians that modern scientists are still trying to unravel. One you probably haven't heard concerns modern high-voltage insulators—and Egyptian water pots.

The high-voltage transmission lines from Boulder Dam and other sources today depend on knowledge gleaned from the Egyptians. When you look at a high-voltage transmission line, count the "petticoats" on the insulators, for they will tell you the amount of voltage being transmitted. The key is that each "petticoat" is good for at least 22,000 volts. So, if you count the line from Boulder Dam, it may have ten "petticoats," which means 220,000 volts.

The year was 1930. Herbert Hoover was President of the United States. A huge hydroelectric project out West, the Boulder Dam, was being built. However, the world's greatest dam would be useless as a power source unless the General Electric Company could solve an insulator problem to harness the extremely high-voltage lines that would be necessary. Besides the high voltage of the power lines, provision had to be included for lightning storms, during which millions of electrical volts would strike the transmission lines.

America's future would depend upon vast voltages of electrical energy. But the lack of proper insulators stood in the way. G.E. had been testing insulators in their lab for years, insulators made of every known porcelain, using man-made thunderbolts, but the bushings had failed and exploded—along with daily hopes for a final solution or breakthrough.

The man in charge of the research for G.E. at the time was Gene Eby. After months of frustration, he decided to give his tired, discouraged staff some time off. The division was shut down for an enforced month's vacation, in the hope that out of that rest period the answer would come.

Gene Eby was a religious man and, as he later told the story, the first glimmer of a solution came to him in a dream, after much thought—and prayer. In his sleep he dreamed about that passage in the Bible, in the Gospel of Saint John, where Jesus changed the water into wine, saying, "Know ye not that I have spoken through My Word? Did I not use six big pots? Was it not My Power that changed the water into wine?"

When he awoke, Eby puzzled over the dream, thinking about those "stone" water pots. They had to be unusually large, probably special for a wedding party. To an engineer this suggested that the stone-like pottery was super-strong.

Was that the answer? But where could such pottery be found, man-made and virtually blast-proof?

The next part of the answer came in a telephone call. One of the engineers on the project had gone to Europe during the month's vacation, visiting France, Italy, Greece—and Egypt. He spoke of visiting the newly opened tomb in the desert, the tomb of King Tut, and of bribing the guard with a quarter to let him palm a souvenir, a piece of broken pottery.

Late into that night and the early morning, something nagged at Gene Eby's brain. The first inkling of discovery came slowly. Pottery…man-made…ancient…Egypt…water… jug …

At 4:00 A.M., Eby was on the phone, waking up his friend, whose name was Chermak. "You said you visited a tomb—Tut's? What was the souvenir you stole?"

"Now look, Gene," Chermak said, "you wouldn't be about to get me in trouble, would you, over a measly piece of pottery?"

But Eby wasn't making waves; he was just interested in that ancient piece of pottery. Chermak agreed that the next day he would break off a piece of the pottery and test it at the shop for its chemical composition. He could even have a batch of clay made up from the formula and send it to Eby.

Eby could scarcely control his voice. "Make it in the shape of an insulator. That's a rush order, Chermak! Good night, you angel!"

The rest of the story is history. The "Tut" insulator would not explode. As Eby stood in the lightning lab a week later, he ordered the testers to fire up every available condensor that their transformers could handle. The resulting arc shook the building—but didn't faze King Tut's insulator!

Within the hour the impatient President Hoover had his answer: His mighty gamble on the Colorado would pay off. The world's largest power plant could now safely send its mega-volts across the forbidding Mojave Desert, despite its high-voltage storms. The face of the earth would soon be straddled by high-voltage power lines, protected by the insulators made possible by the discovery of a piece of pottery from an Egyptian water pot, thirty-two centuries old…

BUYER'S REGRET

Have you ever had a case of "buyer's regret," meaning that you have bought something only to discover the same item cheaper and better somewhere else?

It can happen easily. The best way to avoid this situation is to "comparison shop" before you buy. By shopping around you can increase your chances of making the right decision about your purchases, especially if they represent a substantial amount of money.

We had always heard about the spectacular bazaars of Egypt, the shops with their fabulous displays of dazzling merchandise. At one such shop we saw some large, very beautiful metal trays, trimmed with gold and silver and carved in most attractive designs. These trays were about forty inches in circumference. Impressed, we purchased one, the storekeeper quoting a price of $1320 complete, shipped and delivered to our home address. We had the charge put on our credit card.

As we continued through the bazaar, we saw another shop which had the same type of tray, only much smaller and lower in price. One experienced traveler warned us that some of the merchants in these bazaars will sell you a large tray and then deliver a small one, worth only half the price you paid.

Our experience was a little different. When we returned home, even after some months passed, we had not received the tray—but we had received our monthly charge account bill, showing not the balance we had signed for, $1320, but a charge of $1927—an increase of $617!

Because of this dishonesty, we notified the bazaar in Cairo that we were canceling our order. Our bank's credit department was also notified of the reasons for canceling the order. It was fortunate indeed that we had not paid in cash or with a personal check, or we would never have had any recourse.

All of which illustrates the ancient caution, *caveat emptor*— buyer beware, and you will avoid buyer's regret.

After that we decided to do more of our shopping from the wide assortment of fairly priced merchandise in the QE2's own shopping center—the beautiful arcade of shops that is a floating New Bond Street.

EN ROUTE TO HAIFA

Having left one ancient civilization behind, we set our course for another, the historic land of the Bible, as we journeyed from Alexandria to Haifa. It was a time of reflection and daydreaming...

You are sitting in your deck chair, daydreaming. You inhale the sea breeze and order a cool drink from the deck steward. "Going to be a good day," you say as you hand him a five-dollar bill. "The rest is for you." "Yes, sir, it sure is a good day," he says as he hurries off to fetch your drink.

A good-looking girl in shorts passes by. You smile. She smiles back. People are very friendly on the QE2. Your drink arrives. You toast life, deciding to let yesterday take care of tomorrow...all you want is the *now*. The girl, your real girl, reappears and sits down beside you. You raise your glass to her and to life. "Here's to you, here's to me, here's to us, here's to now." She smiles wistfully, not knowing what's going through that crazy head of yours now.

You decide to call your secretary in California on the ship's radio and its costs you $110 for three minutes. She asks why you're calling her in the middle of the night and, by the way, you've got a letter from the I.R.S. In a daze you walk out onto the open deck for some fresh air. "Maybe it's a refund check," you say to a passing seagull.

LOOK CLOSE TO HOME

"We searched the whole world over. Then one day we found happiness in our back yard. We drilled three oil wells and two turned out to be gushers." You may not find oil under the soil, but the lesson we have learned is that a family pulling together and drawing strength from one another can win the battle of successful living.

HAPPINESS

The Eternal Quest of Mankind depends upon...
...The character of your thoughts,
...Some vocation which satisfies the soul,
...The ability to give value to your existence.
For happiness depends upon what lies between the
soles of your feet and the crown of your head.

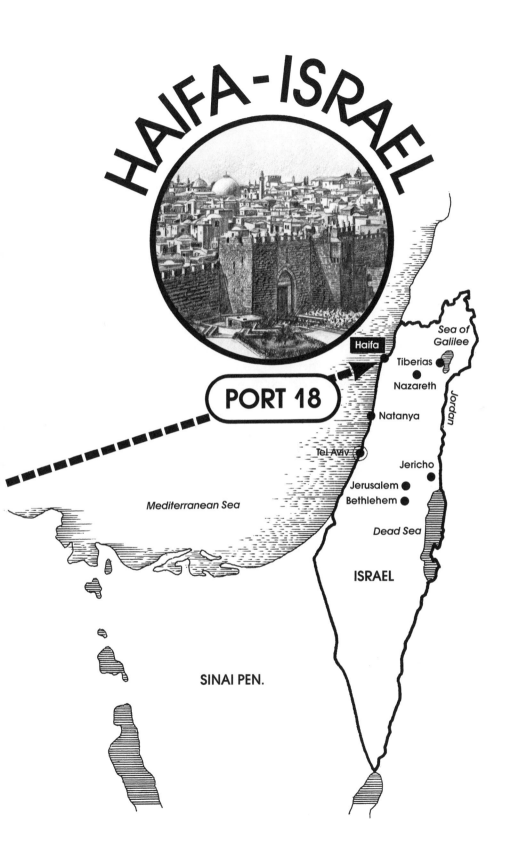

HAIFA-ISRAEL

PORT 18

Haifa

Sea of
Galilee

Tiberias

Nazareth

Jordan

Natanya

Tel Aviv

Jericho

Jerusalem
Bethlehem

Mediterranean Sea

Dead Sea

ISRAEL

SINAI PEN.

HAIFA

We docked at Haifa on a cool morning in March, filled with anticipation of the next two days. It is cool in Israel at that season, and indeed there had been six inches of snow in Haifa the previous week. But it was sunny when we debarked—perfect weather for touring and walking.

An ancient port with a beautiful harbor, Haifa today is both the country's main port and an important industrial city. Driving through the city that morning, we were struck by the modern housing—many of the houses were solar heated—the large number of condominiums, the good roads, and the general air of thriftiness and prosperity. After the poverty in much of the Orient, it looked indeed like the "Promised Land."

Then we left Haifa behind, our hearts lifting with the knowledge that this day we would at last visit Jerusalem ... this day we would walk where Jesus walked.

THE FLOWERING DESERT

As we drove through the countryside, everywhere were fields of growing vegetables, with extensive use of modern plastic "greenhouses" low on the ground. These enable the farmers to plant seedlings much earlier than normal, providing fresh vegetables six weeks earlier than others—in fact, fresh vegetables are grown year-round. However, the ground was full of stones and it must take years to get rid of those stones.

Part of the Carmel Plain through which we rode used to be a swampland until the lands were drained about 100 years ago.

Those parts of the swamp unsuitable for farming because of the brackish water are now used to raise carp. The swamps also attract flights of wild birds of all kinds, and the area is both a bird and fish sanctuary.

Wildflowers bloomed in astonishing profusion along parts of the roadside. Most, we learned, are from bulbs, remaining dormant in summer and blooming from the winter rains. There were tulips, narcissi, anemones, and cyclamens growing wild. Our guide, Rena, pointed out a white shrub, a kind of broom with lovely white flowers, and a beautiful tree with pink blossoms known as the Judas Tree. It is named from the legend that Judas hanged himself on such a tree.

Coming into sight of the mountain ranges of Samaria, the once barren sand dunes abounded in lush stands of vegetables and marvelous citrus groves. The land has indeed been made to "blossom once more as the rose." We drove past fields of cotton as far as the eye could see, and areas where grew olives, grapes, pomegranates, figs, and dates. Israel is literally "the land flowing with milk and honey." And the dates taste like honey with their own special out-of-this-world sweet flavor.

THE KIBBUTZ PLAN

Israel's agriculture has flourished and floundered under the kibbutz plan. What this means, as our guide Rena explained, is that if you wish to become a farmer you must become a member of the community. You cannot simply pick out a piece of land and buy it.

In the kibbutz, each member is assigned an amount of land, and each farms that piece of ground. Each will live in a certain house, have his or her own cattle, sheep, chickens, and livestock. They buy their seed and fertilizer in bulk and help each other in countless ways.

There is no division of property. All income goes into a

common fund. You might raise the chickens for the kibbutz, be in charge of the orchards, or simply wash dishes in the kitchen. All jobs are equal. Everything you bring in goes to the community; the kibbutz provides what you need. It even decides who can travel each year!

There is only one way in which the people are not equal in the kibbutz, and that is seniority—how long one has been in the kibbutz. Someone with forty years has seniority over one who has been a member for only twenty years, and seniority means first choice to build a new house or go on a cruise.

MOUNT CARMEL

Ahead of us rose Mount Carmel. There is a lighthouse on top of it, and a Carmelite church is there now. But Mount Carmel is famous for the story of the prophet Elijah.

It was here that Elijah challenged the prophets of Baal. When their sacrifices failed to ignite after they had prayed all day, upon a short and powerful prayer from Elijah the water-soaked wood burst into flames, licking up everything within reach. Whereupon Elijah had the fleeting Baalites captured and put to death.

In so doing, Elijah brought down upon himself the vengeful wrath of King Ahab and Queen Jezebel, who vowed to leave nothing undone until his fate was the same as the prophets of Baal. Suddenly Elijah became very human, fleeing in terror to the desert. The end of the story is that an angel visitor came to him in the night, and Elijah became reunited with God once more and resumed serving the people in justice.

JERUSALEM

And so we came to Jerusalem, Israel's capital city and the heart of the Holy Land, a city sacred to Moslem, Jew, and

Christian alike. Dating back to early Biblical times, before the reign of King David and the Golden Age of Solomon, its turbulent history is carved in every wall, every street, every dome and tower in its vivid skyline. It is a fascinating mingling of ancient and modern, of sacred places encircled by modern high-rise buildings, filling stations, businesses, and shops.

THE OLD CITY

The Old City of Jerusalem is divided into four quarters. Inside the Jaffe Gate, on the west side, is the Citadel of David, bastion of the city for thousands of years. The southwestern part of the city surrounding this citadel is the Armenian Quarter, inhabited by this staunch Christian people since early times. East of this is the Jewish Quarter, terminating at the Western Wall which encloses Temple Mount, where King Solomon built the First Temple and later generations built the Second.

The northern part of the Old City holds the Christian Quarter to the west and the Moslem Quarter to the east. Though thus divided, the paths of the faithful of all religions cross many times along the narrow, twisting lanes and streets. The rich mixture of peoples and cultures is also visible in the colorful bazaar, with its mingling of all manner of smells and voices, goods and foods.

Damascus Gate, in the north wall of the Old City, is the most impressive of the gates, the work of Suleiman the Magnificent in the sixteenth century. We walked along the busy bazaar streets to the Via Dolorosa and followed it to its eastern end at the Lion's Gate. Nearby is the Church of Saint Anne, built in the time of the Crusades on the site where Anne and Joachim, the parents of the Virgin Mary, lived, and where Mary was born. Next to it are the excavations of the Pool of Bethesda, where Jesus cured the crippled man.

Then it was time to turn back along the Via Dolorosa and,

The Wailing Wall—Jerusalem

beginning at the Franciscan Convent of the Flagellation, follow the Way of the Cross...

What a profoundly moving experience it is to round the first corner along the walk and see the point where Jesus fell under the weight of the cross...to pause at the shrine which marks the spot where Jesus met his mother...or at the little Church of Saint Veronica, which commemorates that moment when Veronica wiped the face of Jesus. Each step is heavy with tradition and memory. Finally, we arrived at the Church of the Holy Sepulchre, which contains the last five Stations of the Cross.

There has been a church on this spot for 1650 years, since Queen Helena visited here in the fourth century and identified the site of Golgotha, or Calvary, where Jesus was crucified. A great basilica and rotunda were built here by Constantine the Great, but these were later destroyed, and the present church dates from the time of the Crusades.

Here is the spot where tradition holds that Jesus's body was anointed after being taken down from the cross, the tomb of Joseph of Arimathea where Jesus was laid to rest, a small crypt cut into the rock of Golgotha. Most of the rock was later cut away, but the stone shelf where Jesus's body lay until His resurrection on Easter Sunday morning still remains, now covered with polished marble.

After this moving walk there was still more. We continued on to Temple Mount, sacred to all three of the Western world's great religions. Then on to the Dome of the Rock, with its richly colored tiles and golden dome, considered by many to be the most beautiful in all Jerusalem. This is the place first made sacred when Abraham prepared to sacrifice Isaac, and later as the site of Solomon's matchless Temple. Legend says that Jeremiah hid the Ark of the Covenant under the same huge, immovable rock. It is also the Moslem's sacred shrine, for Moslems believe that Mohammed ascended to Heaven from this place.

From Temple Mount, we came down and walked through the Jewish Quarter to the Western Wall, or "Wailing" Wall, perhaps the most sacred place in the world to Jewish people. We stood before it as countless millions have over the centuries. Once crowded by old buildings, there is now a broad plaza in front of it, and in the short time we were there hundreds of people came up and not only touched the great stone blocks in the wall but also said a prayer. *There was a holy atmosphere about this place that you could feel. No one can describe the song of the thrush: neither can they describe the power of prayer. It can only be experienced.*

MOUNT OF OLIVES

Our afternoon of sightseeing was almost too full, but there was more to come. We ascended the Mount of Olives outside the city, said to be where Jesus fed the 5000, where the crowds who continually followed Him came to hear His teachings. From here He ascended into Heaven, and it is here that Biblical scholars believe Jesus's feet will first touch upon His return to earth.

From this Mount we looked out over miles of the wilderness of Judea. Below in the valley is Solomon's Pool, the Mormon Center on the side of the hill beyond, the entire city of Jerusalem. We remained for long, unforgettable moments, searching the skyline for familiar landmarks.

When we came down to the lower part of the slope, we visited the Garden of Gethsemane, a visit filled with deep personal meaning and spiritual blessing beyond words to express. We touched with awe the ancient olive trees, said to be at least 2000 years old, and wondered if Christ Himself had knelt beneath this ancient tree. It was a moving end to an inspiring day.

BETHLEHEM

After a refreshing night of sleep at the Jerusalem Hilton Hotel and an early breakfast, we set out for the city of Bethlehem, about five miles south of Jerusalem. It had rained during the night and the day was sharp and crisp, but it soon warmed comfortably under a clear, sunny sky.

On our way to Bethlehem, we stopped briefly at Rachel's Tomb beside the main road. A memorial and a small domed monument dating from the fifteenth century pay tribute to the memory of one of the mothers of the Old Testament.

Bethlehem is still a small town, with a population of about 30,000, but it is set dramatically in the Judean hills about 2600 feet above sea level, with its church towers and minarets outlined against the brilliant sky. From the first moment we alighted from our bus, we had a deep sense that we were walking through history. Bethlehem's roots pre-date even Biblical times. Here David was born, and Bethlehem became known as the City of David. And here Mary gave birth to Jesus, making this little town immortal for all Christians.

At the center of town, on what is called Manger Square, rises the Church of Nativity, one of the oldest in the world, although it has gone through several changes. The present church was built by Justinian in the sixth century. When the Persians destroyed all the churches and convents in the vicinity in the year 614, including those in Jerusalem, this was the only church to escape destruction. It is said that candles have burned in this church continuously for over 1600 years.

And beneath the church, accessible by two entrances, is the cave where Christ was born, a silver star marking the exact place. An old manger can also be seen next to the grotto itself. For any Christian, no moment can be more moving than to stand in this place in awe and reverence.

MOUNT ZION

Returning to Jerusalem, we came to Mount Zion, which rises just south of the Old City near its Zion Gate. Here we went into the imposing Dormition Abbey of the Benedictine monks. Although the present abbey is less than a century old, with a mixture of old and new in its architecture and construction, it is one of the most revered places in this city of churches and temples.

On the opposite side of the abbey is King David's Tomb, directly above the small, unpretentious Room of the Last Supper (not much like the grand setting portrayed by Leonardo da Vinci in his great painting), where Jesus established the first Communion service.

THE NEW CITY

We lunched at noon at the Holy Land Hotel, where we had also eaten lunch on our first day in Jerusalem. We enjoyed a very good baked chicken and rice curry, with a fine salad—after being assured that it is safe to eat green salads here, something that can't be said everywhere one travels.

Afterward we drove through the New City of Jerusalem, its modern buildings contrasting with those in the Old City. We passed the Knesset, the very modern Israeli Parliament, set on a hilltop, and finally stopped at the Israel Museum. The largest in Israel, its buildings are strikingly modern, especially the unusual Shrine of the Book, which houses one of the most priceless discoveries of this century, the Dead Sea Scrolls—a story worth recalling.

THE DEAD SEA SCROLLS

The Dead Sea Scrolls are one of the most important archeological finds to validate the authenticity of the Old Testament. They were first discovered in 1947, near the village of Qumran on the shore of the Dead Sea, which is directly east of Jerusalem. They were found when a Bedouin goatherd threw rocks into the mouth of a cave where some of his goats had strayed. Hearing a crash, like the sound of pottery breaking, he investigated the cave and found some sealed clay jars in which papyrus scrolls were stored.

The precious scrolls, one by one, came into the hands of reputable scholars who excitedly identified them as copies of the Book of Isaiah—the exact Scripture from which Jesus read when He was first asked to speak publicly in the synagogue.

Later, most of the Old Testament Scriptures were discovered and translated. It is believed that the copyists were members of the religious sect called the Essenes. Ruins of their community have since been unearthed not far from the Qumran caves. The Essenes foresaw the possible annihilation of the sacred writings and set to work to preserve them by copying them onto scrolls and sealing them in the clay jars. These were then hidden very successfully in the rocky caves nearby.

THE WAY TO NAZARETH

Early in the morning, we left Jerusalem for our return to Haifa, with Nazareth as the principal destination of this segment of our tour. We visited an olive tree wood factory where they make and sell many useful items, including bowls, plates, and book-ends, all crafted in beautifully polished olivewood.

As with so much of Israel, every name was familiar from the pages of the Bible. We went through the Pass of Megiddo, where New Testament scholars predict the Battle of Armageddon will transpire.

Nazareth is a quiet Arab town whose name, we were told, means "white lily." Here is where Jesus grew to manhood and where He learned the carpenter's trade at the bench in Joseph's shop. We visited the old part of Nazareth where there is a water trough running down the middle of the street, which our artist sister Marguerite painted when she visited here. We went to the Church of the Annunciation, where the Angel came to announce to Mary that she would give birth to the Saviour of the world.

Old Nazareth Street Scene

We passed Cana of Galilee, a short distance from Nazareth, famed as the place where Jesus performed His first miracle, changing water to wine at the wedding feast.

And so, with our guide Rena and the bus driver Abraham leading the way, we sang our way back to the sea. Rena and Abraham sang Israeli songs, and soon the whole busload joined in. It was a happy moment, the end of a happy visit to the land of the Bible.

There was so much more we would like to have seen—the modern city of Tel Aviv, the little town of Bethany where Jesus came to visit in the home of Lazarus, the River Jordan, the Sea of Galilee, and the mineral-laden Dead Sea where nothing can live but everything can float. Yet, we had seen much that would live with us in memory.

LEAVING THE HOLY LAND

This is a practical age. We demand proof and demonstration. Our approach is a pragmatic one. Theories will be tolerated only for experimental purposes. They must produce results or be rejected.

All of this has had its relevance to Christianity. Just as history demands facts, psychology insists on seeing the effect of belief on action, so the world demands a corroborating life of professed Christians. Good preaching may show the reasonableness of Christ's claims, but only good living will demonstrate His power.

CONTEMPLATION

The QE2 is a good place for contemplation, especially in certain parts of the ship. Take the reading room, for example. It is so quiet here that you can hear your heart beat. Time spent in reflection here banishes the cares of the world. When there is a lot of hush you can think and plan ahead. You get fresh ideas, a new outlook. Here are some thoughts that came to me.

IMPORTANT WORK REQUIRES SILENCE

To deeply THINK, CONCENTRATE,
and PRODUCE IMPORTANT WORK,
be alone…isolate yourself…
no distractions…solitude…
plenty of hush.

MAN'S FINEST HOUR!

The QUALITY of a person's LIFE…
is the RESULT of CONVICTIONS to high IDEALS,
DISCIPLINE of WORK and of PROBLEMS,
HIGH STANDARDS and CHARACTER,
FAITH in GOD and LOVE with COMPASSION.
COURAGE to fight LIFE'S BATTLES…
even with some defeats.
When he has done his BEST, worked his HEART out
for NOBLE CAUSES, and lies battered and exhausted
on the field of battle—
THEN he is VICTORIOUS.
THIS IS MAN'S FINEST HOUR!
FOR TO BUILD A MAN…IS LIFE'S
GREATEST PROJECT—FOR EACH OF US!

ISTANBUL-TURKEY

PORT 19

Black Sea

Istanbul

TURKEY

Izmir

Denizli

Mediterranean Sea

Haifa

EN ROUTE TO ISTANBUL

What a litany of names echoed from the past as we sailed across the Mediterranean, passing the island of Cyprus! The next day, at about noon, at the entrance to the Aegean Sea off the southwest coast of Turkey, we passed the Isle of Rhodes. From around 280 B.C. to 224 B.C., at the entrance of the harbor of Rhodes, stood one of the Seven Wonders of the World, the huge bronze statue of the god Apollo. You squint your eyes, but it has disappeared like other childhood dreams or maybe it's just hidden in sea mist and will be there when you return some day.

Threading our way among the many islands of the Aegean by nightfall, we were entering the Dardanelles, sailing past ancient Gallipoli and on to the Sea of Marmara.

During the day we refreshed our knowledge of Turkey's ancient history. This territory between the Mediterranean and the Black Sea has seen the rise of three major and many lesser kingdoms. At its zenith in the fourteenth century B.C., the Hittite Empire in Asia Minor rivaled Babylonia and Egypt. From the fourth to the eleventh century after Christ, the Byzantine Empire dominated. Three centuries later, the Turkish Ottoman Empire began its sweep from Anatolia around the Mediterranean Sea. But gradually, the proud Ottoman Empire collapsed, until by 1918 it had shriveled to a powerless remnant. Then, Turkey became a republic after the pattern of Western nations. Since then it has known an up-and-down status among nations of the world, and is on a noticeably unsure footing with the USSR, right next door.

Turkey is rich in ancient folklore as the site of two of the best-known Biblical legends: the Garden of Eden and Mount Ararat, where Noah's Ark came to rest after the Flood. Traditionally, the Garden of Eden was said to be in the area lying between the Tigris and Euphrates Rivers, flowing southward from Turkey into Syria and Iraq. Mount Ararat (16,696 feet) in eastern Turkey, near the boundary of the USSR and Iran, is thought to be the place where the remains of Noah's Ark will be found. "And the Ark rested in the seventh month, on the seventeenth day of the month, upon the mountains of Ararat." In recent years, however, this research has been halted by government officials on the alert against suspected spy activities.

Morning brought us to Istanbul at the mouth of the Bosphorus, gateway to the Black Sea. The city was formerly known as Constantinople, for the Roman Emperor Constantine chose this peninsula, site of the ancient city of Byzantine, as the meeting point of Europe and Asia. Trade flourished. Furs, timber and slaves flowed in from Black Sea ports, grain and textiles from the Mediterranean. Raw silk came from China, spices from India, gems from Ceylon, and gold from Africa. Constantinople became the wealthiest city in the world. It was a place of colorful mosques and great churches, magnificent palaces, baths, and bazaars. The Crusaders marveled at "so rich a city."

And for the next two days it was ours to explore!

ISTANBUL

The city of Istanbul spans the Bosphorus, a narrow neck of water that divides Europe and Asia, so parts of the city are on different continents. The European side is again split by another long thin sword of water known as the Golden Horn, and to the south is the Sea of Marmara. The city rises from the harbor to sprawl over seven hills, and its ragged skyline, especially in the old city, is pierced by hundreds of domes and minarets.

The Mosque of Suleiman the Magnificent—Istanbul, Turkey

At about 10:30 A.M., we left the QE2 for our first tour of Istanbul. The weather was very cold, about fifteen degrees above zero, and we could see every breath go out in white puffs before our faces. But we had bundled up well and kept warm and comfortable. Everyone we saw on the streets was bundled up in overcoats, caps, mittens, and scarves. Our bus was very comfortable, riding smoothly along the crowded, twisting, climbing streets. It was a Mercedes-Benz. If you're going to go by bus, we thought, it might as well be in a Mercedes!

Crowds of people were everywhere, jamming the railway station to go to Europe, spilling across the bridges that connect the two parts of the European side across the Golden Horn, bringing traffic to a crawl in streets filled with cars, carts, buses, and people, all apparently ready to veer off in any direction at any moment.

Noise is part of Istanbul's ambiance. Calls to prayer rise from hundreds of mosques as soon as the sun is up. The cries of street vendors compete with the clatter of horses' hoofs, the singing of beggar musicians along the sidewalks, the hooting of boats and freighters on the waterways, and the blare of automobile horns. Many drivers, it seems, never take their hands off the horns.

Everywhere was the color red—the soil, the red tile roofs, the brick facings of buildings and houses. The city is a mingling of old and new. Many condominiums under construction, packed very close together, were the newest. The guide explained that there is a movement into the city of peasants and farmers, and many of the new houses, erected hastily on government ground, are called "built-in-one-night houses."

Also new is the Bosphorus Bridge, by which we crossed to the Asian side of the city. *It is one of the longest suspension bridges in the world, and the first permanent span in history that connects the continents of Europe and Asia.* It marks the historic channel where King Darius of Persia (of Biblical fame) lashed boats from shore to shore during a campaign in the sixth century B.C., enabling his troops to cross the waterway.

Driving to the top of Comlica Hill, we stopped for a spectacular view of the old city on the European side and the Bosphorus to the north. There were many fishing boats, ferries, and other craft in the busy waterway. Any nation can use the Bosphorus, we were told, though there is a varying toll charge.

We stopped for lunch at the Ziya Restaurant, one of the many fine waterside restaurants overlooking the busy Bosphorus. We had one of the best meals ever: a delicious bouillabaisse soup, green salad, red cabbage, shredded rutabaga, excellent sea bass, and fresh fruits for dessert.

TOPKAPI PALACE

After lunch, we were on our way again, crossing over the crowded Galata Bridge across the Golden Horn to the older part of the city and one of its prime tourist attractions—the Topkapi Museum in the Sultan's palace. We were not alone, for Turkey is seeing a tremendous growth of tourism. During the day we encountered English, German, Dutch, Swiss, French, Scandinavian, and Italian visitors, exploring the city's museums, mosques, and winding streets with us.

The Topkapi Museum, set high on a hill overlooking the city, is famed for its fabulous display of jeweled artifacts, four rooms of emerald and ruby encrusted swords, daggers and guns with jewels, and jewel boxes. There is a pair of solid gold candlesticks that stand three feet high, each weighing 100 pounds. Equally impressive, if more subdued, is a display of Ming China, and blue and white porcelain from the fourteenth century.

The palace in which the museum is housed is a city in itself. Most impressive are the elaborate harem and the Sultan's grand apartments, seemingly dedicated to the proposition that 200 can live as cheaply as one.

THE BLUE MOSQUE

Any tour of Istanbul's mosques and churches must include Hagia Sophia, which has been called the greatest monument of Byzantium, and the Suleymaniye Mosque. But the grandest of them all is still the huge Blue Mosque.

The dome of the Blue Mosque and its many needlelike minarets dominate the old city's skyline. We took off our shoes and went inside in our stockinged feet. Men and women pray separately here, men on one side and women on the other. It is an exquisitely beautiful edifice, with its azure blue tiles, enormous columns, and many beautiful windows, the most beautiful in this city of 500 mosques.

THE SULTAN'S PALACE

On our way to see the Grand Bazaar, we drove by a tall wall enclosing one of the Sultan's grand palaces, built in 1853. It is said to have 265 rooms, all furnished very richly as in its heyday. Soldiers regularly patrol the walls and walkways, and rightly so, for the palace's fabulous artifacts are legendary: walls covered with tons of gold paint, enormous crystal chandeliers, the largest in the world, as well as priceless carpets. But it might as well be empty, for no one lives in the 265 rooms, no one walks on the handmade Turkish carpets, no one admires the priceless wall hangings. The palace is even closed to visitors.

THE GRAND BAZAAR

Next we visited the Grand or Covered Bazaar in the old city. This is one of the world's largest covered markets. Spread over fifty walled and roofed areas, it houses 4000 shops, at least 500 of which specialize in gold jewelry. Here you can find treasures for any purse from 5¢ to $5000.

Grand Bazaar—Istanbul

As we walked through the Bazaar, we were not disappointed. It looked just as an Oriental bazaar ought to look, with shops on all sides with every kind of merchandise imaginable: diamonds, leather goods, copper, brass and silver articles, and jewels of all kinds. We entered one place that sells Turkish rugs to compare quality and prices with those at home and then ducked into another stall to buy some Turkish delight, the sweet soft candy.

We finally emerged from the Bazaar, sated with noise and color, crowds and confusion, into the streets with their own milling masses, the cries of street vendors, the blaring traffic. As we returned to the QE2 in the gathering darkness, we felt that we had truly had a taste of the enchantment of exotic Istanbul.

LOCAL CUSTOMS

We regretted not having time for a Turkish bath ashore, but decided to take one back on board ship. Sitting there, letting the fatigue of crowds and shopping sweat out of us, we decided that *the Turkish bath is one of Turkey's great contributions to relaxation, not to mention cleanliness.* There are said to be about 350 baths in Istanbul today, and they are still a popular part of life for both men and women. In the old days, allowance for bath money was sometimes even written into the marriage contract.

Another marital custom involved divorce. All a man had to say was, "I divorce you" three times! We're glad that this custom didn't spread around the world quite as fast as the Turkish bath!

EN ROUTE TO YALTA

Leaving Istanbul in the late afternoon, the QE2 joined the busy traffic of fishing and other boats through the Bosphorus and emerged into the Black Sea. The Black Sea takes its name from the stormy days that render its water black, boisterous and foreboding. Fortunately we encountered no storms. The weather was cool, but brisk and invigorating.

Stretched out in your deck chair, a doctor friend passes by and you discuss health with him. He tells you that a long sea voyage can sometimes be better than medicine. It is a natural way to health and well-being, especially when fresh, clean ocean air is supplemented by nutritious food.

You nod your head in agreement. Encouraged, he continues: "It is easy to forget that at the turn of the century there was very little cancer. We lived closer to nature and did not use so many synthetic devices and harmful chemicals. We ate more highly fibered, less refined foods. We walked more and obtained more physical exercise."

"There was not so much stress," you say. "People were more carefree and didn't have the daily tension of freeways, and certainly not the extreme pressure characteristic of today's business life. Everyone was not reaching for the brass ring and ready to strangle each other to get it."

"Cancer has become one of the prices modern man pays for his way of life," he agrees. "One cardinal finding of researchers has been the lethal hazard of cigarette smoking *when combined with* the foul air of our cities."

With that he hurries off, afraid to be late for a bridge game. You think over what he's said.

PHILOSOPHY FOR SUCCESSFUL LIVING

1. Do the *best* you can *each day.*

2. *Think* and *plan* first, then *do* secondly, then *enjoy* the *fruits* of your labor.

3. Do not waste *time,* for time is the *raw material* of *life.*

4. Live *constructively* and *optimistically.*

5. *Live* to *enjoy* the money you make.

6. Abide by the *Golden Rule*—Matthew 7:12.

7. Abide by the *Sermon on the Mount*—Matthew 5, 6, 7.

8. Nothing in life is *static;* one must *learn* to make adjustments.

9. Never fear defeat. *Live confidently.*

10. Always look for the *good* in the other fellow; no one is perfect.

11. Think *well* of yourself, as the world takes you at your own estimate.

12. Beware of *thirst* for the wrong kind of pleasures; cut off wrong pleasures and replace them with the *real pleasures* of life.

13. *Understand* the Law of *Cause* and *Effect.* You will suffer if you violate it. It becomes your greatest friend if you understand it.

14. Every *excess* has its *effect,* its *aftermath,* its *hangover. Everything* that exceeds the *bounds of moderation* has an *unstable foundation.*

15. *Future:* This is the kind of thinking you have to engage in: Figure out what is going to happen in the future, then figure out how you can participate profitably in it. *Present thoughts* determine your *future.*

16. *Contentment:* Most of us are more *in need* of a deeper sense of contentment with life as it is than we are of a deeper understanding of life.

17. *Happiness* depends not on things around you, but on your *attitude.* Everything in your life will depend on your *attitude!*

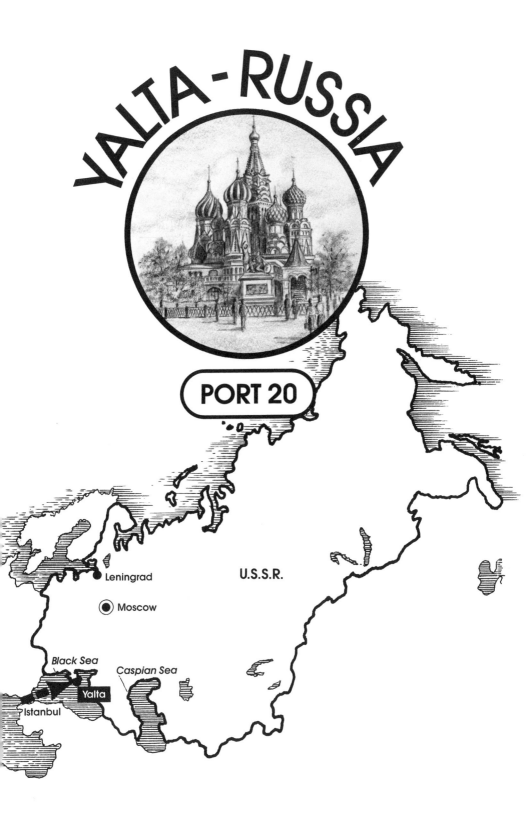

YALTA - RUSSIA

PORT 20

U.S.S.R.

Leningrad

Moscow

Black Sea

Caspian Sea

Yalta

Istanbul

YALTA

We had looked forward to our Yalta visit, to discover the balmy Crimean coast which had lured Russian czars away from the bitter winters of Moscow and Leningrad, to visit the Chekhov Museum and the house where the great writer once lived and wrote, to see Livadia Palace, once a summer residence of the last czar and the place where Churchill, Roosevelt, and Stalin met at the 1945 Yalta Conference.

Well, every adventure is full of surprises or it wouldn't be an adventure. So it was when we reached Yalta.

Our first surprise came when we emerged on deck that morning to see what the weather was like. When we opened the outside door, a gust of freezing cold swept in. From the starboard side we gazed on high, snow-covered mountains—a beautiful but unexpected sight. These mountains, we learned, shield the Crimean coast from Russia's harsh winters. If this was balmy and springlike to a Russian, we thought, what must their winters be like!

We took pictures of the mountains, breakfasted, dressed warmly, and assembled early in the Queen's Room to get our launch tickets. While we filled out the required currency declaration (all visitors to the USSR must declare all funds and valuables they bring with them), tenders arrived from the port of Yalta. We were among the first group of 200 passengers out of 700 planning to visit Yalta or take one of the shore excursions into Russia.

Then the delays began.

Long conversations ensued between the ship's officers and

Russian officials. We had already exchanged our money for Russian rubles. Now we learned that we must get out our passports and boarding cards. Two stern-faced Russian officers took the passports and cards, giving us a small brown receipt book printed in Russian. Then those of us in the first group to go ashore boarded the tender.

Or some of us did. After the first fifty or so passengers were aboard, clinging to our seats as the tender bobbed up and down in the freezing cold, the line was stopped. Another delay. Then the unexpected announcement came: The Yalta tour was off. The QE2 was going to raise anchor and leave port!

A TRIBUTE TO THE CAPTAIN

It was evening before the full story was told. By then the uproar of protest and inquiry had died down. And by then, Captain Robert Arnott was a hero to the QE2's passengers.

This was our first encounter with the Russian Bear, and it was not a friendly one. The Russian port authorities had presented one obstruction after another. The money exchange and currency declaration, we learned, were normal procedures for entering the USSR. But, in spite of prior special arrangements made for the QE2's visit, Russian officials on the scene had delayed until "official permission" for landing had been given.

Another obstacle was the insistence on individual visas for each passenger going ashore. And even after this hurdle had been cleared and the first fifty passengers were already in the tender, a new demand was made: Only 200 passengers out of the 700 planning to debark would be allowed ashore.

Captain Arnott's decision was immediate and firm: "All or none! Raise anchor!"

That evening, when Captain Arnott entered the dining room, the band struck up a martial welcoming fanfare, and he was given a standing ovation. His decisive good sense in handling a prickly situation was clear. We were now all friends and shipmates and, like shipmates everywhere, we knew we had to stand together or hang separately.

AFTERMATH

After we left Yalta, we soon discovered that we had acquired an escort. Three ships of the British Royal Navy pulled up near us and saluted. The ships then stayed with us throughout our time in the Black Sea, until we had once more passed through the Dardanelles into the Aegean Sea. It was a welcome sight to look out and see those three ships, a clear sign that we were under the protection of the Royal Navy.

There was much speculation about the reasons behind the Russian actions. This was, however, a time of considerable international tension, brought on by the Russian invasion of Afghanistan. The decision by the United States to boycott the Olympic Games and to impose other sanctions may have contributed to the unfriendly reception of the QE2 at Yalta.

All this is mere conjecture, of course. The real reason was undoubtedly another triumph of Russian bureaucracy. It was probably decided that the Union of Soviet Socialist Republics would not be safe with 700 prosperous-looking capitalists roaming about. And so we had to eat our caviar on board in our old, familiar Columbia Dining Room! *Quel dommage!*

A FESTIVAL OF LIFE

Early each morning, the room steward slipped a copy of a four-page flyer under our cabin door. Prepared by Cruise Director Brian Price and Social Director Bern Meckel, the day's "Festival of Life" outlines the schedule of events. There is truly something for everyone, from morning till night. No dull moments unless you are dull. It's all there—and just for you. Sample a day on the QE2:

1. *Bon appetit.* The times are given for meals served in the various dining rooms and there is a schedule for Early Bird Coffee, hamburgers and frankfurters, and Midnight Buffet, for nibbling (or feasting) in between.

2. Thomas Cook's daily information pertaining to the tours available at the next port.

3. For the athlete, a listing of sport clinics of all kinds, to perfect everything from your swimming to your golf swing.

4. Many card parties, plus lectures and instruction on bridge and backgammon.

5. Shuffleboard and table tennis tournaments.

6. Anyone for bingo, trap shooting, or horse racing?

7. Scavenger hunts for those under 16.

8. Wife and husband hunts for the unmarried of all ages, continuing daily (and nightly) above and below decks.

9. Yoga or jogging for health with Eric Mason.

10. Lectures on the lives of great artists.

11. Lectures on the various ports where the ship docks, ably presented by Sheridan H. Garth.

12. Movies: titles, times shown, running times and ratings.

13. Panel games, such as "What's My Line?"

14. Anyone for languages? Jean Adra helps you learn French.

15. Fashion shows.

16. Dance classes and arts and crafts.

17. Preparation for the next party or costume ball.

In addition to all this, there are investment lectures, beauty experts to make you up or massage you, music to soothe you, and instructors to teach you everything from how to write letters to how to read palms. The activities go on and on. Whatever you want is there and a little bit more. Finally, there is much entertainment offered each evening and you always know ahead of time what is in store for you in the various lounges, nightclubs, and casinos. You may get tired—but they won't!

ADVENTURES

You meet many wealthy people on the QE2 who tell you that they don't feel well unless they're traveling on the water. They speak of the excitement and satisfaction of new adventures and their eyes light up. Travel is their passion. They delight in daily discoveries, the serendipities of living in different cultural climates. Their way of life is to take at least one long cruise every year. Life for them has always been one adventure after another, and as they get too spoiled to go out looking for it on their own, they have it delivered in one kaleidoscopic package via a luxury suite on the QE2. One of these suites is so luxurious that it costs $150,000, another is a mere $80,000. If these people awaken at 3:00 A.M. and decide that they want a bathtub filled with Dom Perignon and a casserole of Iranian caviar, they get it, all with a polite bow and absolutely free. This in itself is an adventure of a sort.

What is adventure if not new, intense, distilled experiences? All of us need adventures, and as you sit on the sundeck eschewing the caviar and just being glad to be able to chew a hot dog, you think about some of the things you would like to do next. Some of your dreams you've already realized, and taking a trip around the world is one of them. You've visited the Holy Land, the Pyramids and the Sphinx, Cairo, the Taj Mahal, you've ridden a camel and an elephant, you've been to Hawaii (Nature's Paradise), and you've seen the wonders of the Orient. But there are more dreams, more goals, and you decide it would be fun to list them:

1. Take a boat trip up the Nile to see the old temples of the kings.

2. Visit Rome, the Cistine Chapel, and the Vatican library. Drive through Italy, stopping at Venice, Milan, Florence, and Sienna.

3. Visit Paris, the Louvre, and the Eiffel Tower. Imbibe something cold on a hot day on the Champs Élysées. Drive through France, stopping at small inns and sampling local wines with no watch, only a calendar.

4. Visit and enjoy the wonders of Switzerland, the Matterhorn, Lake Geneva, the Jungfrau. Look down at the world and up at God.

5. Visit London, Trafalgar Square, Piccadilly Circus, and the museums. Drive through England and Scotland on the wrong side of the road.

6. Visit Lake Louise and Jasper National Park. Walk on the Columbia Ice Fields with a flask of brandy in case you get lost.

7. Take a ride in the Concorde, London to Washington. They say it's like riding on a broomstick.

8. Drive through every state and visit the principal cities of the United States of America. Eat lobster in Maine, fried chicken in Dixie, and seafood in New Orleans.

And...and...

It's all right to dream. Really it is. It's how all good things start and many end.

When you were young and didn't know any better, you collected things. Now you collect *experiences.* This is what life is all about. When you get older and can't do things, there will be time enough to stop and just collect dust.

Today? What are you doing to live life to its fullest today? You're resting. Sifting dreams of a better tomorrow.

DREAMS

A man is no greater than his dream,
his ideal, his hope, and his plan.
Man dreams the dream...and fulfilling it
is the dream that makes the man.

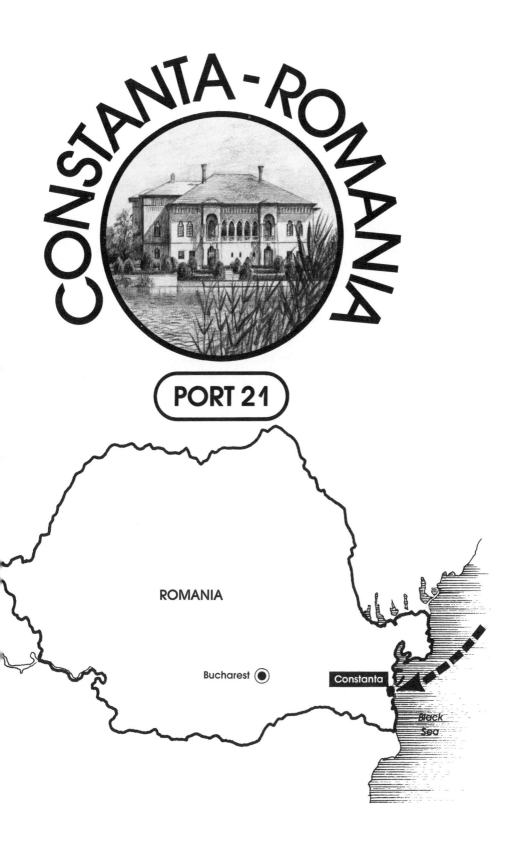

CONSTANTA - ROMANIA

PORT 21

ROMANIA

Bucharest ⊙

Constanta

Black Sea

CONSTANTA

While others among the QE2's world travelers elected to fly inland to Bucharest, Romania's capital, for a day of sightseeing, we chose a more relaxed morning tour of the ancient seaport of Constanta and, a short distance up the coast, the popular seaside resort of Mamaia.

It wasn't a day for frolicking at the seashore, however. The temperature was about thirty-five degrees, the wind sharp and piercing. The streets were barren, almost no one was up and about, and those who were outside bundled up in fur hats, fur coats, and mittens. Our guide told us that it was actually the ski resort season in the mountains. Constanta is more of a summer resort. We did see some people working on the roads and in the fields, the women working with shovels alongside the men.

Constanta's history goes back some 2500 years, when it was founded by the Greeks and known as Tomis. Alexander the Great camped here, and there is a legend that the Argonauts, returning from the search for the Golden Fleece, stopped here.

Looking at the bleak and cheerless countryside, you duly note that history records only short stops or camping here and you decide that those ancients weren't going to get caught in this place. The cheerless atmosphere follows you inside a department store. All stores are government owned and operated and are called, fittingly enough, "company stores." Both clerks and customers are grim and unsmiling, and you decide that they are the losers who live here, reminding you of the atmosphere many other travelers have reported on visits to Eastern European Communist countries.

It wasn't all bleak, however. Culture is very much appreciated behind the Iron Curtain and our morning tour was highlighted by visits to the Archeological Museum, housing artifacts of ancient Romania, and the aquarium, housing a collection of apparently nonedible fish. Among the more spectacular edifices were the Opera House, very large and ornate, and the Genoese Lighthouse.

If some of us were chilled by the morning's outing, that soon changed when we stopped for lunch at the Casino Restaurant. Here we found warmth in the atmosphere, the food, and, best of all, the people.

We were met at the door by a trio of musicians playing accordions and a violin. There followed an exceptional meal, and what abundance! For the first course came bread, rolls, and butter, and three kinds of wine, all you could drink without charge. After that came a fish course with rutabagas, and many different cheeses with raw vegetables. The fish looked vaguely familiar. Next, they brought on baked chicken, veal, cabbage, and a cornmeal dish. For dessert there was fresh fruit, crêpes suzette, cognac, and coffee. In short, just about what they must have figured any capitalist has for lunch.

To top it off, a special program of folk music and dancing had been arranged. An ensemble of thirty native dancers in authentic costumes danced and sang, and everyone was soon caught up in the lively spirit and forgot about the beach, the department store, and even the aquarium. The troupe serenaded us with Romanian music and songs, then graciously swung into "God Save the Queen" and "God Bless America." The audience joined in, singing other popular American songs and, because it was Saint Patrick's Day, there were Irish songs—all in all, a welcome and happy sound—God save the Irish!

Our lunch and songfest lasted a full three hours and sent us all back to the Queen feeling better about ourselves, humanity in general, and our Romanian comrades in particular.

That night, as we and our Royal Navy escort sailed out again across the Black Sea, there were Saint Patrick's Day celebrations aboard the QE2, catching the happy spirit of the afternoon, as strains of "My Wild Irish Rose" and "Danny Boy" rang out across the darkness of the bar, and anyone who thinks that the Irish don't drink on Saint Patrick's Day was not among those present that night, 'tis sure.

EN ROUTE FROM CONSTANTA TO ATHENS

We had been away from home for over two months, and some of the passengers were getting restless and complaining. It is so easy to complain about the weather, the food, or the services. Any sea captain, waiter, or steward will tell you that this is common in the later stages of a long ocean voyage.

Complaining is a disease of our age and, like other diseases, it can be contagious. This is what seemed to be happening. As authors of several books, we were asked to write something for the QE2 Times. We all know that *our negative thoughts are destructive. Every day we need good, positive thoughts to live by,* whether we are on land or sea. *Good thoughts are mind conditioners and act as a tonic for mind and body.* They are the best antidote for anxiety and depression. They lighten human burdens, help keep your spirits *up,* and bring contentment. Thinking that the captain and crew were doing a splendid job, we decided to jostle the grumblers...So we wrote the following essay on appreciation.

The waiters and the room stewards told us how effective these words were. They helped both the passengers and the crew to enjoy every day more, to see the good side of life, and to keep looking up!

APPRECIATION

Stinginess is not a matter of money alone...So—

Let us not be stingy with our appreciation when it is justly due.

Or with our words of praise where praise is due.

Or with encouragement when one has tried and failed.

Or with commendation when a job is well done.

Or with understanding and sympathy when another has been hurt.

Or with our service, even where sacrifice is required.

Or with acts of love and kindness for those toiling ones we meet along life's sometimes stormy way.

Everyone likes to be told that he is respected and appreciated and liked. "I like you because..." and be ready to give definite reasons.

If you have but a word of cheer to give, speak it while the one is near and able to hear.

Angels come to visit us and often we know them only when they are gone.

IN HOMER'S WAKE

We were once again on the Aegean, cruising past the islands in the wake of Homer's heroes, past Lesbos, which claims both the poetess Sappho and the great storyteller, Aesop. We felt a new warmth from the sun as we neared the shores of Greece.

Your adventurer's heart is filled anew with anticipation. Thoughts of Corinth, Mycenae, Athens, the Parthenon, the Acropolis, color your dreams. On a cruise ship, it's easy to be whoever you want, live in any age you choose. And you choose that Golden Age in the fifth century B.C., when the glory that was Greece exploded in a sunburst of achievement in arts and architecture, in science and philosophy, that many historians feel has never been matched before or since.

You remember reading somewhere that if you want to get a real perspective on things, you have to explore their beginnings. That's where you're headed now, you think, back to the real beginning of European civilization.

MOTTOES OF ANCIENT GREECE

Know thyself.

Seize occasion.

Industry is all.

The mean is best.

Look to the end of life.

The most of men are evil.

Haste, if thou wouldst fail.

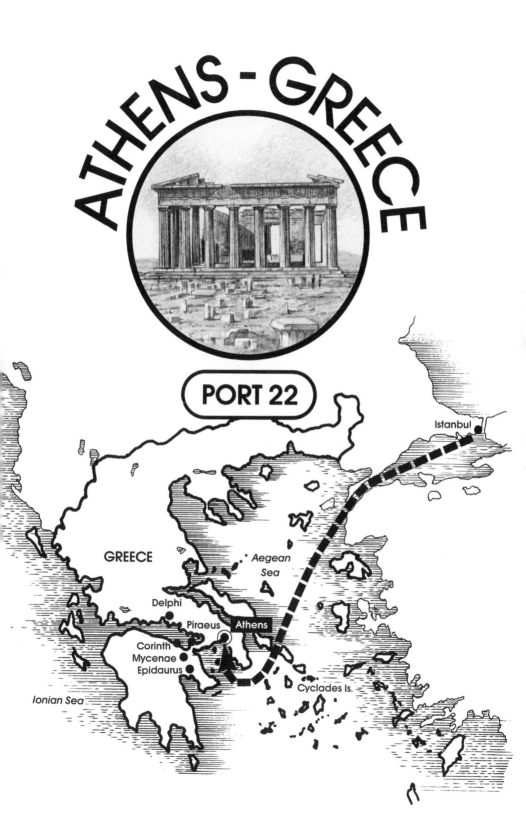

ATHENS - GREECE

PORT 22

Istanbul

GREECE

*Aegean
Sea*

Delphi

Piraeus   Athens

Corinth
Mycenae
Epidaurus

Ionian Sea

Cyclades Is.

The Acropolis—Athens, Greece

ATHENS, GREECE

The sky was an impossible blue, everything mirror bright and sparkling when we docked at Piraeus, the port city of Athens. This natural harbor was first developed in the fifth century B.C. and it built up such a huge commercial trade that it dominated the entire Aegean Sea. Today the port is still thriving. We berthed in the heart of the city, towering over the shops and jetty nearby.

The active harbor has facilities for great ocean liners, oil tankers, and smaller trading ships. From the top deck we could see the shipyards of the great Greek shipowners and the huge marina where hundreds of yachts were anchored. Beyond the larger port, we could pick out the fish restaurants and taverns around tiny Mikrolimano Harbor.

Two miles away was Athens itself, ringed by mountains, open only to the sea. Your heart suddenly seems to be in your throat as, through the morning mist, you discern the hazy outline of the Parthenon.

But the glorious Acropolis will have to wait. First there's a tour bus waiting to visit other historic landmarks in the Greek countryside.

DAPHNE

Our first stop, not far from Athens, was the eleventh-century marvel of Byzantium, the monastery at Daphne.

It was in the fourth century that Constantine the Great, the first Christian Roman Emperor, decreed that Christianity was to be paramount in all the domain. He thus ushered in a Byzantine period that would flourish for more than 1000 years, until

Constantinople was overrun by Turks in the fifteenth century. Though the setting is gone, the jewels remain in the form of lovely Byzantine churches in Greece and Italy, and Daphne is one of the finest surviving examples.

The Byzantines "invented" the best way to set a dome gracefully over the central cube of a church. They also developed the concept of four wings extending outward from the center, thus having the whole church form the shape of the "Greek cross."

The first church at Daphne was built on the ruins of a pagan shrine in the sixth century. Destroyed a century later by invaders, it was finally replaced in the eleventh century by the present gracefully domed, richly ornamented edifice we see today.

Daphne, we learned, was also the name of our tour guide for the day, and it was she who told us that Daphne means "Laurel," coyly explaining that in Greek mythology Laurel was Apollo's sweatheart.

CORINTH

Under the brilliant blue sky, an enchanting landscape unfolded—craggy snow-covered mountains and deep green valleys...hillsides dotted with grazing sheep, goats, and donkeys hauling carts loaded with oranges...gypsies camped by the roadside...turquoise seas...and, as the road dipped near the coastline, the summer homes of wealthy Athenians. Everywhere there were white-blossomed almond trees and large, silvery-green olive groves. The olive trees, we learned, last for centuries, so one plants them for following generations to enjoy.

Corinth is situated on the narrow isthmus that joins the Greek mainland to the Peloponnesus. On the east is the Saronic Gulf, to the west the Gulf of Corinth. Corinth, the old capital of southern Greece, at one time had a population of 500,000. It prospered in ancient times because it was easier to haul goods, even ships themselves, across the four-mile neck of land than to sail all the way around the Peloponnesus, a dangerous voyage of some 200 miles.

Today, with a canal cutting across the isthmus for ships to pass through, New Corinth is a thriving seaport with prospering industry. But it was the old city that had lured us here. Old Corinth was dominated by the Temple of Aphrodite, the goddess of love, and in her name Corinth was known as one of the most voluptuous of cities, with 1000 prostitute priestesses serving the goddess. It was the city's sinful reputation that brought the Apostle Paul here to preach in A.D. 51.

Atop a hill overlooking the old city stands a series of stark, lonely pillars, all that is left of the sixth-century Temple of Apollo.

THE PELOPONNESUS

Crossing the narrow isthmus, we arrived in the Peloponnesus, the home of warlike Sparta to the south. Almost nothing remains of this famous place, the sparse legacy of a people more interested in fighting than in building monuments. Eastward on this same peninsula is Olympia, the site of the first Olympic Games.

We stopped for lunch at a wayside inn, one of the serendipities of the Greek countryside. Here we enjoyed a hearty lamb stew with lima beans and stuffed cabbage and, as a special treat, the sweetest ripe oranges, freshly picked from nearby groves.

Then it was on to the site of Mycenae. This is southwest of Corinth on the Argolis promontory, and was once a city of great power and wealth, the capital of King Agamemnon. The beehive tombs, the Lion's Gate, and the remains of the palace offer a glimpse into what must have been a magnificent early civilization.

As the afternoon waned, we retraced our steps, crossing the isthmus to the mainland and following the coastal road along the

Bay of Salamis, thinking how much of history this tour had enabled us to relive in a few hours.

That night, Greek friends from Athens, Gerry and Mary Metaxatos, came down to join us for dinner on board the QE2. Gerry is a former general and surgeon in the Greek Army and Mary, his wife, is a Greek missionary.

The QE2 allows two guests per passenger to dine on the ship, provided you make arrangements beforehand.

We explored the ship together and dined in the Columbia Room, bringing a warm and hospitable end to a memorable first day in Greece.

THE ACROPOLIS

Athens, in its Golden Age in the fifth century B.C., was built to surround the hill on which stands the Acropolis. Even today, the modern city of Athens, with its broad boulevards, sleek apartment buildings, superb hotels, and sprawling residential areas, is dominated as no other city in the world by the glories of its past towering above it. Here are the surviving monuments of classical Athens, the cradle of democracy, a society dedicated as perhaps no other has been to the ideal of intellectual and spiritual freedom, of reason and moderation, of the full flowering of man's physical, mental, and spiritual nature.

Our tour bus worked its way through modern Athens's round-the-clock traffic jam, all of us filled with awe and anticipation.

Finally, we arrived at the base of the rounded, rocky hill and climbed its sloping paths, breathless with excitement. The word "Acropolis" means "the highest part of the hill," and when we reached it, clambering over broken slabs of stone and white marble, the whole city of Athens lay spread out below us.

Looking around, momentarily silent, you remember what the composer Richard Strauss had said about the Acropolis, that it reminded him of a symphony by Beethoven.

Only four buildings remain of the elaborate system of temples built to honor Athena, the protectress of Athens and the virgin goddess of wisdom, but they are enough to usher us into the Golden Age of Pericles, of Plato and Socrates, of Herodotus, Thucydides, and Hippocrates.

We entered through the massive gateway called the Propylaea, with its beautifully simple Doric columns. To our right was the small, white-marbled temple of the Wingless Victory. Off to our left and lower down were the slender Ionic columns of the Erectheum, beyond the Porch of the Maidens, resting on the heads of the Caryatides, gracefully-wrought stone maidens serving as the pillars.

But it was the main temple—the Parthenon—that drew our feet inexorably toward it, as it has drawn countless others down through the centuries. We climbed toward it, marveling at its soaring grace and wonderful symmetry, splendid against the bright blue of the sky. Its appearance of symmetrical straight lines is an illusion; it has almost no straight lines at all, everything subtly curving to correct the optical distortions a really straight line would produce.

The interior of the temple is roped off now. Over 2 million tourists come here every year, our guide Daphne told us, and their steps were wearing away the marble base. So we stood outside and walked around, trying to imagine ourselves here on that day in 438 B.C., when the Parthenon was dedicated.

"We are lovers of the beautiful," Thucydides wrote, quoting Pericles. "There are mighty monuments to our power which will make us the wonder of this and succeeding ages." And the Parthenon is the mightiest of them all.

MARS HILL

From the Acropolis we could see Mars Hill, a huge rock below us on the northwest approach to the Acropolis. The Apostle Paul was brought here so that the council could hear him preach the new Christian religion. When he arrived in Athens, he went through the Agora, the marketplace, and saw on his way many temples and altars dedicated to various gods and goddesses. One of these was an altar dedicated to the "Unknown God," and Paul took this as the theme for his sermon, for he had come to introduce the Athenians to this Unknown God.

SIGHTSEEING IN ATHENS

There was much more to see on our last day in Athens. To the north of the Acropolis, at the base of a steep cliff, stands the Agora, the marketplace where Socrates taught and where he was later compelled to drink the hemlock. It was the central meeting place for Athens in the Golden Age, a place of business as well as philosophy and debate.

On the other side of the Acropolis are the ruins of two of the famous open-air theaters—the amphitheater of Herodus Atticus and the even more notable Theater of Dionysus—where the Athenians came to hear and see the plays of Sophocles and Euripedes, Aristophanes and Aeschylus.

Modern Athens is a rich feast in itself, and one should not come here without allowing enough time for just sitting in Syntagma Square at the center of the city, at one of the many sidewalk cafés among the orange trees. The main shopping streets are nearby, so this huge square (also called Constitution Square) is a good jumping-off place. The National Museum is another must, with its treasure of classical art and antiquities.

Most delightful of all, after the wonders of the Acropolis, is the old quarter, or Plaka as it is known. Some call it touristy and perhaps it is, but the smells and sounds and colors of Greece are here in its steep and twisting narrow streets. There are many little shops and noisy bouzouki tavernas, a profusion of fresh flowers for sale, and sidewalk stalls where you can sample delicious lamb kebab. Sure, it's crowded and overripe and maybe even a tourist trap, but it's not to be missed.

It took many years of traveling around the world to finally learn that when some supposedly sophisticated person refers to something as "touristy," it doesn't necessarily mean that it's bad. Tourists aren't dumb. They usually pick out the *best.* It would be amusing to see these "sophisticates" take a trip to places devoid of tourists. They'd end up in the South Pole with an audience of amused penguins asking for their autographs.

Here are some other things that are not to be missed:

In *shopping,* look for peasant arts and crafts, textiles from Mikonos, embroidered blouses, and tablecloths. The colorful wool carpets are world-famous.

In *food,* try moussaka (mincemeat and spices), dolmades (meat and rice in grape leaves), the ubiquitous lamb kebabs, and the crumbly goat's cheese called feta (especially in salads).

In *drink,* no one should leave Greece without drinking the native wine called retsina. Being resinated, it has a tangy, different taste. Ouzo, the aniseed-flavored aperitif, is another taste that will linger with you, or perhaps even prevent you from leaving.

In *entertainment,* of course, you must go to one or more of the popular tavernas. Fill your ears with the blare of the bouzouki music and fill your stomach with tasty food and delicious wine, all for three or four dollars. The entertainment, which is free, will probably include a belly dancer, and before the evening is done, the customers join the show by participating in native dances. And, if you really want to get in the spirit, you can buy some plates from a waiter to smash at the feet of the dancers while the floor shudders and the windows rattle and the music blares and the crowd shouts and…there's always tomorrow to clean up the mess…for that's Athens.

> *Glistening Athens,*
> *violet crowned,*
> *Bulwark of Hellas,*
> *far-renowned…*
>
> —Pindar

EN ROUTE TO NAPLES

We were now back on the Mediterranean Sea, sailing toward Naples. This was a good time for another infusion of *inspiration* and *motivation* for *successful living.* The people who put out the *QE2 Times* seemed to be happy enough with the first article we wrote and wanted more—something about happiness, they suggested. So we stopped at the bureau on Two Deck and left this short essay.

TEN STEPS TO BRIGHTEN YOUR LIFE

1. Begin the day in a calm and cheerful mood. Say, "This is going to be a good day. I am going to be calm and cheerful right now."

2. Try smiling at others—make believe your underwear is tickling you. A smile is contagious and you will feel better as others smile at you.

3. Count your blessings—list them one by one. Did you ever realize the real wealth you have?

4. Enjoy this day with beautiful thoughts and pleasant memories. Live life one day at a time.

5. Be adventurous. Try walking and see new neighborhoods, new buildings and parks, new scenery.

6. Give a friend a phone call or write a letter. Tell them you were thinking about them, encourage them—encouragement is oxygen to the soul.

7. Be a happy person, see the bright side of life, shun the gloom. Having a cheerful, loving attitude lends itself to your best health.

8. Do a good deed, buy a book or give something beneficial to a loved one.

9. Give of yourself, offer your services to a hospital, to a church, help people. The law of giving will reward you tenfold.

10. Do the best you can each day. You are only living when you are useful and constructive.

TRAVEL

Three of the great values of *travel* are...

1. EDUCATIONAL

Travel educates a person by broadening his outlook on life and his relations with people in a way that cannot be learned from books. It brings back pleasant memories that can be lived and re-lived again and again.

2. RECREATIONAL AND PHYSICAL

Travel provides a change of climate and scenery, which is often more necessary for certain ailments than medicine. It aids in restoration of health, refreshment of strength and spirits after toil. Although travel may be considered the richest of all pleasures, it may also be considered a good investment.

3. INSPIRATIONAL

Our objective in traveling should be to inspire, to learn, and to venerate, to improve the understanding and the heart. The world we live in is a fairyland of exquisite beauty. Our very existence is a miracle in itself, and yet few of us enjoy as we might, and none appreciate fully the wonders that surround us.

The world belongs to those who have seen it!

NAPLES - ROME

PORT 23

ITALY

Rome

Adriatic Sea

Naples — Pompeii

Sorrento — Amalfi

Roman Forum and Colosseum in Background—Rome

NAPLES

Italy has reigned for centuries as Europe's most traveled country, regardless of the season. Dr. Samuel Johnson said of it, "A man who has not been in Italy is always conscious of an inferiority." It is also, in spite of rampant inflation, still one of the better bargains for tourists among European countries.

One reason is that so much of Italy is there just for the looking. Great churches—magnificent ruins—spectacular scenery, especially along the rugged coastline—and an ebullient, loving people out to prove that the best things in life are usually free.

One of Italy's most famous vistas is the Bay of Naples, nestled at the foot of Mount Vesuvius, with its mighty cone lost in the clouds, and the city of Naples, climbing in steps upward from the harbor.

Naples is not only a great and beautiful port, but it is also the intellectual and financial center of southern Italy. The city dates back to before 600 B.C., when it was founded by the Greeks as Neopolis, or "New Town." It was captured by the Romans in 326 B.C., and its balmy air quickly made it a favorite residence of Roman emperors.

A landmark of medieval Naples is the Castel Nuovo, built in the thirteenth century. Dominating the main harbor is the beautiful sculptured Renaissance triumphal arch and there's more. Always more!

Twentieth-century Naples has been called the city of pizza, ice cream, and automobiles. Very Italian, very noisy, very musical. The Opera House, founded in 1737, is the largest in Italy. It is a good city for shopping, both in the big arcades, like the Galleria

Umberto, and in the many thousands of small shops along its downtown streets. It's a place to discover the pleasures of al fresco dining at one of the sidewalk cafés and inviting *trattorias* along the seaside Via Carricciolo…to gaze at the Borgia collection of antiquities and the treasures from Pompeii housed in the National Museum…to listen on Sunday morning to the countless bells competing for attention in this "city of churches."

Naples, in fact, has more than 200 churches, and a visitor could well spend his entire time exploring them. Especially noteworthy are the interior decorations and frescoes of the thirteenth-century cathedrals of Saint Januarius and Saint Domenico Maggiore. Nearby is the cell of Saint Thomas Aquinas and San Lorenzo Maggiore, where Boccaccio met Fiammetta.

THE NEAPOLITANS

When you have seen all the buildings, however, you still don't know Naples. That's because the most interesting thing about the city is undoubtedly its people. Lively as well as cultured, the Neapolitans flavor their city as garlic flavors tomato sauce. Neapolitans conduct much of the business of their lives in the streets of Naples—this is their market, playground, workshop, and living room. This makes for an ever-colorful, ever-lively spectacle for the visitor in this giant outdoor theater of a city.

One story exemplifies the nature of the Neapolitan people and their approach to logic. Vittorio de Sica was directing a movie in Naples and employed a good many of the local residents as extras. At the end of one day's shooting, he paid them, and a man who had watched all of the day's filming also presented himself for payment. He reasoned that he had been so interested in the proceedings that he had neglected to go to work that day, so it was only fair that de Sica should pay him. After all, wasn't it de Sica's fault that he did not go to work?

Just as it is asserted that a man who has seen a ghost is never afterwards seen to smile, so in the opposite sense it may be affirmed that no man can be utterly miserable who retains the recollection of Naples.

—Goethe

MOUNT VESUVIUS

To the philosophically-minded, the legend of Naples gives reason to wonder—is the inevitable Law of Cause and Effect always at work? The city of Naples was originally a Greek colony, founded upon the legendary spot where the body of the Siren was washed ashore after she had sung to Ulysses to no avail. Legend has it that she drowned herself in a fit of anger, bringing in the seeds of innate corruption that blasted nearby Pompeii in retaliation.

As we left the congested older part of Naples on our morning tour, we could see Mount Vesuvius straight ahead of us to the left of the highway, rising from a broad, flat plain. The sulphurous steam said to arise from it constantly was not visible this morning. The soil in the area is very rich from deposits of volcanic ash, and the lava helps to hold moisture. There were many orchards wherever we looked—apricots, peaches, almonds—and miles of vineyards, for this is also a famous wine country, with vast areas of terraced acreage for growing grapes.

As we approached it, Mount Vesuvius was a fearfully desolate sight. It was not hard to imagine that terrible day a little over 1900 years ago, in A.D. 79, when the great volcanic peak, then twice as high at 8000 feet, erupted in an awesome cataclysm, completely burying and embalming the old city of Pompeii under cinders, dust, and ashes.

Naples and Mount Vesuvius

THE RUINS OF POMPEII

Some ancient ruins are disappointing to the tourist, demanding a considerable effort of imagination to bring to life a time and place long buried. Not so with Pompeii, for this ancient city was quite literally frozen in time, preserved by the very eruption that destroyed it.

Our guide was another Italian monument, a man of seventy-five named Tony with an ebullient personality and an outstanding set of lungs, whether he was bursting forth in a snatch of song or bellowing a stentorian "Yoo hoo!" to retrieve stragglers in our group. His cry meant "Here I am!" and we heard it often that morning. His admonition was, "Stay with me as one person and none will get lost."

Pompeii, first built 2600 years ago, had been ruled by the Greeks, then the Sumites, and then the Romans. In 1748, when the area was under Spanish rule, a farmer digging a well struck something with his spade…and the lost city of Pompeii was rediscovered.

In the first frenzy of discovery, people carried away everything that was found as fast as diggings could be made. Then, when the Italians took over about 100 years ago, and Italy was united by Garibaldi, an effort was quickly instituted to preserve the ruins, leaving everything as it was in the streets, houses, and shops.

That morning we walked the ancient pavement made by the Romans, and Tony made it all come marvelously alive:

"Here, at the entrance to a shop, the grooves for sliding doors can be seen. Notice the rain basin in the patio. The rain would drain into it from the roof, and from there it ran into a well dug underneath the house. When all the wells and cisterns were full, the water overflowed into the streets. Now the reason for these stepping stones becomes clear; it was a way to walk without getting wet feet.

"Over here is a sacred area where three temples once stood. White marble pieces can be seen between the cobblestones. Over there is a statue of Apollo, nearby one of his sister Diana. In the center is a sacrificial altar and a series of pedestals which held the statues of governors and emperors.

"We come now to one of the main temples, dedicated to the god Jupiter. Nearby is a store that sold togas. We call it Pompeii's Clothing Store.

"The people were trapped where they were in the city. Choked by the gas, they lay where they fell and were slowly buried by dust and ashes. Mud and lava would have crushed the bodies, but the dust and ashes, as they slowly hardened, preserved the skeletons intact. See this man with a belt around his body? He was a slave, a small man, not over five feet." Tony smiles broadly. "Beautiful teeth." He points to his open mouth. "Better than mine."

The way of life of the ancient city slowly unfolds as we walk the streets, peering into Roman baths, entering a wine shop where the big wine jars stand intact behind the counters, the dippers still in them. Close by is a cosmetic and perfume shop with a sign for ladies on one side, men on the other. "A combination barber shop and beauty salon," Tony suggests.

"Here is a drugstore, identified by the insignia etched into the panels. Above us is a water tower, part of the system that supplied running water to everyone's dwelling. And close at hand is an area where corn was ground. See the cone-shaped round stone with a cup on top? And in the oven there were sixty-five loaves, all preserved in stone. It was in the afternoon," Tony says, "so they had already baked their bread."

We look into a doctor's house, where tweezers and forceps are found ready for use…a public justice building, where striking frescoes, their colors as vivid as if they had just been painted, cover the walls…a flower market, where plants grow in the exact places where the same plants grew 1900 years ago. "We identified them by their roots," Tony informs us, "so the same kinds of plants have been planted where these roots were."

"Yoo hoo!" Tony's cry alerts the stragglers. It is time to leave. They emerge from the shops and houses, spilling into the streets and looking up fearfully toward mighty Vesuvius. We see the plume of smoke now, drifting above the cone, and shiver a little...

AMALFI DRIVE

The drive along the coastal road that leads around the Bay of Naples to storied Sorrento and on to Amalfi and Salerno is considered the most spectacular in the world. At every bend is the breathtaking beauty of pink-tiled fishing villages, lush green pine trees, and flowering gardens, all silhouetted against the azure blue Mediterranean.

Our bus hurtles along, the driver navigating a hairpin turn or skimming the edge of a precipice as deftly as he would weave in and out of the traffic in busy Naples. Blithely, he tells us that the road back will be much better since the other side is a foot wider. As he says that, he backs up to let some cars pass on the wrong side. Looking down from our bus window, there is no road to be seen—only steep cliffs and the sea below us. It's an adventurous ride in more ways than one, but then even a taxi ride in Italy can be an incredible adventure.

Always at our side, beyond the tumbling cliffs, is the blue beauty of the Bay of Naples. While only four miles off shore, the romantic Isle of Capri beckons. We pass a nudist colony, one of a number in the area, and men, women, and children wave greetings exuberant enough to put everything in motion—bless their little belly-buttons!

At lunchtime, we stop at a tiny outdoor restaurant by the sea. Its garden is cool and shaded by many trees. There's a good

The Vatican—Rome

local wine, charcoal-grilled fish, a delicious salad and, of course, pasta for an appetizer.

In the sleepy hours of the afternoon, there's a stop at Sorrento, a pretty little resort town balanced precariously on the top of 160-foot cliffs, looking northward across the Bay of Naples. Sorrento could be called a city of shops, but our best purchase was a delicious ice cream cone, which we enjoyed standing in the Mediterranean sun, staring out across the bright blue bay toward Capri.

A ROMAN HOLIDAY

Having come so close (Naples is an easy 140-mile drive on the modern Autostrada), the lure of the ancient city proves irresistible, and you decide to leave the tour and pop up to Rome for dinner.

You arrive on the Via Veneto just in time to buy yourself a new silk tie and scarf. Then you arrive at the Hassler Hotel's rooftop restaurant just as the sun is setting and lights are beginning to illuminate Rome's monuments.

After a delicious meal, impeccably served, you sit back, twirl your wine glass, and drink in not wine but 2000 years of history. They say that Italy is changing. How can it? Who can touch one hair of her marble head?

After dinner, you come back to earth and take the elevator to the lobby. As you step out onto the Piazza D'Espana and the Spanish Steps, you look at your watch. There's still time for a carriage ride through the Roman Forum. The old horse paces off the steps backward into the heart of the Roman Empire. Soon you are passing the old Altar of Vulcan, the Temple of Castor and Pollux, the temple erected to Concordia, the House of the Vestals, the Curia, and the Rostra. Suddenly, the Colosseum is looming above you. It is a relatively quiet night for Rome but you can still hear the roar of 50,000 throats at the games, the thunder of racing chariots, and the bloodthirsty cheers of the gladiator shows echoing in the silence. The driver returns by way of the most perfectly preserved ancient monument in the world, the Pantheon.

Then you are at the Trevi Fountain, throwing your money away in the best of causes—the hope of every traveler to return to Rome.

It's a good memory to carry away...like the strains that evening in the warm darkness of "O Mia Bella Napoli" or in the morning in the clamor of countless church bells, the voices of Naples...

When you are out on the town all day and you finally get back to your cabin on the ship, then you appreciate kicking off your shoes, taking a hot shower, and exclaiming, "What a delight is the bed!"

LAUGH

Always laugh when you can…
It is a cheap medicine.
Laughter is a tonic for your health.
It calms stress, fear, tempers, and
relieves the great strain of modern life.

The Riviera—France

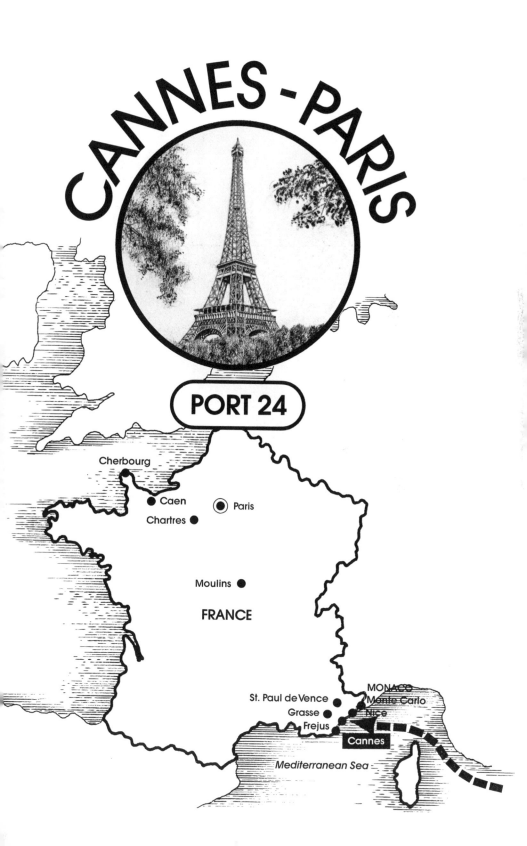

CANNES - PARIS

PORT 24

Cherbourg

Caen

Chartres

Paris

Moulins

FRANCE

St. Paul de Vence

Grasse

Frejus

MONACO

Monte Carlo

Nice

Cannes

Mediterranean Sea

The Casino at Monte Carlo—Monaco

CANNES

Cannes is the most beautiful sea port in the world. The QE2 docks in the middle of a magnificent city that is elegant and full of charm. Visualize the QE2 tied up in the middle of Fairyland. You walk off the ship and the first thing you see are green lawns lined with flowers and sycamore trees, four abreast, running parallel to the sea for miles. Across from the trees is a row of six- to ten-story buildings painted in all colors with matching colored grille work, all buildings of individual designs. Beautiful sidewalk cafés line this boulevard of breathtaking beauty.

Cannes is a resort on the renowned French Riviera, perhaps best known in America for its annual international film festival. The name "Cannes" conjures up a thousand images—glamorous movie stars, elegant shops, pine trees and yachts, enough flowers, fun, food, and *femmes* to make it a continuous, nonstop, year-round carnival. All this adds up to make this jewel of the French Cote d'Azur one of Europe's most popular year-round resorts. *It is said to be possible to enjoy life here more than in any other European resort,* and looking at the beautiful women and handsome men, sniffing the air for a mixture of sea breezes and delicious bouillabaisse, one knows immediately why.

The whole scene looks like a watercolor by Dufy. There are always a sprinkling of yachts in the harbor and an air of elegance in the smart hotels and expensive boutiques that line the flowered Boulevard de la Croisette, along the bayfront, which is the showpiece of Cannes. By night the casino glitters with diamonds and sables. By day the terrace of the Hotel Carlton sparkles with silver service and champagne in fluted crystal.

Just as Brigitte Bardot made Saint-Tropez famous, so Cannes, too, has its discoverer. In 1834, a Britisher, Lord Brougham, then Lord Chancellor, was on his way to Nice for a holiday when an epidemic of cholera halted him. Turning back, he stopped at the little port whose name derives from the canes growing in the nearby marshes. He liked it so well that he built a house here and returned annually for the next thirty-four years. His friends soon followed him, and before his death the poor fishing village had been transformed into a winter haven for the rich and fashionable people of Britain. By 1890, as many as sixty members of the royal houses of Europe were spending their winters here. The reputation of Cannes had been secured.

It's a perfect jumping-off place for other points of interest along the fabulous Riviera, from Saint-Tropez to the west to Nice and Monte Carlo to the east. Nearby Juan les Pins is a smart settlement that is fast becoming popular among young people from a dozen European countries.

TOURING CANNES

As we started our tour and left the dock area, our first impression of Cannes was one of cleanliness and charm spilling over into opulence. Everything was beautifully kept, painted, and landscaped. Even the apartment houses were attractive, with their windowboxes overflowing with flowering plants. We passed the cream-colored Film Festival Palace, adorned with the flags of many nations—the "Pleasure Court" of Cannes—and the Marina, where a hundred luxury yachts ride at anchor among a thousand dutiful sailboat subjects. One of the most elegant areas of Cannes, the Marina is surrounded by beautiful condominiums.

Flowers are one of Cannes's treasures. The rosery has some 4000 plants that flower from April through the end of the year, lending their fragrance to the entire area. There is a thriving flower industry, with some 2500 greenhouses used mostly for growing roses. Every day from two to three tons of flowers are shipped out from Cannes to other cities and countries. Lemon and olive groves are also productive here, as they are all along the Riviera.

Celebrities are another local product. During our tour we glimpsed the home of Greta Garbo, a white house built out on a point projecting into the sea. Nearby, David Niven's house was distinguished by its three arches. On an island in the bay was the luxurious residence of Jack Warner, the movie producer. A castle on the same island was formerly the property of the Duke and Duchess of Windsor, later sold to the Greek shipping tycoon, Aristotle Onassis.

The bright colors and luminous light of the area have lured such great artists as Renoir, Dufy, Matisse, and Picasso, whose daughter still lives here.

Shopping in Cannes rivals the best of Paris. In fact, the choicest shops in Paris just pack up and come here for the late summer months. Along the Rue d'Antibes, a few blocks inland from the Croisette, milady can stock up on jewelry, couturier clothing, sportswear, silver, crystal, pottery, and perfumes. Provencal flowered cotton fabrics are famous. Shops with "duty-free" signs in the windows can save you the value-added tax, which can be as much as twenty percent of your purchase.

SAINT-PAUL-DE-VENCE AND GRASSE

Next morning, a tour takes us along the Cagnes sur Mer, past the Cap d'Antibes, a lovely stretch of the Mediterranean shoreline east of Cannes. Inland, it continues through hillsides lovely with blossoming cherry and almond trees, and finally on into the mountains to the medieval village of Saint-Paul-de-Vence. Rising above the narrow cobblestoned streets made from stones of the sea found on the beaches of the Riviera, is this thirteenth-century church. Nearby is an array of small attractive shops, their windows filled with the paintings, sculpture, and pottery of its present-day artist colony inhabitants. It is a delightful experience to sit by the spray of the fountain in the square at the center of the town on a warm day and let the beauty and atmosphere of the place surround you.

Set in a grove of pine trees just outside Saint-Paul is the Foundation Maeght, an outstanding museum of modern art. Among its treasures are the works of Giacometti, Calder, Braque (including stained glass windows), Miro, and other twentieth-century masters.

We drove on through the picturesque mountains, passing through the hilltop village of Gourdon after navigating the spectacular Gorges du Loup canyon. Then we turned southward toward the sea, and passed through flowering fields to the quiet steep-hilled town of Grasse.

We stopped here, for Grasse has its own claim to fame. In the valley is grown the jasmine used as a base for all perfumes, as well as roses, violets, mimosa, tuberose, and other flowers. *Many perfume factories are here and we doubt that any woman left Grasse without carrying away memories of its quiet charm—and a fragrance to bring back those memories.*

AFTERNOON IN MONACO

We returned for lunch to Cannes. This storied playground on the Cote d'Azur has innumerable exotic eating places, all trying to outdo each other in their preparation of bouillabaisse. You look on hungrily as a steaming bowl of broth is poured over thick slices of crusty bread, subtly combined with olive oil, saffron, tomato, onion, garlic, pepper, thyme, bay leaves, sage, fennel, and orange peel. Another waiter arrives with a platter of lobster and half a dozen varieties of fish to complete the meal.

After this royal lunch, we set off again, motoring along the Corniche toward Monaco. The coastal road is an inviting progression of fishing ports and seaside resorts, with the Mediterranean, calm and blue, always at our side.

Soon we arrived at Nice. Its half-million inhabitants make it the capital of the French Riviera. Founded by the Greeks 400 years before Christ, it, like Grasse, the perfume capital, is a city of flowers. The new town has thirty factories turning out extracts, essences, and perfumes for shipment around the world. The old town, with its narrow streets and colorful flower markets, maintains the charm and enduring appeal that has made Nice one of the largest resort centers along the Riviera.

And then, more dazzling than anything we had seen before along this glittering coast, we came to the tiny, fairy-tale principality of Monaco, one of the world's most captivating international playgrounds.

Surrounded on three sides by France and on the fourth by the Mediterranean, Monaco has been an independent country for more than six centuries. Although it contains only 453 acres and a population of 30,000 (only 4000 of whom are native Monacans), it has a fame that far exceeds its size. For Americans, it is best known as the home of actress Grace Kelly, who became Princess Grace when she married Prince Rainier III, a descendant of the Grimaldi line which has ruled Monaco since A.D. 1297.

The section known as "the Rock" contains the Victorian-style royal castle and the old city with its winding, narrow streets lined with fashionable shops and restaurants.

But the older part of Monaco is dwarfed by the modern opulence of the new city. Facing the spectacular harbor with its marinas dotted with luxury yachts is a forest of high-rise condominiums and hotels, set against a backdrop of rugged mountains.

And then, across the harbor, lies the fabled splendor of Monte Carlo...

MONTE CARLO

Monte Carlo is a district of Monaco, lying across the harbor from the old city. In 1865, gambling was legalized to save

Monaco from going bankrupt. It succeeded beyond anyone's wildest hopes.

The centerpiece of it all is the Monte Carlo Casino, a fitting match for the magnificent Renaissance palace across the way. Unlike the neon glitter of Las Vegas, it is an elegant, sophisticated, honeybee location in which the well-heeled can move through ornate, high-ceilinged rooms, hearing the quiet whir of the roulette wheels and the discreet whispers of croupiers. Although long gowns, dinner jackets, and diamond tiaras have not gone completely out of style, the Casino's players today are more cosmopolitan in both manner and dress…and craps has been added to the traditional games of chemin de fer, baccarat, and roulette.

To one side is the century-old Hotel de Paris, and on the other is the popular Café de Paris. Down the beach there are other spectacular new resort hotels. The most dazzling is the Monte Carlo Sporting Club, an ultramodern complex that includes a disco, a nightclub, restaurants, and its own casino.

But it is to the old casino that you are inexorably drawn to try a spin of the wheel. The sense of style and grace recalls an old-fashioned, more elegant, well-mannered time, and you leave hoping that it will never change, that it will never become "Las Vegas by the Sea."

On the drive back to Cannes, someone recalls the story of "the man who broke the bank at Monte Carlo." It seems he didn't really break the bank, though he did shut down one table on several occasions in 1891. He went away with a small fortune. Everyone thought he had some kind of system, but it turned out that he didn't. He did work one out, however, and came back the next year to break the bank—and went broke.

There seems to be a lesson there somewhere.

TOURING FRANCE

For those who chose to bypass the Riviera and the ports of call in Spain, one of the finest of all the special shore excursions arranged for QE2 travelers awaited: a seven-day motor tour through France, culminating in two nights at the Hotel George V in Paris. (We had many eyewitness special reports of this fabulous gourmet's tour, to which we add our own favorite memories, especially of Paris.)

It was Thomas Jefferson who said, "Every man has two countries. His own and France." And this tour is a splendid introduction to much of France, from the quiet towns of the distant provinces, to the great chateaux of the Loire River Valley, to the capital itself. You drive through spectacular gorges and along the banks of meandering rivers, staying at elaborately furnished hotels and quiet country inns.

Some experts claim that the best of French cooking can no longer be found in tourist-overrun Paris, but it is still there for the tasting in the fine country inns and restaurants. So, to sample it, the QE2's bon vivant contingent set out for the restaurants that read like a gourmet's litany: the Abbaye de Sante Croix in Salon-de-Provence, La Musardiere in Millau, the Lion d'Or Hotel at Mende, the famous Les Freres Troisgros at Roanne, and the chateau Domaine de Beauvois at Luynes.

But man does not live by bread alone. This tour is also a feast of history, architecture, and visual delights, a tapestry of medieval villages and quiet country scenes, of old churches and great cathedrals, and especially of the magnificent chateaux of the Loire Valley.

In the fifteenth century when the British, victorious in war with France, chased Charles VII from Paris, he settled in Tours. The French court and its nobility accompanied him into exile, and competed with each other in building beautiful country chateaux. There's Rambouillet, the summer residence of the president of France, set in a dense forest, and the serenity of Amboise built on the banks of the river overlooking the town. You'll see other fine chateaux everywhere along the way, for every town claims its own in this area. What many believe is the most beautiful of them all is the "Chateau of Six Women" at Chenonceaux. It is built across the Cher River, with magnificent garden approaches. Among the most notable of the "six women" who have enjoyed its beauty were Henry II's mistress, Diane de Poitier, to whom he gave it as a gift, and his wife, Catherine de Medici, who reclaimed it after the king's death. Both historically and architecturally, it is a gem sparkling like a diamond in the emerald-green valley of the Loire.

Just outside of Paris is Chartres, one of the great cathedrals of France. Its gothic towers rising above the low houses and flat terrain make it a most awesome sight. The vast interior is almost 400 feet in length, and it contains some of the finest stained glass windows in all of France, including the famous rose windows above the arched portals of its facade.

Its memory lingers as you cross the last stretch of French countryside and finally arrive at the city on the Seine which everyone loves...Paris.

PARIS

This ancient settlement of the Goths was conquered by Caesar in the first century before Christ. In 451, inspired by a young woman called Genevieve, the inhabitants of Paris resisted the siege of Attila's Huns, eventually driving them away. Saint Genevieve remains the patron saint of Paris.

It was Charlemagne who made Paris a seat of learning, and in the following centuries it grew into the largest and richest of all the great medieval cities of Europe. It became a world center of goods and commerce, music and opera, literature and learning. Needless to say, it still is.

Part of Paris's charm is its changeless beauty. From many vantage points the city looks the same as it must have two centuries ago...the great Gothic cathedrals, the houses with their chimney pots, the quiet-flowing Seine with its graceful old bridges, the narrow streets with their many small shops, the flower stalls, sidewalk cafés and lovely parks. But much of Right

Bank Paris is newer, dating from the middle of the nineteenth century. It was then that Napoleon III (nephew of Napoleon Bonaparte) commissioned Baron Eugene Haussman to modernize the city. Haussman did so by ruthlessly tearing down many old buildings to make way for Paris's famous broad boulevards and park-like squares. Purists and historians still moan about the destruction of so much of early Paris, but the city that Haussman redesigned is a delight to the eye. Today, space is just barely adequate to allow traffic to move across town.

SIGHTSEEING IN PARIS

Paris is expensive in many ways, but a walk along the Champs Élysées, one of the world's great boulevards, is free. So is a stroll over one of the bridges, pausing to look down at the Seine and out at the teeming life of the city. You can see a lot of Paris just sitting at the Deux Margots on the Left Bank, or at the Café de la Paix. Sip a glass of wine or hot chocolate and watch the girls and boys go by. Within an hour, they say, you're sure to see someone you know. Be entertained by the street musicians. It's a fine way to get the feel of Paris without denting your budget.

Half-day Cook's tours (included in the QE2's shore excursion to Paris) will give you glimpses of the must-see highlights of Paris. They include the Arch of Triumph at the center of the Place de l'Etoile, with a dozen streets fanning out from it, the chief one being the Champs Élysées. The Place de la Concorde is where the French Revolutionists set up their guillotine. Loius XVI, Marie Antoinette, and Madame du Barry were among the many who lost their heads here. You should see the elaborate Palais Royal, built by Cardinal Richelieu, and Napoleon's Tomb in Les Invalides. Drive through the lively Latin Quarter and the Marais district, the heart of the fashionable Paris of the Renaissance, where many of the great houses have been restored. And you'll discover scenes of romantic Paris that are familiar from Utrillo's paintings in the winding streets of Montmartre.

In Montmartre, you'll find one of the great cathedrals of Paris, Sacre Coeur, whose great white dome is a landmark. From the terrace of Sacre Coeur you have one of the finest views looking out over Paris. The other cathedral not to be missed (though there are many more) is, of course, Notre Dame de Paris. This is on the Ile de la Cite, an island in the middle of the Seine, and it can be reached by one of the graceful bridges, Pont Neuf. Begun in the twelfth century and completed in the thirteenth, Notre Dame is one of the great Gothic cathedrals of Europe.

Two other musts complete this "instant tour." One is, of course, the Eiffel Tower. Nearly 1000 feet high, completed in 1889, it says "Paris" immediately to almost anyone anywhere in the world.

And then there are the Louvre and the Tuileries Gardens. The Louvre was once a fortress, later a royal palace, and then one of the great museums of the world. It's actually a dozen museums in one, and you would need a dozen longer visits to take in the rich artistic heritage it holds. But even a quick tour will let you see Da Vinci's *Mona Lisa*, Titian's *Man with Glove*, Van Gogh's *Self Portrait*, the *Winged Victory* and *Venus de Milo*, the magnificent Rubens collection, works of Raphael and Cezanne, and countless others.

There is also one other way to see Paris at its best, and that is on a boat trip along the Seine. The QE2's tour closes the first day in Paris with such a cruise and dinner on the Seine. You can also do this in the late morning and enjoy a delicious lunch on board. Either way, Paris is lovely from the river, and you can see the famous bridges in no other way.

It's all the same—it's all that great, big, wonderful place that lovers of life, and just plain lovers the world over, call Paris.

CONCIERGE

Concierge is the French word for a person who serves you by doing small and various duties as an attendant of a hotel or building, one who handles mail, actually a *factotum,* a practical helper. In English-speaking lands they are sometimes called "keys" or "hall porters." Concierges can be men or women, and they usually speak two or more languages.

The concierge is your advisor and helper. He or she obtains tickets to operas and shows, does shopping for you, mails letters and packages, and gets tables at any restaurant or nightclub on the busiest nights.

An important fact for travelers to know is that you don't have to stay in that particular hotel to ask the concierge for help. Concierges are the greatest source of information about a locality that you will ever find.

In Paris, where reservations for such things as dinner, theater, and opera are an absolute must, your concierge is indispensable.

RESTAURANTS WE LIKED

Everyone loves Paris, but everyone loves it in a different way. You can dine at a thousand restaurants, any one of which is outstanding in gustatory pleasures, and every visitor will find different favorites. These are a few of ours.

Perigordine, 2 Place Saint-Michel, is called the "Temple of Gourmets." Besides superb food, it has a nice view overlooking the Seine. We had the most delicious chocolate mousse we have ever eaten in our lives.

Maxim's is world-famous. We liked many other restaurants better, but tourists still consider Maxim's important. That's one reason why it is *very* expensive. Try their wild strawberries.

Joseph's has wonderful food and service. You have a good chance of seeing celebrities here. Try the crêpes suzette for dessert.

Escargot-Montorgueil, 38 Rue Montorgueil, is more than 150 years old. Snails are a specialty, but other choices are fine, too.

Auberge du Pere Louis, 17 Rue de Ponthieu, is a good choice for the night when you see Folies Bergere, since its location is convenient to the theater. Sole meuniere is wonderful, as is the foie gras with truffles.

Restaurant de la Tour d'Argent ("silver tower"), 15 Quai de la Tournelle, is the oldest restaurant in Paris, established in 1582. The specialty is roast duck. Every duck served is given a number; ours was no. 305,291. Our dinner was superb. No wonder all U.S. Presidents eat here when they are in Paris!

VERSAILLES

After Paris, what is there? The next step is Versailles.

The highlight of the last day of the QE2 tour of France, en route from Paris to rejoin the Queen at Cherbourg, was a visit to Versailles, the palace of palaces. It was built by Louis XIV, the Sun King, as his palace, and it took more than half a century to complete. Fortunately, Louis XIV reigned for a remarkable 72 years, so he had time to complete his favorite project.

It is spectacular in size and opulence, from the Great Apartments to the Hall of Mirrors, where the World War I peace treaty was signed. Nothing in France offers a better glimpse of the sumptuous way of life that provoked the French Revolution. You wonder aloud if it was all worth it, and a group of swans swims by nodding their question-mark necks as they go.

While you're still a little stunned by the larger-than-life splendor of Versailles, in the afternoon you have a chance to see another oversize achievement, the famous 230-foot tapestry at Bayeux.

You're still shaking your head in wonder when you reach Cherbourg. Now you have something to compare to the size of the *Queen Elizabeth 2!*

AND MEANWHILE

Back on the QE2, those who did not elect to take the tour of France and Paris have left Cannes and the French Riviera, going to sleep that night off the coast of France, and waking up in Spain!

EN ROUTE TO BARCELONA

On the deck chair next to you is a beautiful lady. Though she is old in years, there is a freshness to her complexion, a youthful radiance and sparkle in her pale blue eyes.

You strike up a conversation with her. She's a mother of two and has three grandchildren. Her eyes brighten even more as she tells you their names and ages. Looking into her unwrinkled, untroubled face, you wonder what secrets she knows. What could she tell you?

After asking about something she's reading, you maneuver the conversation around to ask her, "What do we get out of life?"

She smiles and says softly, "We get out of life exactly what we put into it—but if we know how to go about it, we get that back in great abundance."

Before you know it, she closes her eyes and shares, not something she's read, but the poetry within her:

TODAY

This is the beginning of a fresh new day;
I greet it with HOPE.

Today comes only once, and never again returns; I must
show my LOVE and be KIND.

God has given me this twenty-four hours to use as I will;
I shall have a cheerful ATTITUDE.

I must do something GOOD with this day and not waste it.

This is my day of opportunity and duty; I expect some-
thing GOOD because I am going to help make it
happen!

Today is a NEW DAY in my LIFE, a new piece of road to be
traveled; I must ask God for directions.

Today I will be filled with courage and confidence; I must
show my FAITH in God.

What I do today is very important because I am exchang-
ing a day of MY LIFE for it.

The COST of a thing is the amount of MY LIFE I spend
obtaining it.

When tomorrow comes, this day will be gone forever,
leaving in its place something I have traded for it.

In order not to forget the price I paid for it, I shall do my
best to make it USEFUL, PROFITABLE, JOYFUL.

The seeds I plant today determine my HARVEST in the
future; my life will be RICHER OR POORER because of
the way I use today.

Thank you God for today; I shall not pass this way
again—What I must do, I'll do today!

My, what a way to live each day, what a philosophy to live by!

You find out later that she has spent a life helping others and that she herself has suffered many hardships and personal tragedies along the way.

You hurry back to your cabin to write down her words, hoping you might learn something from her wisdom. You utter a silent prayer that your eyes may be as bright, your skin as unwrinkled and unblemished, your smile as happy, and the love within you as apparent and bounteous when you are her age.

Replica of Ship Sailed by Columbus—
Barcelona

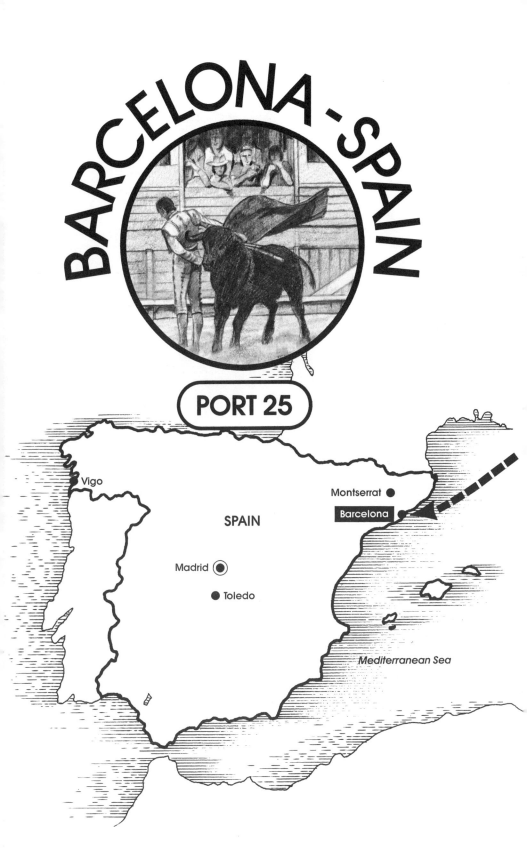

BARCELONA · SPAIN

PORT 25

Vigo

Montserrat ●

Barcelona

SPAIN

Madrid ◉

● Toledo

Mediterranean Sea

Statue Representing Industry, Commerce, Neptune, Maternity—Barcelona

MANY-SPLENDORED SPAIN

Spain has become one of the greatest tourist meccas of our time, drawing some 130 million tourists each year. What is the reason for Spain's success? A cynic might cite its relatively low prices and its reputation for providing the bargain-basement vacations of Europe.

One other reason is the climate on the southern coasts, which lures Europeans from the colder northern countries during winter to bask in the sun of the Costa del Sol and the Costa Brava. But Spain has many climates, for its landscape ranges from snowcapped mountains to arid desert plains to the Mediterranean beaches.

Variety and contrast are part of Spain's appeal. Romans and Moors have occupied the land and left their marks in its architecture and its people. There are fifteen different regions of Spain with as many different peoples, among them the Basques, Catalans, Castilians, and Andalusians, each with distinctly different customs and even different languages.

The gourmet might praise Spain's food, be it Andalusia's gaspacho, an ice-cold summer soup; Castile's cochinillo asado, roast suckling pig; Catalonia's calamarea a la romana, squid fried in butter; or the universally popular paella. Wine lovers might say that Spain's popularity is deserved and cite its colera sherries, tawny ports, or satisfying sangria, the heady mixture of red wine, brandy, fruit juices, sliced fruit, and ice that quenches one's thirst on a hot summer day. They also enjoy the tapas, tidbits of prawns, squid, or sausage that are served as snacks in Spanish bars to tide the hungry tourist over till his eleven o'clock dinner hour.

Still others might say that Spain's reputation rests on its churches, the cultural imprint of Roman and Moor on its architecture or flamenco music and dancing, the color and pageantry of its bullfights, the beauty of its flashing-eyed señoritas, or the charm and elegance of its regally mannered men.

You see, the question is not easy to answer because there are many Spains. It is a land with a cornucopia of pleasures just waiting to supply everyone's favorite thing out of its bounteous riches.

BARCELONA

There was an early morning haze on the water as the QE2 entered Barcelona Harbor. If you squint just a little, you can still see Christopher Columbus traversing the same waters as he returned from his first voyage to the New World. To make it seem more real, a full-scale reproduction of the *Santa Maria* is moored there to greet you.

The 2000-year-old Barcelona is the capital of Catalonia, and is said to have been founded by a Carthaginian named Hamilcar Barca. The Catalans are both fiercely independent and proud of their heritage, so proud that they call themselves Catalans instead of Spaniards. A distinctive Catalan language still survives, combining elements of Spanish, French, and Italian. It is said to be the closest thing to a now-vanished language that was once spoken throughout southern France.

Many aspects of the traditional Catalan culture survive in modern Barcelona. One colorful tradition is the native dance called the sardana, a simple folk dance done in a circle with everyone joining in. During the summer months, the sardana is danced in the squares of the city on Wednesday and Saturday evenings, and at noon on Sunday. Lively as it is, the dance is carried out poker-faced, with great dignity and pride.

Today, Barcelona is the major Spanish port on the Mediterranean, the crossroads town visited by everyone who travels to the popular coastal resort of Costa Brava. Barcelona is also noted for its many elegant bronze statues.

Built on a broad, sloping plain between the mountains and the sea, Barcelona is today a city of more than 4 million, but it is much more "manageable" for the visitor than many other great cities. One reason is that Barcelona is divided into three rather well-defined sections: the Old City which includes the famous Ramblas, the Modern City, and the suburbs, made up of all the small old villages that have gradually been absorbed into the metropolis.

Considered one of Spain's leading cultural centers, Barcelona was one of the first cities in Europe to print a newspaper, the *Diario de Barcelona,* in 1792, and that newspaper is still printed.

THE OLD CITY

The old, medieval sector of Barcelona, with its winding streets and ancient buildings, is centered around the Barcelona Cathedral, the finest example of Catalan Gothic architecture in existence.

A plaque in the cathedral commemorates the return of Columbus from America. Juan, our guide, pointed out the famous crucifix called the Cristos de la Ponda, said to have been fastened onto the top of a Spanish ship that was facing the Turks in battle, and believed by the people of Barcelona to be the reason for the Spanish victory. Beneath the main altar of the cathedral is the elaborate sarcophagus of the body of Saint Eulalia, an early Christian martyr who refused to deny her faith to the Roman governor.

Nearby is the modern Church of the Sagrada Familia. This huge, striking edifice, with its openwork towers, is the work of the

Saint Elena Cathedral—Barcelona

architect Gaudi. Gaudi has left his mark throughout Barcelona, in startling houses with facades that change shape as one views them from different angles, many flats and office buildings, and a park.

Near the cathedral is a fresco by Picasso and a museum containing a broad selection of the famous artist's work.

RAMBLAS

Bordering the southwest side of the old quarter are the tree-lined Ramblas (the name means "places to ramble"), filled with open-air cafés, stalls, and shops of every kind. There is a flower market, a bird market, and newspaper and book stalls. It is also the place to come in the evening for dining and dancing and lively singing. A delightful place to stroll, these wide avenues radiate outward from the Plaza de Cataluna onto a series of all-night shops, bars, and taverns where you can hear the slap of a guitar, the click of heels, and the twang of a haunting flamenco melody coming through the doors as you shop.

THE MODERN CITY

What is today called the Modern City of Barcelona was, in 1850, an area of fields and farms. Now, its wide, straight streets contain a fashionable residential section, a 100-year-old university, and a modern university city, with restaurants and nightclubs. The Consulate is here, as is the Paseo de Gracia, the luxury shopping center of Barcelona.

An interesting monument at the end of one street is dedicated to Montreal, a priest, poet, and inventor. His long poem *The Atlantia* is a well-known recounting of the legend of the lost city of Atlantis. But Montreal is also a hero in Barcelona as the inventor of the submarine, which was submerged successfully for the first time in Barcelona Harbor in 1858.

THE SPANISH VILLAGE

If one could only visit a single city in Spain, Barcelona would lay strong claim to being that one. A reason is the remarkable Spanish Village, for here, as our guide Juan proudly claimed, you can see the whole of Spain in an hour!

Begun in 1924, the Spanish Village was completed five years later in time for the International Exhibition. It is a life-size recreation of the architectural styles and ways of life of all fifteen of Spain's provinces. We began at one end, inspecting houses representative of the north of Spain, and then traveled southward to the southernmost province of Andalusia.

The Village is undeniably touristy, but it still shouldn't be missed. The streets are lined with shops and stalls where Spanish artisans can be seen practicing the age-old trades of their districts. Hand-blown glassware, leather, and wrought iron articles are among the best buys. You might also find a rosary made from the petals of crushed roses, beautiful handmade ladies' shawls, or a bouquet of "roses" that is actually made of seashells.

The Spanish Village is a museum of Spanish history, a display center for the whole range of Spanish arts and crafts, and above all, a place for fun!

DINING IN BARCELONA

Besides sightseeing, Barcelona is the place to savor your first taste of real Spanish food. The Catalan version of paella adds chicken and meat to the usual fish, rice, and shellfish.

MONTSERRAT

People from all over the world make pilgrimages to the monastery at Montserrat, but the QE2's pilgrims had only a short journey from Barcelona, about thirty-eight miles inland to a spectacular range of rugged mountains. Montserrat, the legendary home of the Knights of the Grail, is called the "Holy Mountain." You park below and reach the sanctuary at the top of the mountain by cable car.

The eighteenth-century cathedral is lovely, but especially memorable is the famous boys' choir which sings in the church every day at noon. In the still mountain air, on a clear and sunny day, the voices of those black-haired, dark-eyed boys were like those of angels.

The monastery also has an excellent restaurant, where the QE2's visitors lunched before returning to Barcelona.

EN ROUTE TO GIBRALTAR

I was lying on the massage table in the gymnasium, and Dave was giving me one of his superb massages, when the thought came to me about *happiness*. My mother was one of the happiest people I ever knew. When she laughed her stomach would jump up and down like Jell-O during an earthquake. *Happiness* should be the number one product of our life. So here is my little opus on *happiness*.

HAPPINESS—THE ETERNAL QUEST OF MANKIND

The most important thing to learn in life is how to live. Happiness is many different things. Few people are aware of how many elements go into making happiness.

Make up your mind to be happy. Learn to find happiness in simple things. When the famous French writer, Colette, was dying of cancer and was being interviewed by a newsman, she exclaimed, "What a wonderful life I've had! Those were my happiest days!" Then, after a sigh of remorse, she added, "I only wish I'd realized it sooner."

Our biggest mistake in our pursuit of happiness is not knowing when we have it. *The most important product of our life is happiness and joy.* The fountain of happiness is in the heart. *Happiness is when you feel good inside.* Make this your chief goal—to spend your life experiencing happiness and joy.

The quests of life are many and varied. Among them are the quest for *money* and *possessions,* the quest for *love,* the quest for *truth,* the quest for *usefulness* and *duty,* the quest for *goodness* and for *God,* and the quest for *happiness* and *contentment.*

If it were possible to measure on a meter the happiness of the life a person leads, or the quality of life, we might be shocked by how much we are shortchanging ourselves. Are you low or high on the happiness scale? The quality of your life-style has a profound influence on your health, wealth, and happiness.

Guard within yourself the treasures of happiness which come from kind words, kind acts, kind looks, warm hand-shakes—these are all *acts of kindness.* Lead the life that will make you a kindly and friendly person to everyone around you, and you will be surprised at what a happy life you will live.

The benefits of being happy are many. If you are a salesperson, on your next call see how happy you can be and notice how much easier your negotiation turns out. Your thoughts flow more freely when you are happy and not tense. Your happy attitude is contagious and spills over onto others around you. When you laugh you relax, and when you relax you give freedom to your muscles, nerves, and brain cells. Man seldom has use of his reason when his brain is tense. A sense of humor creates a relaxed environment where reason can act. If you have to work with a difficult person, see how happy you can be, and you will be amazed at how well you will get along with him. The *results* of being happy are *so great,* I can't understand why anyone would want to be unhappy.

Rock of Gibraltar

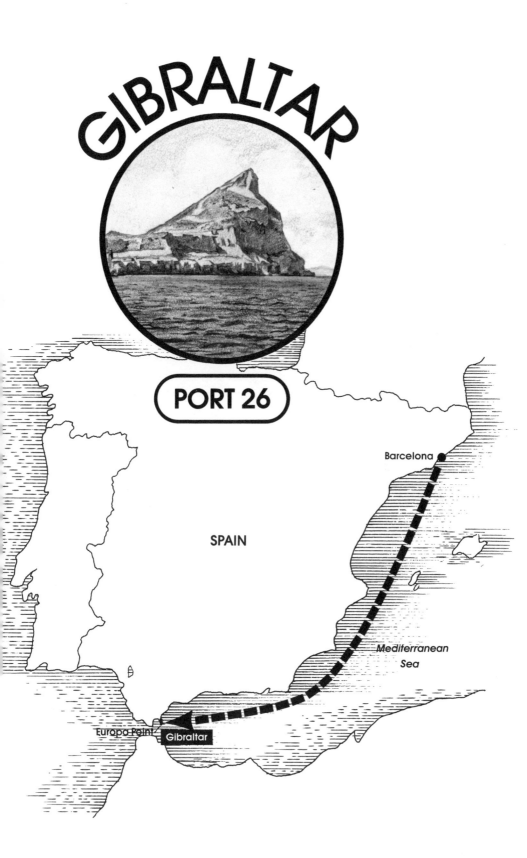

GIBRALTAR

PORT 26

Barcelona

SPAIN

Mediterranean Sea

Europa Point · Gibraltar

GIBRALTAR

Ay, this is the famed rock, which Hercules and Goth and Moor bequeathed us. At this door England stands sentry.

—Wilfrid Scawen Blunt

The Rock of Gibraltar, one of the legendary two pillars of Hercules, guards the straits between the Mediterranean Sea and the Atlantic Ocean. Probably the best known rock in the world, it stands 1396 feet high at its peak and looks out across the straits toward Morocco on the African coast, just fifteen miles away.

The Rock's strategic position is its reason for being. Phoenicians and Romans came here, but it was the Moors who landed at or near Gibraltar in A.D. 711 and went on to conquer Spain. They built a fortress castle on the Rock and fought off the Spanish for centuries. The castle was enlarged in the fourteenth century, but only the main tower stands today as the Moorish Castle. The Moors were finally driven out in 1462, after holding the Rock for over 700 years.

Gibraltar gets its name from the leader of the original conquering Moors, Tarik-Ibn-Zeyad. The Rock was called Gibel Tarik (Mountain of Tarik), which was eventually corrupted into Gibraltar.

A British-Dutch naval force took the Rock in 1704, under the command of Admiral Rooke. By the Treaty of Utrecht (1713), Gibraltar was ceded to Britain "to be held and enjoyed absolutely with all manner of right forever."

That treaty didn't end the strife, however. The Spanish made several attempts to recapture the Rock, culminating in the

Great Siege of 1779-1783, during which a valiant garrison of about 7000 British troops fought off Spanish forces numbering over 40,000. In the end, when the Spanish tried to take the Rock by sea, the defenders destroyed the "unsinkable" Spanish ships by firing "hot potatoes" down on them, red-hot shot that set the ships on fire.

For the best part of three centuries, Gibraltar has remained a British bastion, an important element in British naval power with its commanding position at the entrance to the Mediterranean. During World War II, General Dwight D. Eisenhower established headquarters at Gibraltar for launching the invasion of Africa, and there is an American memorial erected in his honor. The largest of the many caves within the Rock, Saint Michael's Cave, was used as a wartime military hospital.

WHO ARE THE GIBRALTARIANS?

Who lives here? Where did they come from? They speak both Spanish and English, but which are they?

The answer is complex. The cemetery tells the story of the early settlers of Gibraltar after the British occupation in 1704. Family names from Italy and Portugal, Malta and Minorca, Jews from Morocco, British soldiers and sailors who married local Spanish girls—all are part of the heritage of the Gibraltarians. And, while the Spanish influence is strong, the Gibraltarian is actually a British subject and proud of it, owing loyalty to the British Crown.

CITY OF TWO MAYORS

Gibraltar's mixed heritage is seen in many ways. You can have a drink in an English pub or a Spanish bar in the town of Gibraltar, and in either place you may soon learn that Gibraltar has two mayors, neither of whom recognizes the other. One mayor resides in the town hall of San Roque, a village five miles beyond the border between Gibraltar and Spain. The other, of course, is the real mayor of the town of Gibraltar.

All of this points out the continued Spanish desire to assert sovereignty over this tiny peninsula. The British, however, have strong emotional ties to the Rock, even though Gibraltar in the modern world no longer has the same strategic significance that it had in the past.

TOURING GIBRALTAR

Our stay was short, and there was no organized shore excursion from the QE2, but one can see a lot of Gibraltar in a few hours—and it is full of surprises.

We took a taxi, actually driving through the Rock via a long tunneled roadway. During various times of siege and war, tunnels have been hollowed out to create access to gun and cannon ports high up on Gibraltar's face. There are now about thirty-two miles of tunnels called Galleries.

The Caves of Gibraltar honeycomb the huge Rock, caves at sea level or high up, hollowed out by the sea or created by earthquakes. The most famous is Saint Michael's Cave, 980 feet above sea level. It is a huge natural auditorium with a spectacular display of stalagmites and stalactites, enhanced now by artificial lighting. It is even used for concerts and ballet performances. This cave became a major hospital during World War II. There are many other natural caverns: Lower Saint Michael's Cave, discovered during the war when the main cave was expanded, Gorham's Cave, Poca Roca Cave, and many others.

On our drive we passed a fishing village, several popular beaches on both the eastern and western shores of the penin-sula, and a fine large airport. Traffic is stopped when planes come in because they have to use part of the roadway as a landing strip!

For those who think of Gibraltar as only a rock fortress, the town itself is a surprise, with its busy main street crowded with shops and restaurants, its sunlit plaza, government buildings, and intriguing gates that restrict access to the walled enclave.

With its population of over 25,000 and a growing tourist trade, Gibraltar is chronically short of water. One interesting sight is the system of gutters and catchment basins that drain rainfall into cisterns at the base of the Rock, where more than 16 million gallons can be stored. There is also a plant to convert sea water and a number of water wells in the area.

The Gibraltar Museum, on Bomb House Lane, is a must-see in Gibraltar. It is housed in a fourteenth-century Moorish bath, complete with stables and cellars that are still utilized. Displays illustrate the fighting history of the Rock, and there is a Great Siege Room honoring the valiant defense of the Rock by the British soldiers led by General Eliott, the British Governor throughout the four years of the siege.

The Governor's residence today is called the Convent, a name that goes back to 1531, when a wealthy Spaniard gave the Franciscan friars a site on Gibraltar. No one knows if there were ever any nuns living in the Convent, but a ghost is said to haunt the building, described as a nun in grey.

Europa Point is another tourist favorite, for it is the tip of Europe. A medieval shrine stood here, to Our Lady of Europa, and the celebrated statue, deposed several times by various invaders, once again stands in the shrine. A light has glowed at this point in the Lighthouse since 1841. It has progressed from the single-wick oil light first lit that year, 150 feet above the sea, through various stages of evolution to an incandescent light, to an electric revolving system, to the present powerful twin Super-tyfons, complete with red lights and fog signals.

THE BARBARY APES

The Barbary Apes of Gibraltar are not really apes, but a species of tailless monkeys, the only monkeys living wild in Europe today. The name comes from an earlier belief that they came across the straits from Morocco (formerly Barbary) or were perhaps brought by the Moors from Africa.

There used to be hundreds of them on the Rock, but their numbers dwindled as the human population grew, shrinking available space and vegetation and bringing periods of famine. But there is an old Spanish saying: "When the Apes leave the Rock, the British will go." So a tradition has grown up of helping the monkeys survive. British soldiers began feeding them during World War I, and for the past sixty years the government of Gibraltar has borne the cost. There are two distinct packs, each with a recognized leader and its own territory, where they roam quite freely. They are friendly, though they have a weakness for purse-snatching. The Apes are fed twice daily by a member of the Gibraltar Regiment, and the two thriving packs now number between thirty-five and forty. At birth each ape is entered onto the roll of the military garrison.

SHOPPING IN GIBRALTAR

Gibraltar is a duty-free port, and a good selection of the world's goods can be had here cheaper than anywhere else in Europe, from Turkish water pipes to Havana cigars, French cheese, German cameras, Swiss chocolates, Japanese cultured pearls, or French perfume. Most of the shops are crowded onto Main Street and you can get good buys if you are selective.

EN ROUTE TO VIGO

As you depart from Gibraltar Harbor, the band is playing "When You Come to the End of a Perfect Day." You think how fast the trip, like life itself, has passed. Now, even this eighty-day, 30,000-mile world cruise will soon be coming to a close. You wonder if time is a quantity or a quality. Einstein proved that time is not a fixed succession of equally spaced intervals following each other inexorably like a beginning pianist might bang out the notes of "Chopsticks." Time, it appears, is like the rich, accordant notes of a symphony, blending and melding with the emotions of the conductor.

Your experience, too, tells you that time is a quality based on feeling, not watches. When you were a child, summer vacation would never come, and then it was gone so quickly. How quickly all the good moments pass. More than the ticking of an old clock, time seems somehow like the beating of a heart—*your* heart—in time with the stardust of the cosmos.

Your life is never measurable in years, but in *events,* big and small, a succession of inner states of joy and laughter, pain and sorrow, like everyone else. The idea of a number of arbitrarily fixed, succeeding events implies multiplicity when there is really unity. Only a whole personality can measure time, and no part— not even divisions of one's life into seconds, minutes, hours, days, weeks, months, years, and even lifetimes—can stand alone or do the job or tell you how it is to love or search and find, or fight and conquer.

There is no time in the Piagetian sense...It's just the second act, the third beer, the first embrace, the last part of the trip and, seen in this true light, there are never any beginnings or endings, just experiences.

Fisherman of Vigo

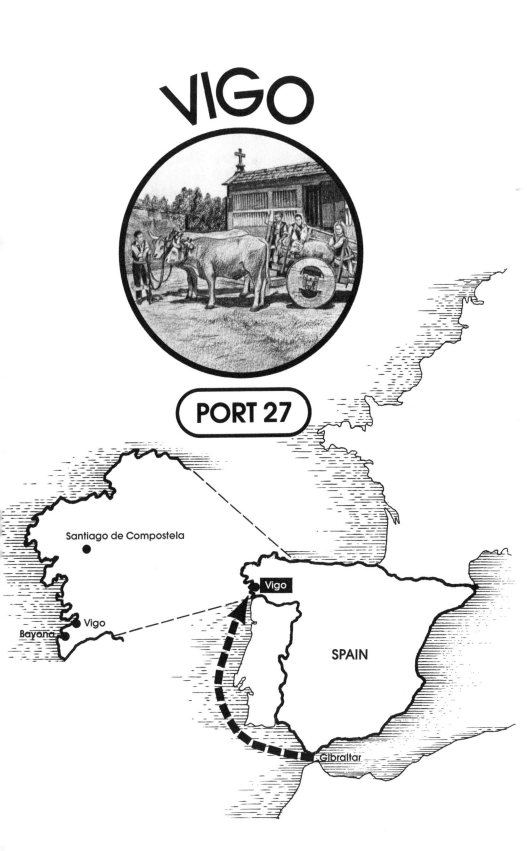

VIGO

PORT 27

Santiago de Compostela

Vigo

Bayana

Vigo

SPAIN

Gibraltar

VIGO

On March 28, a Friday, after traveling north from Gibraltar along the coast of Portugal, the QE2 arrived at the pretty, picturesque port of Vigo on Spain's Atlantic coast. It was raining that morning, and we wore our raincoats as we left the ship, but the rain soon let up and the day turned sunny. The weather along this coast is temperate, a bit on the cool side as it was this day— perfect for traveling.

Vigo, on the Bay of Vigo, is situated on an inlet off the Atlantic, creating a natural amphitheater, with pine-clad hills rising on all sides above the harbor. The busy fishing industry, plus a thriving tourism, satisfy the economic needs of the people. Vigo's rise in popularity as a gateway to historic northwest Spain accounted for the Queen's maiden docking at the port.

The port dates from Roman days, when it was an outpost of the Roman Empire. It is said that the natives fled from the mainland before Julius Caesar's Roman legions to the Cies Islands that guard the bay. In a later dubious claim to fame, Vigo was sacked by Sir Francis Drake in 1585. An interesting legend says that the bay's bottom is lined with gold. This dates from 1702, when a fleet of Spanish galleons carrying gold and silver treasure was attacked and many of the ships sank to the bottom of the bay. The fortune in gold and silver is still there, for no one has managed to recover it.

The town of Vigo is small, it was built on a hill overlooking the bay, and it has two distinct parts: the Old Town, which includes the harbor and the slope down to the waterfront, with winding streets and ancient palaces, and the New Town, at the top of the hill, with modern streets and a business center. The medieval squares and narrow streets of the Old Town are little changed from centuries ago, and they provide a real glimpse into Old Spain.

TOURING AROUND VIGO

As we drove along the coastal route into the countryside around Vigo, it reminded us of the California seacoast along Monterey Bay. It was lovely the way the woodland pines grew down to meet the sea. And as far as we could see were beautiful stretches of sandy white beaches and turquoise breakers.

Agriculture is an important part of local life. "Vigo," we learned, means "fig," and the town was so named because at one time figs were grown here. Now there are other fruit trees. Cabbages are especially common here, which our guide suggested as one of the reasons doctors give for the good health of the native people, since cabbages are loaded with essential vitamins and minerals.

From the look of so many stone houses and even stone fences, we were reminded of an old legend, which probably originated with a farmer. At the time of the creation, so says the legend, the angels were given bags of stones to distribute evenly over the earth, but here and there a whole bag would burst, and down would spill stones, stones, stones. So, to this day, farmers need to continually pick up stones before they can plant their crops. Some of the houses in the Vigo area are built of huge slabs of stone, as they were in ancient Roman times.

Along the roadside we occasionally saw some odd little six-legged houses, approximately four by six feet, bearing crosses. The guide said that these were prayer shrines to certain deities revered by the natives.

At noon we stopped at an ancient landmark called Parador Nacional Conde de Gondomas. Surrounded by a wide medieval wall, it overlooks the bay like an old fortress. We found a nice restaurant there and a large banquet room where we all gathered for a festive luncheon of cheese, salami and sandwiches, potato chips, crackers, beer, wine, and punch.

Then a colorful show was put on for us. About twenty-five dancers in native costume performed a fast and furious, lively and colorful Spanish dance. The little boys and girls in the troupe were especially nimble-footed and a joy to watch.

The countryside here is green and lovely. We even saw palm trees which were said to have grown from seeds brought over from America by early settlers in Vigo. The pretty resort of Bayona, fifteen miles south of Vigo and very medieval in character, is where Columbus landed with the *Pinta* on his return from the discovery of the New World, so the area has more than one "American connection."

The entire countryside, as seen on this pleasant, relaxing tour, gave us something to remember of serene and wholesome living. Even the cows are important to these folk. They are used as work beasts for food and meat, and to sustain life with their milk. Even as we write it is refreshing to close our eyes and see again, in full bloom, the fruit orchards on the hillsides—apples, pears, peaches. And once we saw a lavender wisteria vine in full bloom that had climbed over the tile roof of an old brick house, as pretty a picture as you will see anywhere.

Not far from Vigo, reached on a full-day trip by many of the QE2's adventurers, is the site of ancient Santiago de Compostela, one of the three chief pilgrimage sites of the Middle Ages. Here, in the ninth century, the tomb of Saint James the Apostle was discovered. The remains of the apostle, who brought Christianity to Spain, rest in a silver urn in the magnificent cathedral, with its ornately carved doors and huge naves. The town of Santiago is ringed with medieval monasteries, churches, and hostels used by the pilgrims who literally came here by the millions.

In our modern era of jet planes and great ocean liners that

make traveling a pleasure, it is moving to consider the faith of those who journeyed so far, often on foot, to make their pilgrimages in ancient times.

DIFFERENCES IN PEOPLE

People-watching is one of the pleasures of a long ocean voyage, and we had plenty of time to indulge in it during our days on the world cruise. We are always interested in people and in what they have *experienced* first-hand, for that is right from the horse's mouth, not something they have read about or heard.

People are individual entities and each one has unique qualities. Today, people, organizations, schools, and society in general are trying to press everyone into one mold. People thus lose their individual traits and innate characteristics. The ideal situation is to have each individual express his or her God-given talents *but* keep in *harmony* with others. It is a lesson well illustrated by the crew of the *Queen Elizabeth 2*.

Your ship (for it has now somehow become your ship) functions by using the essential differences between people to contribute to the goal of getting everyone there safe and sound. One person may be good with ideas and innovation, another with diplomacy, another with practicability, another with friendliness and warmth, another with seeing the result of the whole picture (such as the Captain), another with deciding whether the ship should even be built, and if, where, and when it should go.

Differences make for a more satisfying, diversified whole. Even countries and nations have different cultures, opinions, skills, abilities, and national characteristics. The British are noted for innovation, the French for diplomacy, the Dutch for pragmatism, the Italians for warmth, and the Germans for discipline.

People's interests do not always run parallel *but they must keep in harmony*, even though they do not think the same way. The key word is *harmony*—compromise is a way of life. One never finds Utopia or complete agreement. Today, the world has become small indeed, but we must learn to live in harmony with the differences that unite us.

EN ROUTE TO CHERBOURG

Soon we will be saying "so long" to all of the new friends we have met on the QE2 on this eighty-day trip. It will be noticed that every successful person has a host of friends, some of whom have helped to make that person a success, while others have been attracted to him because of his success. No man is great in and of himself; he must touch the lives of other great beings who will inspire him, lift him, and push him forward. Without friends, the journey of life is filled with loneliness. We dropped this little essay off at the QE2 News Bureau on Deck Two. Sure enough, it was in print for the next morning's edition.

A FRIEND IS A PERSON

- With whom you can be sincere.
- To whom you do not need to explain yourself.
- To whom you never need to defend yourself.
- On whom you can depend whether he is present or absent.
- With whom you never need to pretend.
- To whom you can reveal yourself without fear of betrayal.
- Who does not feel he owns you because you are his friend.
- Who will not selfishly use you because he has your confidence.

I Would Have Such a Friend…
And I Would Be Such a Friend.

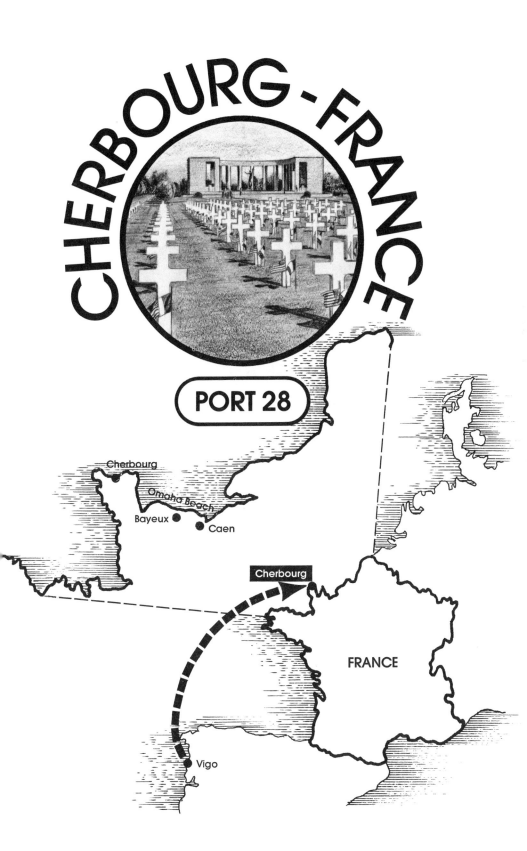

CHERBOURG - FRANCE

PORT 28

Cherbourg

Omaha Beach

Bayeux ● ● Caen

Cherbourg

FRANCE

Vigo

CHERBOURG

After a day of pleasant cruising northward along the coast of France, early on Sunday morning, March 30, we arrived at the twenty-eighth port of call on our world cruise aboard the QE2, tying up to the dock at Cherbourg, France. What a beautiful ship terminal! It was a pretty day to match, bright and sunny with the temperature at about fifty degrees.

Once a tiny fishing village exposed to the furies of the Atlantic, Cherbourg took a giant step toward becoming a major port when Louis XIV caused the building of breakwaters in the seventeenth century, providing shelter for the inner harbor.

The area around Cherbourg is rich in history. From the nearby harbor at Barfleur, William the Conqueror set sail for England in A.D. 1066—one of the few historical dates everyone remembers. Not far away are Omaha and Utah beaches, where American forces landed on June 6, 1944. Mont-St.-Michel is an easy drive away, as are the old cities of Rouen and Caen. Even a brief stay in Normandy offers sights that span a thousand years, not only of French history but of world history.

It was a quiet, peaceful Sunday morning as we drove through the Normandy countryside. Everyone was sleeping but us, we thought. The land was lovely and fertile, with plots of farmland separated by green hedges, so familiar in England. Stables on many of the farms were built close to the houses.

Most of the houses are alike—solid, square, two-story buildings with slanting roofs and two chimneys. The forebears of today's Normans built well, always using stone, and they still build in much the same way with the native granite stone. At the windows were pretty white curtains. The older dwellings that had not been destroyed during World War II's bombing bore white shutters outside. Some of the surviving houses are hundreds of years old, with green moss growing on the tile roofs.

Some houses still stand with thatched roofs, grown over with well-rooted green grass, and pretty vines tumbling down the rough stone walls. We saw a farmer's wife using an old-fashioned water pump at a well beside the back door of her house, working the pump handle up and down, a bucket slung on the spout. She hoisted the full bucket easily and disappeared indoors with it. These farmers are apparently strong and rugged, for we saw a man toting a whole bale of hay with the greatest of ease.

We drove through miles of pasturelands made green by Normandy's frequent rains. This is great horse-raising country, we learned, and we also saw herds of fine dairy cattle every-where—Guernseys, Jerseys, Holsteins, and some we had never seen before, brown spotted with white, and with two-inch dark brown rims around the eyes that made them look like they were wearing spectacles. Because they are a local crossbreed, they are called Normandy cows. This is also a famous cheese making area, source of the famous Camembert cheese.

We drove past apple orchards with horses grazing on the grass that was between the rows of trees—the best way to cut down on mowing grass, winemakers assert. Excellent apple cider and apple brandy come from Normandy, and we were told that both are the best aids for good eating if one is making off with an eight-course meal. Apple cider is served first, after a main meat course. Then comes another round of something hearty with fish or fowl, with apple brandy to do right by it. After a bit of a pause, there is dessert and more brandy.

We didn't have such an eight-course meal when we stopped for lunch at Caen, but we did sample some of Nor-mandy's famous cuisine—and knew we were truly in France!

SIGHTS OF NORMANDY

One of our first stops that morning in France was at Arromanches. Many grim reminders of the Normandy invasion can still be seen in the area, including the remains of the British landing dock that was called Mulberry during the war. In the American Cemetery at Saint Laurent, the columns of thousands of white crosses stir sad memories. At the Invasion Museum in Arromanches, there are vivid exhibits including films and three-dimensional dioramas that recreate the massive landing operation that took place on D-Day in 1944.

Normandy has often been invaded by different peoples, first by the Saxons and later by the Vikings. The Scandinavians came into France around the ninth and tenth centuries. In wooden ships, they tried to invade France by crossing the Seine. So, the beaches along this coast are no strangers to invaders.

But the greatest invasion of all took place on June 6, 1944, when American troops landed at Omaha and Utah beaches. After hard, fierce fighting, the soil was literally saturated with the blood of people fighting for their liberty. It took two months of sometimes hand-to-hand fighting that left 40,000 soldiers dead, before the German army withdrew from Normandy.

We saw moving reminders of those battles at Omaha and Utah beaches. After we viewed the documentary at the museum in the American Cemetery at Saint Laurent, which described the fighting on the beaches of Normandy, we understood why Cherbourg was one of the gateways to the continent that the Germans intended to possess.

At nearby Bayeux, the first town liberated by the Allies in 1944, we stopped to see the famous Bayeux Tapestry in the museum near the ancient Norman Gothic Cathedral. Like many of the churches in Caen and Rouen, this cathedral was miraculously undamaged by the heavy bombing that destroyed much of the towns around them.

The tapestry is an enormous panorama of medieval life and customs, an embroidered scroll said to have been woven by Queen Mathilde. Its fifty-eight scenes portray William the Conqueror's invasion and conquest of England, and the sprawling wall hanging, some 230 feet long, creates a remarkable portrait of the life and times of the Middle Ages, accomplishing in a tapestry what Chaucer did with words in his colorful Canterbury Tales.

There is much more to see on a visit to Normandy. The old city of Rouen was heavily bombed during World War II, but it has been remarkably restored. The city's great Notre Dame Cathedral is worth seeing, as is the Rouen Cathedral with its fifty-six-bell carillons. There is also a famous clock tower that spans the street. But Rouen's greatest claim on history is commemorated by a marker on the sidewalk that tells where Joan of Arc was burned at the stake in 1431.

About 120 miles from Caen, where we had lunch, is one of the marvels of France, Mont-St.-Michel. It was begun a thousand years ago, with most of the construction done from the eleventh to the fourteenth centuries. The town is noted for its omelets (featured at all the restaurants) and it suffers from being one of the top tourist attractions in all Europe, but the ancient fortress-monastery, built into sheer rock on the seacoast, never disappoints. It has been a place of pilgrimage since the Middle Ages. Because one must beware of the tides that can cover the sands around the famous Mont, tide tables can be had almost anywhere in Normandy. Aside from climbing through the town to the monastery on foot, Mont-St.-Michel may be seen at its dramatic best on a boat trip by moonlight.

Our full day in Normandy, filled with grim reminders as well as happier sights, ended with a rush as we returned to Cherbourg, chasing the sun.

HEROES

How highly privileged we are to live in this, our day, with its freedom but plenty of stress and worry. Centuries removed from a beginning where geniuses thought and prayed and worshipped and passed on to us the accumulation of a lifetime of sacrificial work and study.

How much we few owe to the many who have marched in solid phalanx across the centuries, torch bearers for our marching feet, who stumble amid the confusion and darkness of this bewildering present.

How many millions have literally drenched the earth with their blood. Heroically they have passed the torch of freedom from one to the other and kept it burning. We have now received that torch, and it is our high privilege, as well as our duty, to keep it burning brightly and pass it on to the next generation.

Such thoughts seemed especially meaningful to us as we approached Cherbourg and remembered the great sacrifice made in our own time on the beaches of Normandy. Also called to mind were the moving words of a soldier of World War I, in the famous poem, "In Flanders Fields."

In Flanders Fields

by Lt.-Col. John McCrae

In Flanders fields the poppies blow
Between the crosses, row on row,
That mark our place; and in the sky
The larks, still bravely singing, fly
Scarce heard amid the guns below.

We are the Dead. Short days ago
We lived, felt dawn, saw sunset glow,
Loved and were loved, and now we lie
In Flanders fields.

Take up our quarrel with the foe;
To you from failing hands we throw
The torch; be yours to hold it high.
If ye break faith with us who die
We shall not sleep, though poppies grow
In Flanders fields.

EN ROUTE TO LONDON

This trip around the world is a microcosm of life—you get out of it just what you put into it. Your attitude is so important. Look for the good and you find the good. Each day you look forward to a wonderful day...the Wonders of the World...the handiwork of Nature.

As we drew near our destination, the great port of Southampton, we remembered an advertising sign on a car that made us feel good just reading it: *"Spread the Word! Make Somebody Happy!"* Perhaps it was the lingering pleasure of our London memories, or the reminder of so many pleasures we had enjoyed on our homeplace of two months, the QE2, that made the motto ring such a pleasant and meaningful bell. And so we wrote a little accolade to the Queen:

◆—◆—◆—◆—◆

QE2, WE LOVE YOU

You have made our lives healthier and better by your many beneficial services and enjoyments.

May you sail on forever…helping souls like ourselves enjoy God's world.

We hope our fellow globe-trotters have enjoyed this 1980 Around the World Cruise as much as we have.

With our two eyeballs we have encompassed the beauty and wonders of the world, and we have accomplished this on the greatest ship in the world.

Congratulations upon earning the right to realize one of life's fondest dreams!

This Around the World Cruise is an event that will be remembered and cherished for the rest of our lifetime … a delightful and adventure-filled journey.

The greatest souvenirs we will bring home are the enjoyable, pleasant, and treasured memories.

Hope to see you on the next Six Continent World Cruise!

Alfred and Evelyn Montapert

◆—◆—◆—◆—◆

Nelson's Column—Trafalgar Square, London

SOUTHAMPTON·LONDON

PORT 29

ENGLAND

North Sea

London ⦿

❖ Stonehenge

Salisbury ●   ● Winchester

Southampton

Bournemouth ●

English Channel

LONDON

This royal throne of kings, this sceptered isle,
This earth of majesty, this seat of Mars,
This other Eden, demi-paradise...
This happy breed of men, this little world,
This precious stone set in the silver sea...
This blessed plot, this earth, this realm,
    this England.

—Shakespeare,
Richard II

Shakespeare said it all, yet it's almost not enough. Coming back to England is, for the average American, almost like returning home.

We docked at Southampton early on the morning of the last day of March. After getting our passports stamped and ready for departure, we passed a table where we were able to purchase train tickets to London, thus avoiding any wait for coaches going up to the city. London is one of our favorite cities in all the world, and we had two days to enjoy her once again.

If you've ever been to London, returning to it is like visiting an old friend. You don't have to spend weeks to enjoy the visit. Old memories instantly awaken, making the time you have to spend that much richer and fuller.

After a relaxing ride through the green countryside on the train (British trains are rightfully a source of pride), we arrived in London and immediately took a taxi directly to Harrod's, one of the world's great department stores. London is a shopper's paradise, from the hundreds of small antique shops, to the boutique shops on King's Road, to the stores of Regent Street and New Bond Street.

But Harrod's is like London itself; it has something for everyone. They sell everything from safety pins to Rolls Royces, and we had practical needs of typewriter ribbons and paper, cassette tapes, and film for the camera. We had a delightful lunch in the Food Hall and, thus fortified, spent a couple of pleasant hours walking around the store. The food section is something else, strings of white turkeys hanging in the poultry section with their feathers plucked except for a ring of white feathers around the neck, a bewildering catch of every kind of fresh fish and shellfish in the fish section (and smoked salmon at $24.00 a pound), and in the cheese section over 500 kinds of cheeses from all over the world.

We checked into our hotel, the gracious old Grosvenor House. It is one of the Trust Houses Forte chain that operates worldwide, and the hotel is on Park Lane, just across from the Grosvenor Gate of lovely Hyde Park, surely one of the world's most appealing stretches of greenery in the midst of a great city.

That night we returned to another spot which held happy memories from our last visit—the Charing Cross Hotel—for dinner. It is by Charing Cross railroad station, and like almost everything else in London it has a rich tradition. The name comes from the fact that Edward I erected a series of crosses in memory of his queen, Eleanor, who died in 1290. The actual Charing Cross, the last of those he erected, was destroyed in 1647, but that doesn't spoil the tradition. The most recent cross was placed in 1863 in the forecourt of the railway station.

We enjoyed a delicious dinner of excellent French cuisine in the beautiful dining room. An accomplished pianist played familiar songs and old love songs by request, so we lingered another hour, listening and simply enjoying the charm of this unique place before returning to our hotel. We were reminded once again that old buildings and statues are not the only enduring British tradition. There is another tradition of politeness and courtesy, charm and grace.

TOURING LONDON

London is everyone's great city, endlessly fascinating, always holding out surprises around the next corner, up the next winding street. It was Samuel Johnson who said, "When a man is tired of London, he is tired of life; for there is in London all that life can afford."

First called Londinium by the Romans who founded it 2000 years ago, its population today is some 12 million in Greater London—a far cry from when Julius Caesar landed near Dover Cliffs and the trumpets of Roman legions first sounded over the land. London was established as a port, and the Thames River winding through the heart of the city still provides much of the city's character and atmosphere.

London is an overcrowded, teeming city, always changing. Skyscrapers transform the skyline now where they were once forbidden. Yet it is also enduringly the same. And the jangling life of the city is relieved more than in any other great city by its lovely parks. There are in fact some 40,000 acres of parks, including Hyde Park, Regent's Park to the north in the Marylebone district, Green Park, and Saint James Park closer by, buffering Buckingham Palace. These lovely oases and hundreds of smaller parks and gardens soften and ease the noise and crowds of the city, adding to its beauty. There is a lot of life in the parks, too. From the Grosvenor House, we could stroll a few blocks north to the famous Speaker's Corner of Hyde Park, opposite Marble Arch and at the beginning of fashionable Oxford Street.

Huge and sprawling and heavily trafficked as it is, you can see a lot of London in concentrated areas, by taxi or bus or even on foot … so let's take a couple of our favorite tours.

You must go by Buckingham Palace, of course, and if you can arrange it, be there at 11:30 in the morning for the famous Changing of the Guard. This fairytale spectacle takes place at that hour every day in summertime, and in winter as well if the Queen is staying at the Palace. It's a colorful example of the pageantry that is so much a part of England's love for its royal tradition.

To see more of the heart of London, you cross the park from Buckingham Palace to Hyde Park Corner (you'll see the Wellington Arch) and then turn back onto Piccadilly, where the Londoner shops for a new car. As you make your way past the Royal Academy, Fortnum and Mason's, Hatchard's Bookstore, past a thousand taxis and cars and buses, you arrive at Piccadilly Circus. It isn't really a circus at all, but a circle around which much of the city revolves, one of the most familiar intersections in all the world, just as Times Square is a familiar sight even to people who have never been to New York.

Take Coventry Road west from Piccadilly Circus and you are in the heart of the theater district. London is a city of theaters, a playgoer's delight. There are over fifty legitimate theaters, not just here but across the Thames in the area of Waterloo Station and elsewhere. Their names are legends in the world of the theater: Haymarket and Drury Lane, the Royal Opera House and Covent Garden, the Old Vic, the National Theatre, Garrick and Glove, Palace and Palladium.

But back to the tour: Turn south at Leicester Square and you'll come to Trafalgar Square, another famous view, with Nelson's Column and the admiral's famous statue looking down. Saint-Martin's-in-the-Fields is a lovely old church, not as well known as Saint Paul's and Westminster Abbey, but well worth a visit.

If you continue south from Trafalgar Square, you'll find yourself on Whitehall, moving into the center of British government activity. Pass by the Admiralty and the Horse Guards and you'll come to one of the most famous short streets in the world, and one of the most famous houses, at No. 10 Downing Street.

Cut over to your left at Bridge Street after passing the Government Offices, and you'll come to the Victoria Embankment along the Thames. And you'll be in sight of Big Ben, one of the world's most famous clocks (perhaps *the* most famous). You're within hearing of Big Ben anywhere for ten miles around. Here, too, are the great Houses of Parliament, overlooking the river.

And just across the street on the inland side is another of London's great attractions—some think its greatest—Westminster Abbey. It is a fitting climax to this brief tour, one that packs a world's worth of sightseeing into within a few miles.

WESTMINSTER ABBEY

Westminster Abbey has rightly been called England's Pantheon of Geniuses. No other temple of fame in the whole world equals it. Would not 1200 years of consecrated prayers account for much? The Abbey is said to have begun as a Benedictine abbey in the eighth century. As Westminster Abbey, it was consecrated over 900 years ago.

Who can look unmoved upon the tombs and statues of England's heroes and not feel the presence of the great men who virtually made and shaped the history of the Western world? How inspiring to again walk the Aisle of Statesmen, reading the names of William Pitt, Benjamin Disraeli, William Gladstone, Sir John Herschel, Sir Isaac Newton, and others whose contributions so enriched mankind the world over!

We linger in the Poets' Corner, said to have started from an idea of Chaucer, while memories of our schoolbook friends flood in: Robert Browning, Alfred Lord Tennyson, Sir Walter Scott, Ben Jonson, Milton, Shakespeare, Dryden, Macauley, Bulwer-Lytton, Charles Dickens, Robert Burns, Coleridge.

We stand beside the grave of David Livingstone, intrepid and dedicated Scottish missionary and explorer in Africa in the nineteenth century, and realize the heritage with which this great man of God has endowed the past century's missionary movements in all faiths.

A thought continually runs through the backs of our minds as we review the record of these illustrious mortals: "That's great! To have an honored place in the halls of Westminster Abbey..." But is it not infinitely greater to have a place in God's Hall of Fame, like that held by Moses, Abraham, Gideon, David, and Paul, whose keynote for admittance seems to have been simply based on *faith?*...

> *Wealth dies,*
> *Health dies,*
> *You yourself must die.*
> *Only fame survives*
> *If properly achieved.*

CITY OF LONDON

We had more time our second day in London to walk the familiar streets. London is rightly named the "City of Pride," for cleanliness and order prevail. But it is also the city of memories, and there is no better way to evoke them than to visit the old City of London.

This is another part of London where you can see a lot in a concentrated area. If you're coming from the west side, take the Strand from Trafalgar Square, which brings you onto Fleet Street, the picturesque hub of England's newspaper empire, probably the most famous such street in the world.

Two of the must-see attractions in this area are Saint Paul's Cathedral, with its mighty dome, and the "bloody tower"—the Tower of London. But there is much more.

The City, or the Square Mile, contains twelve of London's

thirty-two boroughs, and its old walls were once the walls of London. The population of this area was almost wiped out in the Great Plague of 1664-1665, in which more than 70,000 people died. And just a year later, in September 1666, the Great Fire destroyed most of the City.

After the fire, some planners wanted to change the twisting warrens of streets into an orderly plan, but the people would have none of it, sticking to their traditional ways in the British manner, rebuilding the city along the old Roman streets and with the same twists and turns. Today, that is part of the lasting charm of this older part of London.

You can find just about whatever you want in this part of the city. There's literary London, for instance, and you can visit the houses where Dickens and Samuel Johnson wrote, and find pubs honoring the memories of Samuel Pepys, Johnson and Boswell, and others. Ye Olde Cheshire Cheese is one of the most delightful pubs, and we carried away a delightful memory of sitting there, in the chair said to have been Dr. Johnson's favorite spot, while we enjoyed a marvelous lunch.

Books are one of our passions, and London is a city of bookstores, old and new, large and small…but especially old and small. It's a marvelous place to browse and search for old volumes. One of our problems in visiting London is that books are heavy, and we must carry them or ship them back home. We have to keep reminding ourselves that we can't take everything with us that we'd like to have and read!

We took time for a nostalgic look at the Old Curiosity Shop, immortalized by Charles Dickens. The building mercifully survived the air raids of World War II, so a number of Dickens's mementoes can be seen: the empty chair before his desk, beside it a huge metal wastebasket, and bookcases filled with sets of books. A glassed-in Dickens Shrine displays his personal photographs and handwritten notes and letters. We stood before the original fireplace, and learned that upstairs another fireplace has been restored.

The spirit of the place remains. The shop itself is still used for the same purpose it had in Dickens's time, with all kinds of "old and curious" articles for sale.

Saint Paul's Cathedral, atop Ludgate Hill, is a wonderful landmark, visible from many parts of the old City. It burned along with some 13,000 houses in the Great Fire, and it was after that fire that Sir Christopher Wren built the new Saint Paul's, in a gracefully proportioned style that influenced architects for centuries afterward. When you are in London, be sure to pause here in this ancient citadel of faith.

If you walk east from Saint Paul's, you will come upon Saint Mary Le Bow. *A Cockney is anyone born within the sound of the bells of Bow Church, so you'll know you're in the heart of Cockney London.* And if you continue east for a short distance, you'll find yourself suddenly in the financial heart of the city. Here are the Bank of England and the Stock Exchange, the Royal Exchange, and, a bit to the east, Lloyd's of London.

Go south now, toward the Thames. Along the waterfront are the colorful Billingsgate Fish Market and the Customs House. But your destination is the Tower of London. It's actually not just one tower but many, a complex overlooking the Thames, built by William the Conqueror to secure the city.

If the Tower seems gloomy and forbidding, that's because it has known some gloomy times since William the Conqueror first built it as a prison. Such famous personages as Anne Boleyn, Catherine Howard, and Sir Walter Raleigh lost their heads in the Tower, and the future Richard III had his rival prince-nephews killed here.

But, to relieve the somber atmosphere, you can take a look at England's Crown Jewels while you're here. Saint Edward's Crown, made for Charles II and weighing seven pounds, is a velvet cap surrounded by a golden circle and arches studded with jewels. The present Queen Elizabeth II wore it for her coronation. The lighter Imperial State Crown, worn more often, has 3000 jewels, including the huge Black Prince ruby worn by

THE POST
OFFICE
TOWER

LONDON

Henry V at Agincourt. The magnificent royal sceptre has the most dazzling jewel of all, however, called the First Star of Africa, a 530-carat diamond, the largest cut stone in existence.

Near the Tower Bridge over the Thames, you can end this look at old London in a special way. Instead of taking a taxi back through town, you can take a motor launch, leaving Tower Pier and following the Thames along London's banks to Westminster Pier, as kings and conquerors and London's own river people have gone before you, century after century, for 2000 years.

The Post Office Tower—the tallest building in London—has a wonderful revolving restaurant at the top. It revolves once every half-hour, giving diners an ever-changing panorama of London. All that view and gourmet food, too!

We timed our table reservation so that we would arrive just before the millions of lights came on all over London. We were there for dinner one evening at sundown and it was a most inspiring sight, watching the sun go down and cast a golden glow over the city, and later on seeing the lights come on section by section. We thought of the World War II song, "When the Lights Come On Again All Over the World."

The time to see the lights is when they're burning.

They're burning now!

Believe me, this is a sight you will never forget as long as you live!

LEAVING LONDON

Our stay in London ended all too soon. It was April 1, and we thought of that famous line, "Oh, to be in England, now that April's here!" The glimpses lingered as we drove...Westminster Cathedral, Harrod's, Mason's Department Store with the Queen's Crest, the huge gray edifice of Scotland Yard. We saw Saint Marguerite's Church, where Winston Churchill was married, and nearby the bronze statue of Sir Winston. We also saw the magnificent fifty-two-story Post Office Tower.

As we drove, our kaleidoscopic view of the city included glimpses of the Horse Guard, Trafalgar Square with Lord Nelson's statue, Buckingham Palace, and the Court of Saint James where ambassadors of other countries stay. As we drove past the Hyde Park Hotel, the grass in Hyde Park was the most beautiful green we'd ever seen anywhere.

We passed the Queen Mary Hospital, and drove past what seemed to be miles of race tracks, until once more we were passing beyond London's permanent green belt into the lovely fresh green of the open countryside. Enjoying every mile of it, we passed through verdant pasturelands where herds of Holstein cattle grazed, marveling always at the fresh greenness of the land, the lovely gardens large and small, the beauty of Surrey, and the charm of the old market towns of Hampshire.

SALISBURY AND STONEHENGE

A full-day excursion from the Queen leads into the lovely country of Wiltshire, a quiet, peaceful, and idyllic countryside that brings you to the old town of Salisbury, about twenty-five miles from Southampton.

The medieval buildings, the inn, the many fine houses dating from the seventeenth and eighteenth centuries, and the clean and pleasant streets and shops are an irresistible lure to the new visitor, as the river was to Izaak Walton, who fished here with the Bishop of Salisbury. A delightful place to stop (including overnight) is the White Hart Hotel, a venerable inn, warm and cozy, rambling on many levels, and as comfortable as its service is courteous and friendly.

Salisbury Cathedral was built in a single generation in the thirteenth century, except for the spire, which was added in the next century. It is Britain's highest cathedral spire, and it is one reason why the famous painter John Constable painted the Salisbury Cathedral over and over.

Near Salisbury is one of England's great houses, Wilton House. This palatial manor has welcomed royalty down through the centuries, as well as such greats as Ben Jonson, Spenser, and John Donne, the poet who reminded us "for whom the bell tolls." During World War II, this was also headquarters for General Eisenhower and the Supreme Allied Command. Besides the house itself, with its rich furnishings and paintings, the extensive lawns and gardens are an outstanding example of English gardening on the grand scale.

Just a stone's throw away, so to speak, is one of the world's great mysteries, Stonehenge. Built 3500 years ago on the Salisbury Plain, it still keeps the secret of why it was built there. Set in a circle, the great stones are a somber, silent echo of a lost age. Once seen, their stark image against the sky will never leave you.

EN ROUTE TO NEW YORK

Leaving Southampton, we shared mixed feelings with many of our fellow passengers aboard the *Queen Elizabeth 2*. There was nostalgia for all that we had seen and enjoyed together for the past two months, and a tug of regret that it would all soon end. Yet there was anticipation, too, for we were going home, reaching the end of another journey.

Some of the QE2 passengers had already left, electing to take the Concorde home. It leaves from Heathrow London Airport at 1:30 in the afternoon and arrives in New York at 10:30 in the morning of the same day. So you eat your lunch in London and then eat your lunch again in New York, a case of fooling the clock made possible by outrunning the sun between London and New York.

As England slipped slowly behind us on the horizon, we thought of our friends winging their way through the air at a speed faster than sound, but we did not envy them their speedy flight, for all the prestige of being able to say, "I've crossed the Atlantic on the Concorde." For the truth was that we cherished our last few days of luxurious ease on the splendid Queen.

The five days between Southampton and New York also give you time to ask yourself, "Was the trip a good investment?"

Before you left you had a stack of money. Now you have a stack of dreams to last you through a lifetime.

Before you left, you were tired, maybe not in the best of shape. Now you *feel* like a million dollars even if it has cost you a few thousand to get that feeling.

Certainly, it was a gamble to plunk down all that money for the trip. It seemed a wild extravagance at the time, but was it?

You remember what a cagey old stock trader told you once: "You never get a dividend without an investment."

You've made the very best investment anyone can make—in yourself—and you will reap the dividends a hundredfold in a thousand quiet moments when, just by closing your eyes, you can conjure up the vision of a Japanese shrine, the Taj Mahal, the Pyramids, the Acropolis, Saint Peter's, Westminster Abbey...

There are many forms of wealth, you decide, and now you are richer, not poorer. For, having made the investment, you have a lifetime of dividends ahead of you that your banker or stockbroker will never know about or possibly never understand.

WHAT DID YOU LIKE BEST?

We were often asked, "What did you like best about the trip to the many wonders of the world?" It is not an easy question to answer, for so many memories crowd in upon us. But we'll take a stab at it...

1. *The Pyramids* were deeply impressive. They showed us the truth that the old kings believed in life eternal, something we have lost sight of today. They are also remarkable in the revelation of the skill of the ancient Egyptians in building monuments that have lasted down through the centuries. The Pyramids are the last of the Wonders of the World.

2. *The Taj Mahal* was incredibly beautiful, the most magnificent tomb in the world. It was a monument built by the ruler Shah Jehan to show his love for his wife, and here too is another king who believed that life on earth is only a transient stay, and that future life, eternal, is the one that really matters.

3. *The Holy Land* was very meaningful. To walk the streets and climb the hills where Jesus walked was a moving and thrilling experience we will never forget.

4. *Athens* was all that we had dreamed, putting us in touch with so much of the culture and history that have come down to us from the wise men of Greece's Golden Age.

5. *Naples and Rome* belong on any list of the best, especially the great ruins that bring back so much of Roman times, the mighty Colosseum and the Forum in Rome, the remarkably preserved ruins of Pompeii.

6. *London* is our favorite city. Our grandfather came from Norwich, England, our grandmother from Scotland, so we have deep emotional ties to this "sceptered isle," and a great affection for this city full of history and heroes.

7. *The QE2* itself belongs on the roster of things we liked best—the quality of life aboard the ship, the matchless British courtesy of service, the character of men like Eric Mason and our Captain, Robert Arnott, the warmth and gaiety of social life, the ease and grace of the mighty ship—all these have become cherished memories.

8. Another *big dividend* we received from this trip was improved *health* and well-being. Our *health* is our greatest asset. We arrived home the picture of health, refreshed, invigorated, radiant, and ready to handle anything that comes our way. It is *health* which is real wealth, and not pieces of gold and silver. The ground-work for all *happiness* and *life* is *health*. So, if *health is wealth...we have it made!*

A WORD OF THANKS

We were invited to a special cocktail party by Vaughn Rickard, who is ambassador-at-large for Cunard Lines.

Since we are independent freelance writers and in no way connected to the Cunard Lines—except as lucky passengers— we are able to give our free expression of this wonderful eighty-day cruise on the QE2.

We would indeed be ungrateful if we did not mention the wonderful services and nice gifts given to all of the full-cruise passengers:

Bowl of fresh flowers in our cabin when we embarked
Two giant-size deck towels
Special QE2 crock of expensive Scotch whiskey
Invitation to the Captain's Cabin
Two fancy folding umbrellas
Chocolate clover-leaf candies (about a one-pound box)
  on Saint Patrick's Day
List of full-cruise passengers, in simulated leather covers
Beautiful silk orchid in glass pyramid case which now
  adorns our home
Two silver memorial plates of the 10th Anniversary
  Cruise, struck by the London Mint—they will be
  keepsakes
Queen Elizabeth's 10th Anniversary World Cruise Book

Once again, what can we say? Words are a rickety vehicle on which to haul emotions, but never have we been so fully aware of the observation as we are at this moment when we try to find words adequate to describe our gratitude to the entire staff of Cunard Lines for their many gestures of kindness. We fear we shall be compelled simply to say *"Thank you!"* from our hearts with all the power of deepest emotion.

Thank you is the best phrase at our command. We are grateful and appreciate your services and your *gifts of giving*, and we are proud of you.

AND A WORD FROM A FELLOW PASSENGER

Finally, it's the last party, the last dance, the last of so many lovely things. Suddenly it's time to pack, something you'd done very little of on this trip.

Do you still remember how?

The mood was aptly captured by another passenger in a little poem printed in the final issue of the *QE2 Times*.

THE LAST NIGHT AT SEA

The last night at sea, oh, the last night at sea,
Everybody is busy as busy as bees.
I thought I was packing with the greatest of care,
Until I spied all that stuff on the chair.

Then it's unpack, repack and once again pack,
Until I am lame with a crook in my back.
But the packing is done, the keys in my hand,
What a wonderful feeling, oh, but it's grand.

'Til I open a drawer—it's filled with more junk.
I even doubt if I'll find room in my trunk.
I rant and I rave, throwing all on the floor,
And carefully repack once more.

Now the packing is done, I did it myself.
Believe me, I feel like a jolly old elf.
But wait just a minute, I could scream up the wall.
I did it, I did it! Packed my passport and all.

Gaile Guggenbuhl (Cabin 4173)

SUMMING UP

Now that we have made our trip around the world, we must confess that it was a priceless experience. The world belongs to those who have seen it. The advantages of travel last throughout life, and often as we sit at home some bright and perfect view of Honolulu, Hong Kong, Jerusalem, Athens, London, Paris, or Rome comes back to us, awakening pleasant memories of days wisely spent in travel.

Looking back over the years, there have been more blessings than we could ever catalog. For each and every one we are eternally grateful. And each and every one has been a spur that we may be worthy of all that we have received at His hands. We truly thank God for the opportunity we had to take this Around the World Cruise on the QE2.

Now, this great journey nearly at an end, it's time to say goodbye to ship and friends. We cannot fully express our emotions any more than you can capture the song of a mockingbird. Emotions are like music; they mean something beyond words and sense...something truly of the spirit.

We leave it to another fellow traveler, Leslie Carroll of Sacramento, California, to say it for us.

PARTING

What is more rare
On coming to an end
Than the silent tear
As we leave our good friend.

Volumes it speaks
Though not a word
Thunderous the silence
And nothing is heard.

Yet high it's scored
On memory's chart
And forever imprisoned
Within the heart.

COMING HOME

It was on a Thursday night in winter, January 17, that the QE2 slipped down the Hudson toward the open sea, and we bade goodbye to the Statue of Liberty.

And now, on Easter Sunday, April 6, we felt the same shiver of pride. There she was! The Statute of Liberty! Outlined against the sky on this spring evening, she was far grander and more beautiful than any pictures of her.

We knew the story behind this great Green Lady, how the French artist, Frederic Auguste Bartholdi, was commissioned to design a gigantic statue as a gift from the French people and their new Republic to the Americans, how the great pedestal was laid on August 5, 1884 (paid for by Americans), and the statue itself unveiled on October 28, 1886 (paid for by Frenchmen). We knew the story of her dimensions, too: height of 152 feet, weight of 450,000 pounds, so huge that forty people could stand in the head and a dozen in the torch.

But the lady with the torch held high is more than all the dates and numbers of her past to an American coming home. She is a beacon of welcome, and to us, at the end of our pursuit of all the world's wonders, she remains the greatest Wonder of the World, always there to remind us of the ideals that we as free Americans hold so dear.

It was mighty good to be home!